THE ART OF INVESTING

The Art
of
Investing

by **Philipp H. Lohman**

A Stuart L. Daniels Book

HAWTHORN BOOKS, INC.
Publishers
New York

THE ART OF INVESTING

Book Design: MARTIN J. BAUMANN

1 2 3 4 5 6 7 8 9 10

CONTENTS

Part I—Why Securities as Investments?

Part II—What Equities or Equities Equivalents?

Part III—What Bonds?

v

Part IV—What Strategies and Tactics?

THE ART OF INVESTING

Part I

Why Securities as Investments?

CHAPTER 1

The Second Trillion Is around the Corner.

Will You Get *Your* Share?

The Gross National Product, or GNP, is the country's annual output of goods and services measured in monetary terms. It does not include laundry done in the home, or food cooked or cakes baked by devoted wives. It does include the wash done by a commercial laundry, meals eaten in restaurants, and cakes bought at the bakery, as well as major industrial products.

In 1950 the GNP was $285 billion. By 1965 the total had reached $685 billion, but only five years later, by the first quarter of 1971, the GNP was running at an annual rate of more than $1 trillion. By approximately 1982, it is estimated, the GNP will reach an annual rate of $2 trillion. Think of it! It took several hundred years to reach one trillion, and in a little more than ten years we'll add another trillion to it.

These are figures of current, not constant, dollars, and they reflect inflation. But production in real terms, the GNP in constant dollars, went up 50 percent during the 1960s and will probably show another 50-percent real rise over the next ten years. Ask yourself if you were 50 percent better off in real terms in 1970 than in 1960. If not, you probably made some errors somewhere along the way. These pages should help you avoid the financial mistakes that so many people have made and continue to make, and should show you how to get *your* share of these future gains.

Prerequisites for Getting Your Share

The best way to get your share is to master at least the fundamental principles of the art of investing.

"Investing," like so many other terms, is a word with many meanings. In our sense it means that you put money in a private or public business to realize a share of its profits. The evidence you have done so is a negotiable piece of paper known as a security. The moment your income exceeds your expenditures, you have become an investor, no matter where you put the difference—unless you hide it under the mattress or in a cookie jar. The question then arises: What is the best way to use, to invest, this money or any other funds you have in conformity with your situation?

The solution is derived from three basic factors:

One, the establishment of a proper investment objective and the development of investment decisions in accordance with it.

Two, the selection of available investment media to serve the best interests of the investor.

Three, the use of certain tools and strategies to come out ahead of the game.

There are many opportunities in the investment field to make more money than you had ever thought feasible. This book points out the risks, pitfalls, and proper approaches to the goal of accumulating wealth.

Begin reading a little more. It is amazing how many people subscribe to expensive financial services but won't buy *The Wall Street Journal, Forbes, Financial World,* or Standard and Poor's *Outlook. Business Week* can give you a lot of ideas.

Above all, go through life with open eyes and ears. Listen to what other people are saying. Watch for what they buy or don't buy. Sometimes you can do a surprising amount of effective "research" while going about your weekend shopping chores. If a surprising number of people are saying they will buy a particular car, this might be a guide to buying or holding the stock of that company. If anybody gives you a "tip" or investment advice, listen and then check it out. After a while you will see how ridiculous rumors are, and you will become increasingly resistant to waves of optimism, outright euphoria, pessimism, despondency.

Don't let anybody kid you. Don't kid yourself. There is no shortcut to making money. You have to work at it. Do you have to do all the chores around your house or yard? Hire somebody to do some of them and spend that time reading in your den. You will be working for yourself at far, far higher wages than the guy you hire.

The Art of Investing

Investing can never become a mechanical science. Basically we live in an irrational world. It can become very costly at times to formulate rational investment decisions in such an environment. To illustrate: If I read that a lot of people are concerned about a new international monetary crisis, I might buy gold stocks even though I think there is no basis for such fear. But I would also sell them before newspapers report the "crisis" is over. I would also sell the gold stocks short, knowing from past experience that before long disgusted "investors" will sell their gold stocks since they don't seem to be going anywhere. As more sellers appear, gold stocks will once again approach their low for the year. Sporadic rumors that our laboriously built international monetary structure will collapse and that gold will go to seventy or a hundred dollars an ounce are examples of unadulterated Venetian canal water.

Formulate a rational investment decision and then apply it irrationally in conformity with market trends. When people compare the stock market to a dice game, I think they are referring to this irrationality. But if my analysis of an industry, a security, a market situation is rational and I can understand the irrational behavior of others, I'll benefit from it. This is the reason the professional advises, "Never argue with the market."

What is a stock worth? The amount somebody is willing to give you for it—no more and no less. Market price is often determined by outrageous greed, dreams, hopes, fear, or panic. One of the very few axioms in Wall Street that hold water is this: "The best way to go broke is on inside advice and information." The president of a company can enthusiastically give you all kinds of information about his company's plans and the new products it is going to market. However, if investors and professionals don't see success ahead, that stock may sit like a hunk of lead or even go down five or ten points. Let me add two thoughts. One, trading on inside information is definitely frowned upon by the Securities and Exchange Commission. Two, the death rate of developing new products is very high. Moreover, the time span to exploit a new product is shrinking; before long, a competitor comes to the market, usually with a better product.

Investing will also remain an art rather than a science because we are trying to predict what a company might do in the face of a rapidly changing economic, political, and social environment. We have become very impatient, and good investment results also require, at times, patience. Perhaps the news reports that an Arab country is stymieing a large oil company that operates there. Threats of expropriation are uttered, and financial losses are predicted for these companies. Should I sell my oil stock? No. This is all hogwash. The country needs those companies to sell its oil. After a handful of "paytriotic" colonels have squeezed them as hard as they dare, an agreement is announced. The Western Europeans who need the oil have to pay a higher price. My oil stock, since the announcement of the agreement with pictures of smiling faces all around, now goes up. If I am a trader, I can usually make four or five points on such news items. When reading newspaper stories, remember that journalists will always get a better story if they play up disagreement and play down agreement. More papers are sold that way. The larger the circulation, the larger the advertising revenue.

Fundamentals told me that Eastman Kodak at $80 was a good stock to buy in 1970 for long-term growth. It looked as if my judgment was correct when it went to 84⅜, but it soon went to 57⅞ that same year. Yes, I was right, EK is a good stock to buy for the long pull, but I goofed when I bought it in 1970 in the teeth of the irrational gale that started to blow.

Not all stocks will double in value between now and 1982

as the economy doubles in size. Some will do a lot better than others. The trick is to find out which ones. That is pure art, combined with some scientific reasoning.

Wanted—A "Safe" Investment

In March, 1971, a poll commissioned by *The Wall Street Journal* showed that of those interviewed who had traded stocks during 1969–1970, 28 percent said they wouldn't buy stocks again. One disillusioned "investor" said, "It isn't funny to lose money—I'd rather put my money in safe investments."

To that piece of wisdom, I should say, first, that scared money never made money. Second, dear "investor," there is no such thing as a safe investment in this world. The sooner you accept this fact, the better off you will be, because you will learn to cope with this fact intelligently.

If a disappointed investor caught in a bear market puts money in the bank for the long pull, he will get less interest than many a high-grade bond pays. However, investing in any debt security, or any fixed-income security, exposes the investor to continuing erosion in the value of money.

Look what we want: national economic growth at a good clip, high and expanding employment, and reasonable stability in the value of the dollar. Unfortunately, these goals are mutually exclusive. The more we push the economy to higher levels of operation, the higher will be employment and the higher will be the pressure on prices. Apparently, the country has decided that for continued growth at a good clip we are willing to pay the price of a certain amount of inflation.

The best inflation hedges are good growth stocks in companies that have financial leverage, that is, have bonds and preferred stocks outstanding. As prices rise, bondholders and preferred stockholders don't get any more, so that the company's increased dollar earnings accrue to the common shareholders. For the long pull, to protect yourself against inflation, the answer is common stocks. There are times, however, when bonds should be bought.

Money in a savings account is not working for you. Get rid

of that idea. If you buy a good stock and the company earns $2 a share and pays a $1 dividend, the other buck is plowed back and continues to work for you as long as you are a partial owner of the company.

Have you ever considered that inflation, by making your salary check higher, puts you in a higher income tax bracket? Why buy relatively high-yielding stocks that will further increase your taxes? If you must have a second income, buy a tax-exempt municipal bond. If you don't need the second income, buy into a growth company that plows back most or all of its earnings, and let the money really go to work for you.

If this whole investing business scares you, look for professional advice to plan your investments, if not all your financial affairs. Sometimes professional management can be obtained very cheaply by buying the shares of a so-called closed-end investment company. There will be no load charge, as would be the case in buying into a mutual fund. You might even buy the shares at a discount from net asset value, something you can never do with a mutual fund. But don't let the load charge dissuade you from buying into a *good* mutual fund. There are also a number of no-load mutual funds.

Additional Hints for Practicing the Art of Investing

Some further thoughts when picking your anti-inflation common-stock protection: Buy into corporations that have relatively low labor costs. Such companies tend to have a large capital investment, thus high fixed costs, and show decreasing unit costs as the volume of output expands. I much prefer the aluminum industry to the copper industry. The chief cost in aluminum is electric power; in copper, it is wages.

Invest in companies that have flexible pricing structures. There are usually political reactions when basic industries such as steel or automobiles raise prices. Utility pricing policies are regulated by law and, at times, hampered by conflicting jurisdictions at federal and state levels. New products can be priced flexibly. If demand is elastic, more revenue and profits devolve when prices are cut. If demand is inelastic, even a higher price could increase profits. A company like the Perkin-Elmer Corporation, with its analytical instruments, is a good candidate because emphasis on high-quality performance also permits price flexibility. Just wait for the day, not too far off, when these instruments are hooked up to mini-computers. Other firms in the flexible-pricing-structure category are those that make surgical and other medical equipment, testing and measuring tools, and office equipment items, from computers to copiers.

In the service area, flexible prices can easily be instituted. In the 1970s a lot of advertising and other business service companies, including private security service companies, will go public. The larger ones should do quite well. Some stocks in these categories are already traded in listed or over-the-counter securities markets. Chains of beauty parlors, nursing homes, and funeral parlors deserve a good second look despite some bad experience in the 1969–1970 bear market.

The consumer price index of medical care went from 79.1 in 1960 (1967 = 100) to 129.3 by midsummer of 1971; that of health and recreation, from 85.1 to 122.6. This was an appreciably higher rise than was registered by the overall consumer price index.

Investigate cosmetics, toiletries, and any other business that stands to benefit from increased leisure time. The four-day week is spreading. Avon, Eastman Kodak, or Black and Decker are good illustrations of such companies.

Don't Marry Your Stocks and Don't Have Prejudices

When stocks have served their usefulness, they should be sold. Sometimes a stock runs a race and comes in first but, like an athlete, is tired out. Get rid of it and get into something that promises another good race. Sentiment has no place when it comes to investing money.

In this ever-changing economy, moreover, there is no room for prejudice. I might buy into a glue factory if I thought the price was right. After all, I don't have to live next door to it. Not long ago, a manufacturer of dress patterns would not have been considered an ideal candidate for listing by some of the stuffy people of the New York Stock Exchange. Today the Simplicity Pattern Company is a highly respected entity on the trading floor. It has an enviable earnings record. Simplicity has sewed up more than half of the $150-million pattern market, and its 1970 sales were substantially ahead of the preceding year's record. Its 1970 earnings were about 20 percent higher than in 1969. Not many corporations fared that well.

Home sewing is a $3-billion industry today. Business in this area is good when the economy booms and equally good when it is dragging its feet. Seemingly, it is all part and parcel of our changing social environment. A lot of women crave creative outlets, and home sewing is one way of satisfying this desire. Today's living also demands more changes of clothes, and home sewing allows greater flexibility, not to mention savings on clothing expenditures. Whatever the cause for the boom in home sewing, you would have done far better in 1967 to invest money in the Simplicity Pattern Company than in the mighty U.S. Steel Corporation or the gigantic Alcan Aluminum Company.

The higher per capita disposable income goes, the more we are inclined to step up spending on services. Those connected with health and recreational activities and financial needs will take more and more of the consumer dollar.

Other Forms of Investments

Although this is a book on the art of investing in securities, I should say something about other forms of investments.

Stamps. As a philatelist, I can say with conviction, "Forget about it," unless you really know something about philately and the quirks of philatelists. The spread between bids and offers is very high. You will find that you always pay the retail price when you buy, but when you want to sell, it is invariably at wholesale prices. The bid may be as much as 50 percent below the offering price or even more, and the liquidity of the investment often depends on the whims of collectors.

Paintings. A well-known British gallery estimated that

paintings by Monet gained 1,100 percent between 1951 and 1967, and Renoirs, 400 percent. You could probably have done just as well or better by investing in Jersey Standard or IBM during these years. Moreover, Jersey paid a very nice cash dividend throughout these years, and the spread between the bid and the offer is a great deal less with securities than with paintings. The selling commission is also a lot less. Besides, there is no SEC in the painting business, and you can easily get stuck.

Real Estate. If you know what you are doing, fine. But a developing urban blight could reduce the value of your property substantially. Real estate does enjoy some unique tax advantages. You may depreciate the property when actually its value is increasing, and carrying charges such as mortgage interest and taxes receive favorable treatment from the tax collectors. However, real estate does not enjoy the liquidity possessed by actively traded securities, and commissions are higher than New York Stock Exchange commissions.

Instead of outright real estate commitments, you might well take a good look at real estate trusts.

Real Estate Trusts

In 1960 the Congress created REITs, real estate investment trusts, in an effort to make capital available to real estate promoters and builders. Since then four general categories of these trusts have developed.

The first form was the pure REIT, an equity trust, which invested in real estate depreciable property. Income, partly tax-exempt, was distributed to shareholders. The trust's income is derived from rental income of acquired properties and from capital gains of properties that were sold. It was something new, and investors didn't particularly go for it.

The second type is the MIT, the mortgage investment trust. It goes in for construction and development loans. Its revenue comes from interest and fees. The pioneers were First Mortgage Investors and Continental Mortgage Investors, both now traded on the New York Stock Exchange. Both these trusts have shown a steady earnings growth, and investors seem to like them.

The third type is the trust that provides long-term and even permanent financing at relatively high interest rates. At times there is an equity kicker in the deal. Investors like this type of trust. Connecticut General Mortgage and Real Estate Investors, listed on the NYSE, are good examples.

Finally there is a catchall category of "mixed trusts." It includes real estate investment trusts that specialize in particular areas such as medical buildings or in a mixture of equity properties and construction financing.

If you like real estate investments and leverage, you might learn about REITs, MITs, and mixtures thereof. But before buying shares, check up on their individual managements. How skilled are they? Is there a professional and highly motivated *team?*

A Word about Antiques

Art objects carry their own peculiar risk. They could be forgeries. There are factories that turn out "antiques." Antiques are also easily damaged. The following may get that point across.

In the 1960s a very charming lady had bought an antique Tiffany glass lamp with a rare, exotic, and valuable blue peacock-feather pattern for $350. She thought of her purchase as another form of investment and was delighted with her acquisition when its sale value rose and rose, eventually to $1,200. Here was the perfect investment: substantial appreciation, and continued enjoyment as she gazed daily upon her beautiful lamp.

Early one morning it happened. Madame's bedside telephone rang. Sleepily she reached over for the telephone and knocked her beautiful investment to the floor. She said later, after she recovered, that it was a sound like the most beautiful chimes. The valuable Tiffany investment was no more. The moral of the story: Stocks and lamps can both go to pieces, but stocks can come back—lamps never.

So treat "investments" in art objects as out-and-out luxuries. Enjoy your Corot or your Wyeth or triangular Cape of Good

Hope stamps, but don't calculate how much they are worth by the offers made for them. Besides, they could all be forgeries.

Scared Money Never Made a Buck

Don't be afraid to make guarded optimistic assumptions. A successful life is based on them. Every generation throughout history, including the present one, has those who say that the world is surely going to the dogs. But so far the dogs have had nothing but a good long wait. The optimists, meanwhile, are the ones who have made money and, some, even great fortunes. The pessimists who hoarded their cash, afraid to give up liquidity lest they need it in the next crushing catastrophe, have been losing a lot of their money to the erosion of purchasing power. You won't get your share by hoarding your money or seeking "safe" investments.

Your Right Arm—A Good Broker

From what I have told you here it should be clear that you cannot leave the management of your funds to an account executive. There are very few who can handle it for you. If you should be so fortunate as to have one of these brokers, treat him well, for he is a very busy man with a seven-day work week. Don't ask him for prices after the market closes; he may growl at you (and you'd deserve it), "Haven't you got fifteen cents to buy the evening paper?" He has more important things to do in your interest than to give you prices or to tell you what the averages are doing.

If your broker wants to sell a stock on which you have made three or four points' profit, don't jump to the conclusion that he has larceny in his heart and is out to earn two commissions. By all means, check his recommendation. There are times when you ought to take your points, run, and go into another stock. Try your account executive out a little. If you find him trustworthy, trust him, and disclose your investment problem to him. Don't give him a rough time with a lot of "but's" and "and's." If you do not find him trustworthy, transfer your account to another firm or hire the professional management of an investment company or investment advisory firm.

Summary

1. The second trillion dollars in GNP should be a reality by the end of 1982. Will you get YOUR share?

2. Start reading more. There is no shortcut to mastering the art of investing.

3. Learn to formulate rational investment decisions and apply them irrationally. After all, this is an irrational world.

4. The process of successful investing will remain an art forever.

5. There is no such thing as a "safe" investment.

6. Money in the bank isn't working for you.

7. The best inflation hedges are good growth stocks in leveraged companies.

8. Buy into companies with low labor costs, and seek out companies with flexible pricing structures.

9. Prejudice in investing can cost you a lot of money.

10. It might be better to buy into a maker of dress patterns than of steel beams.

11. Stocks and antiques can both go to pieces, but stocks can come back—your Sèvres vase never.

12. Scared money never made a buck.

CHAPTER 2

How Shall I Plan My Investments?

Have you ever taken a good look at a sturdy, four-legged table? It will nicely support your next Thanksgiving spread, but it might bend a little in the middle. Your investment program ought to be like that. It too should have four supports and bend a little when extra weight is put on it.

One, *liquid funds* for an emergency, in the form of government savings bonds or a savings account. The loan value of a permanent life insurance policy might also be included. If we should then encounter another depressed market, as in 1970, you won't have to sell securities at an unfavorable price, or at a loss, in order to get your hands on some cash for emergencies.

Two, *proper* life and health *insurance coverage,* and don't forget adequate public liability coverage in case somebody falls over your kid's roller skates. Taking out a suitable life insurance policy is the quickest way to create an estate. But remember, life insurance is designed for protection, and rare indeed is the individual who does not need it. It is a very mediocre investment. Perhaps your financial program can include some term life insurance coverage under a voluntary accumulation program with a good mutual fund. This group life protection is dirt cheap.

Three, *properly financed home ownership.* You will probably carry an insured mortgage in which the amount of life insurance decreases as the mortgage decreases. Let there be a built-in gap between the two. In case of death of the insured, the beneficiary will have the home free and clear, but what happens if a new furnace or roof job is needed? Such unforeseen emergencies could twist a financial program out of shape. Of course, if you live in a rented apartment or house, you can skip this point. However, most people eventually buy an apartment or a house and the two- and three-car family is rapidly becoming a two-home family, with a summer home in the Green Mountains or a winter home in the South, for example.

Four. Now you are ready for *investments* in securities. They should be attuned to your individual investment objective. The investment department store has many sections, and each has many items. You can't possibly know what to buy unless your investment objective is firmly established and you use it as a frame of reference for all investment decisions.

Bits and Pieces Everywhere

These four items make up your overall *financial program.* It must be properly planned so that it hangs together and each part does the job assigned to it. The smaller your estate, the more important is proper financial planning.

Personal economic security is usually highly fragmented, with bits scattered all over, ranging from social security benefits, partly or wholly vested pension benefits, group life insurance, individual life insurance policies, bank accounts, to real estate (with or without antiques and other art objects of value), to a bundle of securities. An integrated program must be worked out and periodically revised as conditions change. Securities investment undoubtedly plays a key role in it. Some flexibility within the investment objective is advisable, not to say necessary, so that our investments can act as a shock absorber, softening the bumps in the road of life that are now and then encountered.

Analyze and THINK

Sit down now. Analyze your needs and formulate *your investment objective.* Once that has been done, paste it into your hat, and every time you take it off, look at it. Don't permit fear, hope, or greed to turn you from your chosen path. It is all too easy to stray imperceptibly from it, so that after a number of trades have been made, the portfolio has little or nothing in common with your original investment objective. In a rising market, investors tend to take profits and then try to find cheap stocks to replace the securities sold so that they can do it all over again— that is, buy low and sell high. This money game works for a while, until the inevitable time in this cyclical securities industry when the market falls out of bed. At that point the quality of the portfolio has been diluted and losses will be high.

There are times when it is wise to get out of stocks completely, regardless of unrealized profits or losses, and take refuge in the storm cellar of the short-term money market or the bond market until a better investment climate has been restored. Even stock money sometimes works best for you when it is temporarily invested in a short-term Treasury bill or top-grade commercial paper.

If the stock deserves to be held, hold it. Let your profits run, and don't fall for the line that the only way we can know that we have made profits is to take them. It makes no sense to shoot the horses that are winning races and to keep the others. But once there are good reasons to sell a stock, taxes should not stand in the way. Many an investor has ridden a stock up and then down again simply because he "couldn't afford to sell" in view of the tax bill. That makes no sense. If there is no other reason to hold a stock than the tax collector, you have a very poor reason for hanging on to it.

What Is your Investment Objective?

With these introductory thoughts in mind, let's now figure out what your wants and needs are. Do you need income? Growth? Perhaps a combination of the two with greater emphasis on income, or the sacrifice of some income in order to achieve greater growth? Or can a general trading account be set up on a cash or margin basis?

If *income* is needed, don't forget that dividends are sometimes cut or entirely "passed," that is, not paid. Do you have flexibility of income needs so that a 10 to 15 percent income shrinkage does not create problems? Or is steady dependable income so needed that it would be better to consider the purchase of high-grade bonds? But don't buy your bonds at the wrong time in the interest-rate cycle. Stay away from long-term bonds when the trend is toward higher interest rates, for they will inevitably decline in price and you will be far better off, both as to income and capital, if you postpone their purchase.

Some investors were very happy to buy the 6-percent A-rated bonds of the Aluminum Company of America when they came out in 1967. That was more than the bank was paying in interest. Had they waited until 1970, they could have bought a 9-percent bond of the same company. In the interval, money invested in short-term government or corporate bills or notes would have brought more than 6 percent. By the end of 1971 the Alcoa sixes were selling at $880 for a $1,000 bond; the Alcoa nines were at a nice premium, at $1,110 for a $1,000 bond.

How much risk is there if you establish *growth* as an objective, with income secondary? Be careful about reaching for "a second income." It might throw you into a higher income tax bracket. In that case, you will be better off to stick to a simple growth objective. When you feel like having a little extra cash, you can always sell a few shares.

Growth companies, in order to conserve cash they need for expansion, often pay stock dividends rather than cash dividends. You can sell such dividend shares and still pay the lower long-term capital-gains tax if the old stock was in your possession in excess of six months. Growth stocks are also frequently split, and this will increase the number of shares in the portfolio.

Sock 'Em Away and Forget 'Em

Many investors are looking for a more or less permanent investment that will give them an acceptable return and appreciation of capital to counteract the decrease in the purchasing power of our money. They also want to feel sure that the investment can be liquidated promptly should the need for funds arise. Can this kind of investment be found? Yes, but you will have to do some looking around to find it.

Let's take an individual thirty years of age in 1938. He could have put $10,000 in Founder's Mutual Fund, which was created in that year. It was set up on the basis of a fixed blue-chip list of forty stocks, and until 1971 the list didn't change. This is the "sock 'em away and forget 'em" investment policy that Wall Streeters scoff at. How well would our young man have done with his money? Very well.

The $10,000 would have been worth a whopping $188,503, on September 30, 1969, a more than adequate compensation for the erosion of the dollar's purchasing power. During the 1969–1970 debacle, Founder's only went down 9 percent, while the average mutual fund slipped 18 percent. In 1971 the fund not only made up the loss, but added to the $188,503 value. The funds holding blue chips made the best recovery. One of the prerequisites for reasonable mastery of the art of investing is not to worry about the stock market's ripples. You can afford to miss them. You can even miss the waves. Just don't miss the tides.

However, don't go overboard on the "put 'em away and forget 'em" technique. Even Founder's Mutual Fund, now a part of Downe Communications, had its clinkers. Over those thirty-some years, money could have been more advantageously invested in securities other than U.S. Steel, Du Pont, Air Reduction, or Union Carbide. Successful *individual* investing requires an occasional look-see in this jet-propelled economy of ours. The program must have a reasonable built-in flexibility, and like successful living, it requires intelligent compromises.

Riding the Ripples and the Waves

A *trader* can make more money than the long-term investor if he takes advantage of short-run fluctuations in the market. Let's say a stock doubles in value over a five-year period. Suppose a trader makes twenty-five trades over five years. His capital could then increase much more than that of the investor, who is in for the long pull. Trading means not only buying and selling the purchased securities. It also means going short at times. If you think a stock is overpriced at fifty dollars and you decide to take your profits, then why not make twice as much and sell the stock short when you get out of it?

Trading raises a lot of questions. Can you spare the time to follow the market closely? Will you neglect your primary business? Have you the temperament to trade, to take risks on the long and especially on the short side of the market? If so, go ahead and trade, and do it in a margin account. You can thus buy over 500 shares instead of 300 shares, or 200 convertible bonds instead of 100. To make money as a good trader requires leverage. But operating with your own capital and borrowed money also means that your risk is greater. Can you assume it, mentally, physically, and above all, financially?

Compromises Must Be Made

Your investment objective has been established. As an investor for income or growth or a predetermined mixture of the two, you cannot buy everything you see that looks good. If you try, sooner or later you will be in serious trouble. You must make certain compromises. The trader, on the other hand, has his mind set on specific goals. He either succeeds in reaching them or fails and licks his wounds.

When we reach out for more income through the purchase of public or corporate bonds, we expose ourselves to a money risk that could spell insufferable losses if interest rates should rise substantially and liquidation become necessary. A compromise in quality exposes the investor to a credit risk. Need for tax exemption will reduce income and still expose the investment to a money risk and possible credit risk. Public bodies *can* default. People sometimes have surprising ideas about this. The well-known financial editor Sam Shulsky reported some time ago that an individual had written him: "I've heard that some municipal bonds pay 10 percent—tax-exempt—and are perfectly safe." Either the inquiring investor read or heard wrongly or the question concerned an unspeakably low-quality bond that temporarily paid such a yield.

Should growth be your investment objective, stability, income, and possibly even tax exemption will have to be foregone. A bond bought on the eve of steadily falling interest rates will appreciate in value. Growth stocks, however, are notoriously volatile, and they pay little or no cash dividends. Even a blue chip such as IBM fluctuated between 387 and 212¾ in 1970 and the yield was less than 2 percent.

There Is Always a Risk Element

All human decisions entail a risk. When we go to a party, somebody's sneeze—forty thousand-plus germs—can give us a miserable head cold. A safari in Africa may expose us to cholera. Crossing streets carries the risk of an idiotic driver running a red light as we cross on the green. Even a one-way street requires looking both ways. There is always a chance of somebody coming from the wrong direction. How many of us, at one time or another, have driven down a one-way street the wrong way? We can to some degree, protect ourselves against these hazards by exercising caution.

Who crosses a street in the face of on-rushing traffic? Such a person would probably buy bonds in the face of an ever-tightening money supply. Don't buy housing stocks or shares in savings and loan associations when interest rates are rising and available savings and mortgage money decrease. Only a congenital idiot will sell a three-dollar stock short. Something can always come along that could drive the price of the stock to fifteen dollars, so that the most you can make, if you are right, is three dollars before commissions. Risk and the reward for assuming it must stand in a proper relationship.

See to it that the odds are reasonably in your favor, and then act. Why commit funds when the odds are against you? It's silly to do so. As long as you adhere to the policy "The odds must favor me," the odds WILL be in your favor to achieve your goal and even exceed it.

Selecting an Issue

Assume you have decided that your investment objective is long-term growth. While additional income is welcome, it is distinctly a minor consideration. After looking at some high-quality equities, the decision is made to buy shares in the Eastman Kodak Company.

The reasons for the selection in the early fall of 1970 would be many:

Market Action. The stock at 61 was close to its historic low of 57⅝. In 1970 it had reached a high of 84⅜ as well as its low. In 1969 the low was 68⅜ and the high, 83⅜. There are over 161 million shares outstanding, and this assures a large floating supply of the stock. A substantial volume is thus traded daily on the New York Stock Exchange, so that the stock could easily be sold should liquidation become necessary.

At 61, EK was selling at a price-earnings ratio of slightly less than 24. Only twice in the 1960s had the stock sold at a lower price-earnings ratio; once at 22, in 1965, and once at 23 times earnings, in 1962. The average on the high side for the decade was almost 35. The odds will always be in your favor if you buy a stock at a low P/E ratio, for as earnings continue to rise and the stock sells at a more normal P/E ratio, the investor has two strings to his investment bow. The favorable price action caused by higher earnings is reinforced by the higher P/E ratio.

Earnings were higher in every year during the 1960s. At a P/E ratio of 24, the stock would have gone from about 19 to about 60 by the end of the decade. Let's be conservative and say that a more normal P/E ratio would be 30. In that case EK would have sold at about 24 in 1960 and at 70 in 1969. These data have been adjusted for a 2-for-1 split in 1968 and 1965 and a 5-percent stock dividend in 1964.

Its cash dividend is small. It was only $1.28 in 1970, giving a yield of about 2 percent at a price of $61. Half of its earnings were plowed back in the six years prior to 1970. Therefore about another $1.28 continues to work for the investor-owners. A dividend has been paid continuously since 1902. Standard and Poor's gives EK an earnings and dividend ranking of A-plus. This is based on scientific weighting of earnings and dividends.

Prospects. Total sales of EK went from $945 million to $2,747 million during the sixties. Net income was even better. It rose from $127 million to $401 million. But it is tomorrow's score we are after. Past earnings are important as a possible trend indicator, but the real emphasis must be put on the earnings for the 1970s. Kodak's capital expansion program coupled with the large research and development expenditures augurs well for the future.

Research and development expenditures were $149 million in 1969. That is better than 5 percent of sales. For worldwide capital expenditures the company budgeted $374 million in 1970, almost $100 million more than in 1969. These sums give assurance that the company will bring out new products and that there will be the facilities to exploit markets and products. As per capita income continues to rise in this decade here and abroad, the demand for photographic equipment and supplies will certainly increase.

Photographic equipment and supplies account for 80 percent of EK's sales. Of this, about 60 percent is believed to go to commercial and professional outlets and the other 40 percent is in a fast-growing amateur market. The remaining 20 percent of sales, over half a billion dollars, is distributed among chemicals, synthetic fibers, and plastics. Private domestic sales were 60 percent of the sales total in 1969, and the government accounted for another 9 percent, so that almost one-third of total revenue, 31 percent to be exact, was derived from foreign sources.

Eastman Kodak has big plans for the 1970s. It wants to go into the instant photography market with its own products by the middle of the decade. Moreover, a 1969 agreement with the Polaroid Corporation gives the company a license to manufacture and distribute the Polaroid Type 108 film later in the 1970s.

Financial Condition. Making beautiful plans is one thing. Financing them is quite another. Does EK have the money to do all those things? Yes indeed. Its net working capital went from $374 million to $885 million during the 1960s. In this period the ratio between current assets and current liabilities never dipped below 2.2:1, very good for an industrial company. Such a financial policy indicates that Kodak will have no problems in carrying on normal business activities, while expanding its sales, and in meeting emergencies should they arise.

Cash generated from internal sources amounted to $3.32 per share in 1969. With over 161 million shares outstanding, this amounts to well over half a billion dollars. In other words, no outside financing was needed to carry out research and development and capital expansion programs.

There is even leverage in the capital structure—about $100 million of long-term debt. Of this amount, $70 million in 20-year bonds was sold in 1968 in the Euro-bond market at a very agreeable interest rate of 4 percent. The debentures are convertible into common shares at $96 a share. Should EK have to take to outside financing, straight or convertible debt, or equity financing, it would find institutional and individual investors most receptive toward its new securities.

How would you have fared had you bought EK at $61 in the early fall of 1970? Not badly. On December 9, 1971, the stock closed at $92¾. You could have taken a long-term capital gain and had money left for a winter vacation. But it would have been better to resist the temptation to sell. After all, the assumption is that your investment objective is long-term growth. And so you will stay in EK. It isn't a bad medium with which to get your share of the second trillion dollars in the GNP. In February, 1972, it traded at 108.

Always Look before You Leap

When buying stocks for long-term growth, do what we did here. Look at market action, earnings, dividends, and P/E ratios. Search for the factors that will support the prospects of future growth. Above all, review the company's financial condition and its internal cash-generating ability. If management must sell new stock because it is saddled with large long-term debt, you will share the bigger projected earnings with others and the new per-share earnings will be that much less, the result of the dilution of the equity. For a good growth rate, zero in on the company that can finance itself primarily out of its own internal sources. A reasonable amount of long-term debt will work in favor of the shareholders.

If the capital raised through the sale of bonds costs 5 percent per annum and the company can earn 10 percent on its invested gross capital, then every dollar of debt will add to the earnings available for the shareholders. And interest costs are tax-deductible items! A good growth company with some lever-age in its financial structure makes a good anti-inflation hedge, besides assuring a nice nest egg on retirement.

After reading Chapter 15, which deals with the tools in-vestors can use to make big money, you might wish to take an-other look at this case study of the Eastman Kodak Company. Get yourself a copy of the annual report of the corporation and ask the kind of questions that were raised here about EK. The report will give you a ten-year history, and the message by the chairman or the president usually presents management's plans for the future.

Candidates for Long-Term Growth

Other candidates for long-term growth are these:

Corning Glass Works
Disney Productions
General Electric
Gulf Oil
IBM
International Nickel
Schlumberger Ltd.
Upjohn Company

Remember that no security should be put away and forgot-ten. Please don't keep securities at home. If anything should happen—a fire, theft, or mysterious disappearance—you will have a dreadful time until you receive another certificate, and it will cost quite a bit because you have to put up a perpetual bond. Securities require watching, but that doesn't mean one has to look at them every week. Once a year or once every two years, re-view your holdings. Maybe you should take your profit and invest in another stock that might grow faster. This brings us to the "opportunity cost," one of the most important concepts in business and finance.

The opportunity cost of an investment decision is the sacri-fice of alternatives foregone by your decision. The opportunity cost of the money in stock A is the dividend and profit (corrected for any differences in risk!) differential that could be earned if the money was in stock B. In other words, if you stay in an issue that grows at a rate of 10 percent a year and could switch to another issue carrying no greater risk with a growth rate of 15 percent, the extra 5 percent is the opportunity cost for staying with the slower-growing company. And 5 percent compounded annually means that that capital will double in fourteen years. Growth-rate differentials are therefore very important.

Growth stocks, even the best, can fluctuate by as much as 50 percent over a cycle of five years or less. If your *income* investment objective does not permit you to take such risks, what should you buy? Answer: A so-called defensive stock.

Defensive Stocks

Defensive stocks are equities whose earnings aren't particularly affected by a change in the economic weather. In a business recession, consumers might not buy automobiles or other durable goods, but they won't give up grocery store purchases. On the contrary, they might spend more time at home, drink more beer, and eat more snacks. They won't turn off the gas or electricity, eat cold food, and sit in the dark. They won't use less soap. Consumption of soap products might go up because the wash may be done at home.

Stocks in food companies, utilities, and in firms that enjoy an inelastic demand for their products, such as soaps and personal care items, make good defensive securities. The stock of a good, large bank might also be included.

Such equities tend to be less affected by the vagaries of the stock market than the typical industrial issues. Therefore they appeal to those investors who cannot assume the risk that even IBM shares carry. Of course, the growth prospects are less than those of the candidates given for long-term growth. But the yields will be better.

A list of defensive issues, with above-average quality and with yields more or less comparable to those obtainable on ordinary bank savings accounts, might include the following:

CPC International, Inc.
Chase Manhattan Corporation
El Paso Natural Gas Company
Great Atlantic and Pacific Tea Company
National Biscuit Company
Reynolds (R. J.) Industries
Public Service Electric and Gas

The concept of a defensive issue is, however, not something fixed for all time; it is constantly changing. For example, utility stocks were not very good defensive investments in 1969–1970. As interest rates rose higher and higher as a result of the Federal Reserve's restrictive monetary policy, utilities went down. Tobacco stocks are probably not as good defensive investments as they once were, because of the health issue. On the other hand, the successful diversification program of the quondam R. J. Reynolds Tobacco Company into food and shipping made it more interesting as a growth medium at a fairly attractive yield. But even with defensive issues, the investor should never ignore earnings trends and financial developments. Declining earnings and a worsening working-capital position can cause as much trouble as with any other security.

Dividend Reinvestment Plans

If you are thinking of reinvesting dividends, you might be interested in companies such as Allegheny Power, AT&T, Dow Chemical, Gamble-Skogmo, or Stewart-Warner, all stocks traded on the Big Board. Shareholders in these companies need only authorize a bank designated by the company to receive their dividend checks. They are then used to buy more shares including fractions for them.

The advantage of this plan is that you pay a lower commission through a bank than through a broker. On AT&T the cost to you will be less than a nickel a share in contrast to $2.50 a share. Moreover, you will save the odd-lot differential, for the bank will lump dividend checks together and buy in round lots over a period of days. The prices paid each day are averaged, and all shareholders participating in the plan pay the same price. As time passes, more companies will surely accept such a dividend reinvestment plan. For the small investor it is one answer to high commission charges.

Areas of Great Future Growth

The following twelve sectors of our economy should do particularly well in the 1970s and beyond:

Banking	Chemicals
Cosmetics and drugs	Electric utilities
Electrical equipment	Electronics
Food processors	Hospital stocks
Household products	Housing
Petroleum industry	Pollution control

Not only are more banking services needed, but banks are also diversifying through the one-bank holding company. We cannot move from the one- to the two-trillion-dollar economy without an expanding chemical industry, without more electric power, more transmission equipment, and more petroleum products. Scientists are now making progress in hydrogen fusion power, tapping the H-bomb, which involves no radioactive waste, pollution, or explosion risk, and fuel costs could drop dramatically, perhaps to 1 percent of the present price of coal.

More people, an increasing rate of household formation, plus greater affluence will mean that more apartments and houses will have to be built and furnished and more food consumed. A new investment area is hospital stocks. The New York Stock Exchange lists several companies (American Medical Enterprises and Hospital Corporation of America) that specialize in general hospital operation. Other hospital stocks are traded on the Amex and in the over-the-counter market. Outlays for health and medical care were about $70 billion in 1970. Drug consumption will also rise, as will expenditures for cosmetics.

Risks will vary in these sectors. Electronics, hospital, and pollution control stocks need careful watching. There will be some new companies that will make it BIG. Others will be absorbed or fall by the wayside. Pioneering rarely pays for the investor.

The United States is increasingly becoming more of a service economy. Gone are the days when most Americans were employed in industry and agriculture. Today less than 40 percent of the work force is engaged in making tangible goods. This means that the service sector is of increasing interest to the investor.

Representative service firms range from Doyle Dane Bernbach (advertising), Allied Maintenance (cleaning services and plane fueling), H. & R. Block (income tax returns), to Hilton Hotels, Leaseway Transportation (everything in motor vehicles), to the diversified services of Kinney National Service.

There are also the so-called rack-jobbers, a $2-billion-plus business, distributing nonfood items to all types of retail stores. Pickwick International sells phonograph records.

With a high crime rate, security services have come into their own. The Wackenhut Corporation or Burns (William J.) International Detective Agency might be mentioned in this connection.

The investment scene is ever changing. It needs alert watching.

Summary

1. Your investment program should have four sturdy legs.
2. Establish your investment objective and stick to it.
3. If you don't watch out, you will stray from your objective.
4. Incorporate flexibility in your investment program.
5. You can miss the ripples and the waves, but don't miss the tides.
6. If income is essential, remember that dividends can be cut and bond prices decline at times.
7. If you're out for growth, maybe you can sock 'em away and forget 'em. Still, an occasional look-see is always a good idea.
8. Try to buy a stock with a rising earnings pattern at a low P/E ratio. Keep your eyes open. It can be done.
9. Search for factors that support indicated prospects of future growth.

Part II

What Equities or Equities Equivalents?

CHAPTER 3

Should I Buy Common Stocks

or Preferred Stocks?

The question whether you should buy stocks has the same answer so many personal finance questions have, namely, "It all depends." It depends primarily on your ability to assume risks. Even the bluest of blue chips, from IBM on down, have declined by as much as 50 percent over a three- to five-year cycle. If you had needed money at the low points and had had to liquidate part or all of your investment, you would have suffered substantial losses.

One of the greatest if not *the greatest* threat to your capital is continued inflation. Just as heavy rains can erode the foundation of your beautiful hilltop home, so inflation can erode your capital structure until it can no longer serve its original purpose. Shares, common stocks, in properly chosen businesses guard very well indeed against this danger.

In view of the nature of preferred stocks, we must rule them out as inflation hedges. They are more in the category of debt instruments, and usually purchased at lower yields than comparable bonds, even though they have no maturity date.

I often have marveled at how people can own common stocks for years and still not understand their nature. The purchase of a share of stock makes the investor a part owner of the company—with all its privileges, troubles, assets, and liabilities. If the company has a million shares outstanding and a net worth of $10 million, then each share has a book value of $10 no matter what the certificate gives as par value. Whether it is par or nonpar value stock, stated value has no meaning whatsoever for the investor. The market price is another question. How much are investors willing to pay for a dollar's worth of current earnings—$10? $20? $50? $60? That depends on investor confidence, optimism, or pessimism.

The Importance of Book Value

The importance of book value is often exaggerated. Taken by itself, it is of little or no help in assessing the intrinsic worth of an *industrial* stock. Invariably a market letter gives the price of a stock, say, 28, and then, in parentheses, the book value of 48. It tends to give the reader the impression, "Gee, that stock is cheap." As the song goes, it ain't necessarily so. One company may keep its assets on the books at relatively high values. Another company, in the same industry, depreciates equipment at a rapid rate; its book value is thus much lower. Some companies do not show valuable patents or trademarks, or else they show them at nominal values in the belief that the income account offers a better clue to value than the balance sheet. A patent may be worth a lot of money today, but tomorrow it may be valueless if something supersedes it.

In other than liquidation cases, book value is only one factor taken into consideration when analyzing a security. Among the many other items—such as earnings and dividends, assets and liabilities, operating statistics, management, labor relations, and so on—the security analyst may give no more than a weight of 10 percent to book value. Yet there is always the exceptional case in which book value is important. Assets, currently not very productive, as measured by a ratio of sales to fixed assets (plant and equipment), might become more productive under better management. Somebody might take over the company and make something out of it.

The preceding does not apply to the common stocks of *public utilities and financial companies.* Here book value is quite important. The rates allowed by regulatory agencies may be largely determined by the value of the utility's assets. Nothing in utilities regulation history receives as much attention as the valuation of property. Financial institutions such as banks, insurance companies, and investment companies are closely supervised in respect to accounting procedures; their assets are primarily evidence of debt or ownership rather than being fixed assets, so that book value here can provide a relevant check on the value that is based on other factors. One note of caution: During periods of high interest rates, there could be a considerable discrepancy between the market value of long-term government or municipal bonds and the value stated on the books of a bank. Life insurance regulatory agencies have also, at times, used arbitrary values in their appraisal of insurance companies when market prices for their securities and real estate were abnormally low.

How to Find Book Value

Look at the balance sheet in the annual report of one of your companies. The book value of a share of common stock is quickly found by taking the total of all the listed assets, excluding such intangible assets as goodwill, trademarks or patents, and deferred charges, subtracting all liabilities and any preferred stock issues. The difference is divided by the number of shares outstanding. Book value could also be found by adding up the common stock outstanding, at par or stated value, any surplus items, and any voluntary reserves such as reserves for unspecified contingencies or plant expansion minus the intangibles. This gives the owners' equity, which is then divided by the number of shares outstanding.

Treasury Stock

There are three terms with which every investor should be familiar: stock authorized, stock issued, and, especially, stock outstanding.

Stock authorized is the number of shares that the company can issue under its charter. Don't be alarmed if the company has 4 million shares authorized and 3 million already issued, and then management declares a 100-percent stock dividend or a 2-for-1 split. Where does the stock come from? No problem. It merely means the charter has to be amended.

Stock issued is the number of shares that have actually been issued. Usually a company wants to have authorization to issue more stock than that already issued, to give it financial flexibility. Stock might be issued in a merger.

The most interesting category is stock outstanding. You might see on a balance sheet: stock authorized, 4 million shares; issued, 3 million shares; outstanding, 2½ million shares. What happaned to the other 500,000 shares? They were reacquired by the company, usually through purchase. It is shown on the balance sheet as a deduction from stock issued. A big wad of "treasury stock" is always of interest to the investor.

Why did the company buy it? Possibly because it was ridiculously low in price and now provides cheap stock that might later be used in a merger with an advantageous exchange for stock of the firm to be taken over. Many companies bought substantial amounts of their stock in the bargain markets of 1970 and 1971. There could be another reason. Treasury stock does not vote and does not receive a dividend. Even if the company did not have an increase in earnings, with fewer shares outstanding, management can report an increase in per-share earnings. Don't misinterpret a reported increase in earnings under such conditions.

The Transfer Agent and the Registrar

When stock is bought, it is recorded on the stock record book of the transfer agent, which may be the corporation itself or, more usually, a bank or trust company. It is an agent of the corporation and responsible to it alone; the transfer agent cancels the certificate of the seller and issues a new certificate to the buyer. But before the new certificate becomes available for delivery, it is sent to a registrar, or to another bank or trust company, for checking purposes.

The registrar's function is that of an auditor. It is to guard the company and its shareholders against an overissue of stock. Financial history is replete with scandals involving the fraudulent issue of stock. The New York Stock Exchange insists that for all companies whose securities are traded on its floor "a registrar for a particular issue of stock listed on the Exchange shall not be identical with a transfer agent for such issue." The company may act as its own transfer agent; it can never act as its own registrar.

Late in 1971 the New York Stock Exchange amended its rules to allow an independent large bank or trust company to act as both transfer agent and registrar for any listed security other than its own *provided* it can assure the Exchange that it has appropriate internal accounting controls. The American Stock Exchange has for some time allowed such dual trust servicing. Such steps were taken by the exchanges in order to reduce the time consumed in transferring shares and thus prevent another "paper jam" as stock trading increases in volume.

Check stocks that were bought in the over-the-counter market. The registrar should always be a large bank or trust company. Unless it is large, shareholders will have little recourse in case something goes wrong.

Today the stock certificate is virtually obsolete. The massive, duplicate activity of transferring and delivering stock certificates presents grave problems to the investing public as well as to the finance industry. Without the certificate, brokerage firms and the trust departments of the large commercial banks would become more flexible, so that in periods of very active markets the "fails" (failures to deliver certificates on the fifth business day) would decrease. When "fails" run into the billions of dollars, as was the case during 1969 and 1970, it is difficult to ascertain whether a brokerage firm is solvent or not.

What will take the place of the stock certificate? Maybe an expanded Central Certificate Service for all brokers, under which transfers can be made easily. Don't be alarmed about the elimination of the stock certificate. It has to come over the next few years for your protection. Just as you keep money in the bank instead of in a cookie jar, so will you keep your stock certificates with your broker. Such bookkeeping is cheaper, safer, and more efficient than the ridiculous shuffling of papers.

The Voting of Shares

Ordinarily, common stockholders have one vote per share. In the past a great deal of nonvoting stock has been issued, but the trend is against it. Under the Public Utility Holding Company Act of 1935, the SEC may not approve the sale of non-voting common stock of a registered utility. Chapter X of the Federal Bankruptcy Act precludes the issue of nonvoting common stock of a reorganized company. Since 1926 the New York Stock Exchange has refused to authorize the listing of nonvoting stock "or of any non-voting stock, however designated, which by its terms is in effect a common stock." The Exchange goes farther than that. It refuses to list "the common voting stock of a company which also has outstanding in public hands a non-voting stock, however designated, which by its terms is in effect a common stock. . . ." The reason for such action is clear: The public would own a large amount of nonvoting stock, and a clique could control the company by virtue of a small investment and the 100-percent ownership of a small issue of fully voting stock.

Cumulative Voting

Under straight or statutory voting a shareholder has the right to cast one vote per share for each director to be elected. Under cumulative voting he may give all his votes to one directorial candidate. Suppose 12 directors are to be elected. A shareholder with 100 shares may then "cumulate" his 1,200 votes and cast them for one director, or cast 600 votes each for two directors, or he may divide his 1,200 votes as he wishes. A minority interest can thus put one or more directors on the board. Under straight voting a bare majority of 51 percent can elect all the directors.

Sometimes a company uses the stagger system. Instead of electing directors annually, only one-third of the directors come up for election each year. Should management lose the election one year, it would still have a two-thirds majority on the board. One can hardly say that it is a good thing for the company or the investor. Long-range plans could be hindered. Another company might shy away from a "staggered" company with which it might otherwise like to be affiliated. Shareholders may have lost confidence in current management, but they can't do anything about it; the old management can't be turned out. Moreover, the stagger system has the effect of requiring greater voting power on a cumulative voting basis to elect a single director. A 10-percent minority could quite easily elect one out of twelve directors if all the members of the board are elected at the same time. If only four are elected every year, it takes over 25 percent of the votes to elect a director. For that reason, managements that oppose cumulative voting or are afraid of tender and exchange offers that might result in a take-over like to bring in the stagger system.

Shareholders should be quite clear on this point. The stagger system makes it very difficult to root out an entrenched management that may not be acting in the best interest of the owners. The shareholder might say, "So what? I can always cast a no-confidence vote by selling the shares." True. But he will sell at a depressed price and might throw away potential values.

Will cumulative voting make managements more efficient, or will it create friction and develop a crippling caution in decision making? The question is not easy to answer. But dislike of cumulative voting is a very poor reason for introducing the stagger system. Some courts have declared that a statute providing for staggering is unconstitutional when it conflicts with cumulative voting rights.

Rights of Shareholders

The shareholders have the right to elect directors, by whatever method provided. The relationship between them and the owners, and their corporation should always be one of fairness and openness. Too many cases on record involving conflict of interests and secret profits corroborate this statement.

The courts give minority stockholders the right to sue on behalf of the corporation to compel an accounting from the board and to recover from a dishonest member of the corporation. Stockholders have a right to examine the company's books provided such a desire is not prompted by mere idle curiosity and provided the disclosure will not be used to the detriment of the firm.

Other stockholder rights include voting, usually with a two-thirds majority, on mergers or voting to cease business operations and make distribution of the remaining property after all prior claims have been met; to pass on any changes in the original contract between the company and its shareholders; to subscribe to new issues of common stock or securities convertible into common, subject to whatever restrictions exist under the laws of the state of incorporation or under the charter.

Outside Directors

Increasing emphasis is being placed on "outsiders" as members of boards of directors. The Exchange will not list a company unless provisions are made for the election of a minimum of two outsiders to the board. Otherwise there would be no difference between a management committee meeting and a session of the board. In the interest of the shareholders, it is good to have outsiders watching the affairs of the company. But if outside directors are just prestige names or cronies of the president who do not care to learn about the company and its industry, then there is little value in the appointment. When an individual is on ten or twelve boards, among them perhaps a major bank, a sprawling insurance company, an auto maker, and a large food-products concern, a conflict of interest can easily arise. The question also pops up: Has he enough time to do justice to each of these companies and their shareholders?

Dividends

Shareholders have no right to dividends until they are declared by the directors. Directors determine whether a dividend shall be paid and decide on its form. Rarely have the courts come to the aid of aggrieved stockholders who felt that they should have received a larger cash dividend. Courts are hesitant to substitute their judgment for that of management unless they are convinced that the directors were actuated by a motive other than the best interest of the shareholders.

Some companies pride themselves on the number of years they have been paying dividends without interruption. This can be misleading. They may have managed to stay on the regular dividend-payers list for decades by paying a pittance in bad years. This is quite different from a company that has been paying a steady or an increasing dividend. It shows, however, the anxiety of companies to retain their investment rating as a good-quality stock. Income-minded investors are willing to pay a higher P/E ratio for the stock of corporations with stable dividend records than for those with an erratic payment record.

Investors feel at times that a company with a large surplus should pay a larger cash dividend. This could be erroneous thinking, since there is no relationship between surplus and cash. Surplus is an evaluation account; it is determined by the value placed on the assets. Unless the company has ample cash resources, the surplus, the retained earnings have already been used; they are in the buildings, equipment, inventory, and so on. If a company is otherwise sound, there is nothing improper in borrowing money to pay a dividend.

Stock Dividends

When a stock dividend is paid, the surplus account is decreased and stock outstanding is correspondingly increased. There has been no change in the equity position of each shareholder. But if that is so, why give a stock dividend? There are several reasons for it:

In case of a 10-percent stock dividend, shareholders now receive dividends not on 100 shares, but on 110 shares. Their cash income is now higher. Moreover, cash is retained in the business. The rapidly expanding firm often has liquidity problems and deems it inadvisable to increase its cash drain by declaring large cash dividends. By paying dividends in stock, the owners receive something and are kept happy.

Stocks sell, at times, at very low P/E ratios, so that new

stock issues are difficult to market without undue dilution of the equity. On the other hand, management may not be able to add to its debt without inviting undue restrictions on its managerial freedom of action, so that the next round of financing must be common stock. An unreceptive stock market can make retained earnings a very important source of funds for a company. Stock dividends are then compulsory reinvestment of funds belonging to the owners. But if the money is put to good use, the rising per-share earnings and the higher price of the shares should compensate for that.

We can hardly say that compulsory reinvestment of earnings is bad for shareholders. One dollar of retained earnings is easily the equivalent of $2.25 paid in cash to a shareholder in the 50-percent income tax bracket. If the company were to sell new stock, he would only have one out of two dollars to reinvest and the other $.25 would be eaten up by the cost of floating the issue.

A large stock dividend of 50 or 100 percent might mean that management wants to see a lower price for the stock. In a rising market high-priced shares are often traded far less actively than lower-priced stocks within the popular trading range. The high-priced stocks then lag behind others in price appreciation, and this engenders less enthusiasm for the stock, so that its price is, consequently, further depressed. This is bad if the company should consider the sale of new stock. Instead of $90, the stock is about $45 after a 100-percent stock dividend. The lower price attracts investors and traders, and before long, expressed in terms of the old stock, the market price becomes higher. This is particularly true if the company announces an increase in the dividend rate with the 100-percent stock dividend and if investors are optimistic about the earnings outlook for the company. A 2-, 3-, or even a 5-percent stock dividend has, as a rule, little if any influence on the price of the stock.

Taxability of Stock Dividends

Since there has been no change in the equity position of the shareholder, a stock dividend is not taxable. But a distribution of common stock to preferred stockholders or of preferred stock to common stockholders is considered by the tax authorities as income and taxable as such. Here a change has occurred in the ownership position of the stockholder in the corporation.

If the common stockholder should sell his stock dividend, he would be taxed on a long-term capital-gains basis on any portion of the selling price that represented a capital gain to him. It makes no difference what shares are sold, provided the original stock was bought six months or more before.

If a stockholder has the option of receiving cash or stock, the stock dividend would be taxable. Distributions in stocks of other companies are also taxable upon receipt, except liquidating distributions and spin-offs (shares of stock of a subsidiary).

After prohibition became effective, in 1920, and again during World War II, some distillers paid a dividend in liquor that provided quite a fillip for their stock. When property cannot be distributed piecemeal, corporate property to be distributed can be put under a trust, and trust certificates are distributed as dividends. As the trusteed property is liquidated, the proceeds are distributed among the holders of the certificates. This type of dividend is generally taxable, unless tax authorities interpret it as a liquidating dividend.

Split-Ups or Split-Downs

As with a 100-percent stock dividend, there is no change in the stockholder's equity position with a 2-for-1 or 5-for-1 or any other split. For accounting purposes, there is a difference. In the case of a regular split, the par or stated value of the stock is correspondingly reduced. This is why we find some rather odd-looking par values. One share of General Motors has a par value of $1.66.

The reasons for splitting a stock are the same as those for declaring a large stock dividend—to reduce the price of the shares. Regular stock splits, as do large stock dividends, usually result in a broadening of public interest and an increase in the number of shareholders, the natural consequence of the greater number of shares available for trading. They tend to make for closer markets, reducing the spread between bid and asked prices.

The market price of a stock tends to rise before or immediately following the news of the split. After a few days the price tends to recede from the high as a result of the larger number of shares now available. Whether this happens, and to what extent, depends also on the company's dividend action.

Stockholders expect an increase in the dividend when a split is announced. The price is very often pushed up in anticipation of an increase rather than of the split itself. If the dividend is not raised, the price of the stock will decline before long because disappointed stockholders will sell. Since a company does not like to lose shareholders, the dividend rate is usually boosted when the stock is split. If you hold a cash-dividend-paying stock and the dividend is not raised when the split is announced, sell it. The odds are that the stock will be down in a matter of weeks.

There are, at times, 1,000-for-1 or even 2,000-for-1 splits. When a closed corporation goes public, the few shares held by the original incorporators, their families, or estates must be split in order to bring the price of the stock into an acceptable trading range and make enough shares available for the maintenance of reasonably good markets. Such a large split occurred when the stock of the Book-of-the-Month Club was listed on the Exchange. The ratio in itself has little significance. The purpose of such a split is to create a stock that will enjoy ready marketability.

Split-Downs or Reverse Splits

Split-downs or reverse splits occur when a company, having fallen among the low-priced "cats and dogs," wishes to increase the market value of its stock.

Stock exchanges sometimes force a company into a reverse split when the value of its stock has fallen below the minimum required for continued listing. Rather than have the stock delisted, the company complies. Good Wall Street houses forbid their account executives to recommend low-priced issues. This makes it difficult for a company whose stock is currently selling at a very low price to obtain good "sponsorship" for the stock. A reverse split may be in order. When properly used, it may be exactly what the financial doctor ordered. Even the best companies may encounter trouble at one time or another, particularly during their early years.

General Motors split its stock in 1920 in a 10:1 ratio. But troubles caused a price decline below $10. In 1924 the directors authorized a 1-for-4 reverse split. This is like changing four $5 bills for a $20 note. By 1927, as earnings improved, a series of regular splits was authorized.

American Depositary Receipts—The ADRs

The equivalent of a reverse or regular split can occur in connection with American Depositary Receipts. In order to facilitate the trading of foreign securities, a New York bank will release against foreign shares that it is holding abroad, American negotiable receipts called American Depositary Receipts or, more commonly, ADRs. Many foreign shares are traded on the Amex or the Big Board as well as in the OTC market on this basis. Japanese investors like low-priced stocks. We don't. For this reason, against every ten shares deposited abroad, the bank may release only one American depositary share. Don't get excited if the stock sells for $2 in Tokyo and $20 in the United States.

On September 17, 1970, the shares of the first Japanese company were traded on the Exchange, the Sony Corporation's ADRs. Each Sony ADR represents two shares of Sony common. Prior to listing, the stock was traded in the OTC market. But each ADR formerly represented ten shares. The reduction to two shares was necessary because Sony's ADRs were heavily held in large blocks by United States institutions. Sony needed the "regular split" to meet the Exchange's listing requirement of a minimum number of round-lot (one-hundred-share) shareholders.

Among foreign shares traded as ADRs on the Exchange are such companies as Unilever and Electrical and Musical Industries of Great Britain. While the ADR holder receives his dividends in dollars, a foreign devaluation will reduce his dividends because the bank receives pounds on its shares held abroad and must convert them into dollars at a lower rate. Investors are sometimes puzzled over the decrease in their dividends under such conditions. Appreciation of a foreign currency has the opposite results.

The purchase of Japanese ADRs is not only a good way to participate in the fabulous expansion of the Japanese economy, but also to avoid paying the interest-equalization tax that Americans must pay when purchasing foreign securities from a foreigner. Now that the Sony shares are traded on the Exchange, they can be bought from American sellers, as can the shares of in Japanese firms. The same thing applies to Brazilian ADRs. They could be a very rewarding investment!

The Advantage of Investing in Common Stock

The value of common shares of a good company can only go up over the years to come. As we approach our second trillion dollars in GNP, sales and earnings will increase. If the earnings are two dollars and the pay-out ratio 50 percent, one dollar is plowed back and starts working for you. The retained earnings make the shares worth more, since a share is a part of the company.

The best inflation hedge is common stocks in companies that own natural resources, below or above the ground, and have leverage in their financial structure. As long as the firm can earn more on borrowed money, or on the senior equity, than it pays the bond or preferred shareholders, the common shareholders will benefit by that difference. Since these payments are fixed by contract, as the company grows and general prices rise, less and less of earnings need be used for interest and repayment of borrowed money, and thus more and more is left for the owners.

Investing in common stocks will be particularly rewarding if they are bought at a low P/E ratio. Suppose you bought a stock that earns $1 at a price-earnings ratio of 10 in the depressed markets of 1970 that normally sold at a P/E ratio of 18. If the company increases its earnings to $1.50 and the stock sells again at its previous average ratio, its price would be $27. This is a double benefit—earnings up 50 percent and the stock up almost 300 percent. Stocks can always be bought, at least once in each decade, at very low or even historically low P/E ratios, because when things are going well the sky is the limit and when they go badly, individual and institutional investors are like lemmings in a suicidal run to the ocean.

Be careful about earnings used in a P/E ratio. To obtain it, the stock's market price is divided by annual earnings, after taxes. What earnings? Last year's estimated current earnings, or the last quarter multiplied by four? Are there nonrecurring earnings included, such as proceeds from the sale of property? Were there heavy write-offs? Sometimes an increase in earnings is due less to the ability of management than to the ingenuity of the accounting department.

Besides income, growth, and inflation hedge, stocks are attractive because they are liquid. They can be sold quickly with a small commission. Contrast that with postal stamps, paintings, or antiques! Beware, however, of thin over-the-counter markets. Bids can dry up fast, as the 1969–1970 bear market proved. This greatly encouraged listing on exchanges, because you can always buy or sell stock in a listed market.

Penny Stocks

Some people claim they have made a lot of money in low-priced stocks. Bought by the bushel, there may be some money makers among them. Bought singly, the odds are overwhelmingly against you. Not all penny-stock promoters are swindlers. But if the stock is sold over the telephone, your chance of losing money is 100 percent. There is a doctor in Evanston, Illinois, who can vouch for this. The doctor received a telephone call in 1968 from a Canadian broker who breathlessly described a mining company in Saskatchewan. He said the stock was a cinch to go up and was riskless. Without seeing a financial report or prospectus, the doctor bought twenty thousand shares of Lynbar Mining at three dollars. Within six months the stock was down to five cents and the SEC, charging violation of the registration and antifraud provisions of the Securities Act, obtained an injunction suspending the trading of Lynbar in the United States.

Insiders' Trading of Stocks

Read the column "Changes in Stockholdings Filed with Exchanges, SEC," which appears periodically in *The Wall Street*

Journal. Under the Securities Exchange Act of 1934, as amended in 1964, all public corporations with net assets of one million dollars or more and five hundred shareholders or more must register with the SEC. This requires the company to file financial reports with the Commission, conform to the proxy rules of the SEC, and disclose all trading in the company's stock by insiders (officers, directors, and owners of more than 10 percent of the stock). If insiders buy and sell their stock at a profit within a six-month period, it can be recaptured by the company. All it takes is one shareholder's suit.

These insider trading reports make interesting reading. Why, for example, did the chairman and president of Capital Cities Broadcasting (NYSE) increase his holdings to 82,894 shares in 1970? Why did the chairman of Hartfield-Zodys (Amex) up his holdings to 146,546 shares in addition to his wife's 85,702? Why did the president of Com-Share (OTC) reduce his holdings by 50 percent? Always look around. Quite often what you see, far more than what you hear, can help you make money.

A final word: Don't reach for dividends and don't buy them. The highest yields can be dangerous. Often stocks show their highest yields just before the dividend is either cut or "passed" (not paid).

Don't buy stocks just before a dividend date and sell them shortly thereafter, hoping to make a fast buck. On the ex-dividend date, the price of the stock is reduced by the amount of the dividend. If it is 30 cents, the reduction will be ⅜ of a point, 37½ cents. On the Exchange, stocks go ex-dividend (or ex-rights) on the fourth business day preceding the record date. The record date is the day set by the company on which all shareholders whose names appear on its books will receive the dividend. Buying dividends can be very profitable for the broker, rarely ever for the investor.

Preferred Stocks

Preferred stocks are hybrid securities, a cross between bonds and common stocks. They carry some voting power like an equity and a fixed return like a bond. They have priority over common stocks as to income and, usually, also a prior claim to assets in case of liquidation. But the preferred stockholders' rights are inferior to those of bondholders; they occupy a senior equity position.

Par Value. Most preferred stocks possess a par value of $100 or less. Some industrials and utilities, like Budd Company and Union Electric Company, have no par value. In that case the dividends and the asset priority are stated in terms of dollars. The Budd preferred is a $5 preferred, and the asset priority is $100.

Cumulative Provisions. Preferreds issued today are usually cumulative. Should a $6 dividend be passed this year, nothing can be paid on the common and $12 would be due next year. The dividends accumulate, but without interest. The arrearage must be paid before anything can be paid on the common; this constitutes pressure on management to clean it up. But don't bet on its being paid in cash. Usually such claims are settled by corporations paying out a little cash, and most or all of the arrearage is lifted by giving the preferred stockholders new securities with substantially lower market value than their claims. In other words, the company undergoes a recapitalization.

The opinion is prevalent that if directors decide to use earnings for capital improvements and pass the dividend on a noncumulative preferred, the claim to dividends is gone for good. Not so. In *Cintas v. American Car and Foundry* (1942) the decision was handed down that a noncumulative dividend cumulates if it is earned and not paid out. The preferred stockholders, in this case, were judged entitled to receive net profits of several previous years before any dividends could be paid on the common. This interpretation is a return to earlier legal principles that held that a company's profits are analogous to a trust fund held by the corporation for the benefit of the noncumulative preferred stockholders. So don't let anybody do you out of your dividends on a noncumulative preferred if the company earns them.

Participation. The participating preferred has become a rarity among newly issued securities. Why should the preferred shareholders be given a preferred position in regard to earnings and assets and then, to boot, share any remaining profits? Common shareholders don't like that kind of preference. In that case it is better to make the preferred convertible and sell it at a lower dividend rate.

Call Provisions. Public utility and industrial preferreds are almost always callable, with the call premium ranging up to 10 percent for the utilities and up to 20 percent for industrials. If it is an industrial preferred, it usually has a small sinking fund (amortization) requirement; utilities ordinarily carry no such provision.

Contingent Voting. The nature of a preferred stock depends on the contract between the company and the preferred stockholders. The Exchange requires that preferred owners have the right to elect at least two directors upon the default of the equivalent of six quarterly dividends. The default need not be consecutive. The contingent voting right remains in effect until the arrearage has been removed. It also insists that at least two-thirds of the outstanding preferred must agree to any charter or by-law amendments that would materially alter their rights. But voting and protective provisions vary a great deal. Illinois Power gives the preferred one vote with the right of cumulative voting for directors. In other cases, after failure to pay four quarterly dividends, preferred owners can elect a majority or the entire board of directors. This can be dangerous for common shareholders. When considering a preferred, find out what your protection is against future bond and other preferred issues.

Other Types. Companies sometimes have issued series or classes of preferred. Sold at different times, they have different dividend rates, and the contracts can differ considerably. Some series or classes enjoy different priorities in earnings; others rank evenly. In case of liquidation all outstanding preferreds are usually grouped together. Other companies have classified stock, A and B. The B is a regular common and the A usually a nonvoting, cumulative, callable, and sometimes participating preferred.

The Cleveland and Pittsburgh Railroad Company, operated under a lease by the Penn Central, has a noncallable $50 par 7-percent guaranteed stock outstanding. When our big railroad systems were put together, the parent companies would take over the entire physical facilities of a small line under a long-term lease. The rental fees were in the form of guaranteed dividends on the common. These dividends, or rental charges, are fixed charges for the lessee, like bond interest. This type of common stock is really a high-priority preferred.

Investment Characteristics. The return is usually limited, as in a bond. But a straight bond has greater priority, and failure to pay interest is an act of default; passing the preferred dividend carries no such penalty. A bond will also yield more today than a comparable preferred.

High-grade preferreds are, like bonds, subject to a money risk; should interest rates go up, their prices would go down. Both have the same purchasing power risk.

The right to buy new equity securities of the company is very limited, and so is the participation in management. There is usually no sharing in the future prosperity of the company; no inflation hedge exists.

For all these reasons, preferred stocks are not very attractive for the individual investor. But for the *corporate* investor, preferred stocks are good investments. Since the preferred dividend is not tax-deductible for the paying corporation, the corporate dividend recipient enjoys an 85-percent tax exemption on the dividend income from all industrial preferreds and most utility preferreds. This also applies to common stock dividends. But if a company has temporary idle surplus funds, it is better to put the money into high-grade preferreds and catch a few dividend payments than into common stock that fluctuates too much. Why buy fully taxable T-bills, commercial paper, or bank CDs, when an 85-percent tax exemption beckons on the preferred? Corporate investors have bid up the prices of preferreds, so that they yield less today than bonds.

Summary

1. Common stocks of growing, leveraged, natural-resources companies are good inflation hedges; preferred stocks are not.

2. Par value has no meaning for the investor. Book value could be quite interesting.

3. A big wad of treasury stock is always of interest. It might

foreshadow an acquisition or higher per-share earnings—at least temporarily.

4. A registrar is very important for your protection.

5. The stagger system of voting may mean you can't root out rascally directors. Cumulative voting, for good or bad, means minority representation on the board.

6. With outside directors there could be a conflict of interest.

7. Large stock dividends and splits make for more active trading of the stock.

8. Neither a split-down nor a split-up changes your equity position.

9. ADRs can help you to avoid the interest-equalization tax.

10. Reported insiders' trading of stocks can make interesting and profitable reading.

11. What earnings are being cited? Don't let them sell you a penny stock on the telephone.

12. Preferred stocks are today not for individuals, but the 85-percent tax exemption makes them very attractive to corporate investors.

CHAPTER 4

What Are the Chances for the Small Investor?

One of the hard-headed gnomes of Zurich's Bahnhofstrasse in the summer of 1970 looked thirty years ahead and asked, "What will the economy look like by the year 2000?" His answer: "The annual per capita GNP in the United States will be $10,000, calculated at the 1970 purchasing power of the dollar." Japan, he rated second, with a per capita GNP of $8,600. His very reasonable assumptions: Our present economic growth rate will continue more or less uninterrupted: no global war, only small wars fought with conventional weapons.

You shake your head in amazement and disbelief? Well, what would you have said to a forecast in 1940 that GNP by 1970 would rise from less than $100 billion to $1 trillion? Even if we discount price level increases, that was quite an accomplishment. Moreover, our quantitative indices say little or nothing about the qualitative changes that have occurred in both goods and services. And long-term economic forecasting has become remarkably accurate.

As far as the economic climate is concerned, the chances for the small investor have never been better. But he has to follow the rules for small investors if he wants to survive and grow. A lot of small investors lost their hard-earned savings in the bear market of 1969, or worse yet, sold out at the bottom in 1970. They swore they would never again go near the stock market and would henceforth put their money into the bank or United States Government securities. From their point of view, not only is this a regrettable decision, it is compounding a mistake.

The discussion in this chapter assumes that you have followed the steps suggested in Chapter 2 for planning your investment program and that you have money available to be invested in equity securities, in common stocks, or, possibly, in convertible securities.

How shall you buy them? Through purchases of odd lots? Using the New York Stock Exchange's Monthly Investment Plan (MIP)? Through an investment club or one or more open-end, mutual, or closed-end funds? Should your money be accumulated in a savings account until such time as a round lot can be bought? Should you hold off buying when the market is high and then jump in with both feet when it has come down? Let's examine each possibility.

What Stocks Should I Buy?

At the beginning of your investment career, stick to mundane stocks. Don't buy the exotic offerings in companies with scientific-sounding names. Buy into NYSE-listed, seasoned companies. Later, when you have made and taken profits, you can risk small amounts of your profits on such companies. New industries that will develop are not as easy to predict as what the GNP will be ten or more years from now, as you can see from the experiences of the past.

Here are a few predictions made by "authorities" in 1900 as they looked ahead into the twentieth century. Professor John Trowbridge, of Harvard University, predicted a nationwide network of trolleycar lines that would bind the states and territories together. Suppose you had bought into streetcar companies? Professor Simon Newcomb, the great astronomer, compared the talk of a flying machine to squaring the circle. What bugged him particularly was the "aeronaut's" landing. "How shall he reach the ground without destroying his delicate machinery?" Yet in less than fifteen years, Imperial German zeppelins were bombing London. And even the zeppelins didn't survive.

By 1908 Wilbur Wright had flown seventy-five miles in a little less than two hours. Predictions about the future of the aviation industry were then made. From here on, people could even fly at night. How? That's simple. You just threw overboard a trailing line equipped with electronic gear that rang a bell when it hit anything. That would be the warning signal to the pilot to fly higher. Would you have liked to buy stock in the company that made these essential trailing lines?

Some younger readers will be around when we cross over into the twenty-first century. Whenever man approaches such arbitrary milestones (when the Dow-Jones industrial averages touch 1000 it won't mean anything either!), he feels called upon to predict. Just wait for some of these wild predictions, but keep your hands on your good stocks and your pocketbook.

The investor-pioneer can make BIG money, if human hoggishness lets him get out when he has a nice profit. But this is hardly the proper investment procedure for the small, beginning investor. The pioneering stage in the growth of an industry is to be avoided by the rank-and-file investor. This is an opportunity only for the venture capitalist, the pure speculator, who can afford to lose. Earlier in our history, some of the royal blue chips of today wound up in trouble and a lot of money was lost. Westinghouse Electric went into receivership, and the General Electric Company was saved from a similar fate by the intervention of J. P. Morgan.

Oil, Building, and Electric Company Stocks

These are the types of stocks you might consider as your first investment candidates, not necessarily in the order given. Buy any or all of them.

The Oils. Why buy an oil stock like Mobil Oil Corporation? For one thing, it is a financially strong company and has shown a steady growth in earnings and dividends. For another, the company is in an expanding business.

At this time, when our nation's energy requirements have jumped, coal and gas production is declining. Sudden, new, stringent safety rules have closed a lot of coal mines. An unrealistic rate policy of the Federal Power Commission has made prospecting for new gas supplies not particularly attractive, so that natural gas reserves have fallen from a twenty-three-year supply in 1954 to a thirteen-year supply today and will probably go lower before the old reserve position is reestablished. New tax laws passed in 1969, designed to make oil exploration a little less interesting for people in high tax brackets, have also hurt gas supplies. An important by-product of the search for oil is natural gas. When there are fewer exploratory wells drilled for oil, less gas is found. Meanwhile we are experiencing a rapid, probably too rapid, build-up of gas users to a point where the unthinkable occurs. Utilities refuse to accept new gas customers, and electric companies start to worry about the adequacy of their coal and gas deliveries.

Nuclear energy cannot bridge the gap for years to come at any rate. As far as one can see now, oil has a great intermediate-term future. It is available and can be quite easily desulfurized before burning to meet even tight pollution standards.

Phillips Petroleum and Amerada Hess have important crude production and low-cost refining operations in the Caribbean. Some desulfurization facilities have already been built; others are planned. So oil is a very viable possibility for investment.

The Building Industry. The country needs more housing badly. If we are to meet our national goal of adding twenty-six million new and reconditioned homes in this decade, we have to get going.

Boise Cascade, producer of building materials, has entered the market for factory-built housing, land development, furniture, and engineering services. Georgia-Pacific has been called "the premier growth company" in the building industry. It is also the largest plywood producer, besides being important in paper and pulp production.

Johns-Manville has its corporate fingers in most construction markets—from asbestos fibers to cement pipes, fiber glass, and carpets. JM has tremendous reserves of asbestos in Canada, a strong financial position, and capable management, organized in depth.

As a long-term investment, stay away from the mobile homes industry. Although it will expand for a few more years at a good annual rate, it is a temporary answer to the low-cost, mass housing problem. Mobile homes have quite a few limitations. To mention two: a definite shortage of parking space and increasingly stricter zoning restrictions.

As a concomitant, air conditioning will grow at a substantially higher rate than mobile homes, and its growth has staying power. Either as part of a new construction project or the remodeling of existing facilities, air conditioning is becoming a standard item. Write for annual reports to Carrier, Fedders, or Trane Corporation.

The Electric Companies. The country needs more electric power. Nobody wants brown-outs as a steady diet. If we are to double our GNP by the early 1980s, more electric power will *have* to be produced. Tremendous amounts of capital are needed to finance the new plants, and you will pay through higher utility bills for facilities installed to reduce air pollution. So you might as well get something back in the form of dividends and capital appreciation.

In addition to the utility that serves your area, take a good look at Illinois Power, Ohio Edison, Houston Lighting and Power, or Gulf States Utilities. El Paso Natural Gas has some very appealing long-term growth prospects. Among other things, that company will import liquid propane gas from Algeria using a fleet of cryogenic tankers, and market it on the east coast. That should add a pretty penny to its earnings as the 1970s progress.

Dollar Cost Averaging

Don't hold off buying when the market is, in your opinion, high. No one knows how high "high" is, and you could easily miss out on opportunities to buy at a price that turns out later not to have been so high after all. It probably would have been very costly to make a lump-sum investment in 1969 or in 1970, when you thought securities were cheap, and then to have watched the averages going down another fifty or more points. No. Don't try to outguess what the market is going to do next. Use a formula investment plan known as dollar cost averaging.

This is a method under which a constant amount of money is invested in a specific security at predetermined and regular time intervals, such as monthly or quarterly. You don't pay any attention to the price. When the first of the month arrives, you buy your stock. You are in for the long pull and you know you have a good, generally up-trending stock.

Let's say that you have just about $100 to invest monthly, and the stock you have chosen is Amerada Hess. In 1970, when the stock was 20, you bought 5 shares. When it rose, the next month, to 25, your $100 bought only 4 shares. At 33, only 3 shares. If it declines in the next month to 25, you would again buy 4. At 50, only 2 shares. In other words, under dollar cost averaging the investor benefits from temporary downswings in the price of the stock by being able to buy more shares than his dollars buy at a higher price. Result: His average cost will ALWAYS be lower than the average price he paid for the stock. To illustrate:

	Amount Invested	Purchase Price	Shares Bought
Investment takes	$100	$ 20	5
place at the	100	25	4
beginning of	100	33	3
each month.	100	25	4
	100	33	3
	100	50	2
	$600	$186 (or $31 a share)	21

The average purchase price was $31 per share. The average cost to the investor was $28.57—or $600 for 21 shares. Accumulate cash dividends in a savings account, and perhaps once a year use them to increase your holdings. Amerada Hess paid a 2½-percent stock dividend in July, 1970, and again in 1971, in addition to a small cash dividend. By the middle of spring, 1971, AHC was 63½! At Christmas, 1971, it was 42.

The Rules of Dollar Cost Averaging

This simple investment plan involves no computations of any kind. The rules are also very simple:

1. This is a long-term proposition, not an in-and-out trading system.

2. You should have a steady flow of income so that the $100 (or whatever amount) is available and can be invested regularly so that the plan need not be terminated when stocks are really low in price.

3. Don't select a stock that is on a continuous downward trend. The stock should represent an expanding company in an expanding industry.

4. Willpower is required to act contrary to emotions or alleged common sense.

5. As the number of shares increases and cash dividends get larger, use them to acquire more shares at the next purchase.

After you have acquired a hundred shares, take a good look at the company and the industry. If the outlook is still good for both, continue with the plan. If you can do better in a stock in another industry or the same one without increasing your risk, make the switch. But don't do it merely on a temporary downswing. Remember, this is a long-term proposition.

Results of Dollar Cost Averaging

Studies that have been made on the results of dollar cost averaging, based on the behavior of the Dow-Jones industrial averages, reveal rather satisfactory results. A survey of five-year investment programs for the years 1929–1951 shows that no consecutive five-year program resulted in less than a 12-percent annual gain. If you had invested $1,000 a year during 1943–1952 and reinvested the dividends as they came in, you would have had almost $24,000 at the end of this 10-year period. This is quite impressive when you think of the low rates of interest that prevailed then. On the average, AAA corporate bonds brought no more than a 3-percent return in this period.

What about Diversification?

If you are concerned about a lack of diversification, there are several ways to obtain it and still retain the fundamental advantages of dollar cost averaging. You could buy a closed-end investment company listed on the NYSE such as the Lehman Corporation and thus obtain not only diversification, but also professional management. The Lehman Corporation did far better during the 1969–1970 bear market than many mutual funds, and there is no load charge. If you dollar-cost-average a stock like LEM over the long pull, you are bound to buy it at times at an appreciable discount from the net asset value per share. At other times, closed-end funds have a habit of selling at a premium. But remember, you will buy more when a fund sells at a discount.

Another way to have diversification would be to buy into companies that are themselves quite diversified, in terms of both geography and products. Cleveland-Cliffs Iron Company is one that meets this description. It also has a very large investment portfolio. You could also buy into an insurance holding company that controls, among other interests, a casualty and property insurance company with over one billion dollars invested in a balanced portfolio of common and preferred stocks and bonds. Still another way to have diversification would be to buy three stocks on a quarterly basis. Put a hundred dollars in stock A in January, April, July, and October. Buy stock B in February, May, August, and November and Stock C in March, June, September, and December. This is a very fine plan, particularly if more than a hundred dollars can be invested every month.

The individual stocks I have suggested are all in an uptrend, and you should do quite well. See what the company and the industry are doing about once every two years. There is a lot to be said for diversification. On the other hand, if I have good eggs in my basket, I can watch my basket.

The Costs of Dollar Cost Averaging

What is the cost of investing $100 a month? The minimum NYSE commission for that amount is $6 plus a surcharge of 50 percent or $9. A sales load of 9 percent is rather steep. It is the maximum that mutual funds are permitted to charge under the Investment Company Act of 1940. But there is another way an individual investment program of dollar cost averaging can be more economically effected.

Suppose $100 is put into a bank savings account over a period of 6 months. At the end of the period, say, on the first of July and again on the first business day of January, $600 worth of stock is bought. The commission now would be $11 plus the 50-percent surcharge of $5.50, or a total of $16.50 as contrasted with $54 in commission charges if $100 is invested monthly. But hold on. Assume that the bank pays you interest at the rate of 5 percent per annum. Since there would be an average balance of $300 on deposit over a 6-month period, the interest received would come to $7.50, so that the net cost to you of investing semiannually would be $9—$16.50 minus $7.50—as compared to $9 a month if monthly investments of $100 each are made.

The studies that have been made on dollar cost averaging show that if a long enough period of time and a growth stock are involved, the results of semiannual investing do not differ materially from those obtained when funds are invested monthly. The savings are substantial: $2 \times \$9$ or $18, versus $12 \times \$9$ or $108, or a savings of $90 a year. That adds up to quite a number of additional shares over a 10- or 20-year period.

In addition to the stock exchange commission charges, which go to your brokerage house, there is an odd-lot charge for the odd-lot house that handles the execution of the odd-lot orders. This odd-lot charge is called a differential and amounts to $.25 a share if the stock bought is $55 or higher, and $.12½ a share if it is 54⅞ or lower.

Suggestion: Let the money accumulate at the bank, and punctiliously, on the first trading day in every 6-month period, buy $600 worth of the stock selected—regardless of price.

The NYSE Monthly Investment Plan

Another effective way the small investor can purchase common and preferred stocks listed on the Exchange, provided they are traded in round lots of 100 shares, is by opening a Monthly Investment Plan (MIP for short). Ask your broker to open an account in your name or as a joint account with your wife.

United States citizens permanently domiciled, aliens on an immigration visa, and Canadian residents are eligible. An MIP account can be opened by an adult as custodian for a minor if the Gifts to Minors Law in his state permits the gift of money. If your state does not permit it, you as donor would have to maintain the MIP account in your name and then periodically transfer shares as they are accumulated to a custodial form.

Monthly or quarterly payments from $40 to $1,000 can be made. The commission charges will be higher ($9 a month per $100 invested) than under my suggested semiannual do-it-yourself investment plan. You may well ask, "Why should I open an MIP account?" The best answer I can give is "For convenience." All you have to do with MIP every month or quarter is write a check and put it into an envelope which is provided. Let's figure what an MIP account on a quarterly investment basis would cost.

The cost for investing $300 every quarter is $10.50 minus $3.75 interest, which your average balance of $150 each quarter would draw at the bank, or a net cost of $6.75. You might consider the small additional expense worth the convenience. The do-it-yourself semiannual plan costs $18 a year, and the quarterly MIP plan, $27 per year. Besides the convenience, there is another advantage. All purchases and reinvestments of cash dividends in partial shares are figured to four decimal places. Under a do-it-yourself investment plan, no fractional shares can be bought. But for a monthly investment plan, the charges are monstrous for the investor, and for the firms involved they are not really high enough to pay expenses.

If you wish to pay the high monthly charges, you can, under MIP, dollar-cost-average three stocks at $100 per quarter for each, just as you can do under your own program. An investor can have as many MIPs as he wishes. Each account has its own number, and when the check is mailed, he must indicate how much of it is to go into each numbered account. If your payment is received by the odd-lot house Carlisle DeCoppet and Co. before 2:00 P.M., the order will be executed on the Exchange at the opening of the next business day. If your payment is received after 2:00 P.M., it is executed the day after the next business day.

You can do anything with an MIP account that can be done with a regular account, except execute rights. Rights will be sold at the market as soon as possible and the proceeds credited to your account. Stock dividends and split-ups are also credited to it. If the stock dividend is in shares of an issue other than the one in the MIP, the securities are sold and the proceeds credited. In case of a merger—for example, when the Douglas Corporation merged and became McDonnell Douglas —the account is automatically changed to the new stock. Your company's annual and special reports to shareholders as well as proxy-soliciting material for management, or for any other person authorized to solicit proxies, will be mailed to you.

When a customer wishes to terminate his account, he has two choices. He may ask that his fractional shares be sold or that a sufficient fraction be purchased to round out to a full share. The full shares can then be registered in his name or the joint names and mailed to him, or the certificate can be mailed by the odd-lot house to his broker for his account.

Over three hundred corporations have set up MIP payroll-deduction plans to allow their employees to buy stock. If your company is good enough to devote your life to, why not also your dollars? Under a company-sponsored MIP plan the company pays the commissions, and purchases are made in round lots. Result: Your dollars buy more shares.

Buying Stocks through an Investment Club

Many a big investor of today had his start as a very small investor with an investment club. Such a club usually meets monthly to discuss securities to be purchased with the pooled small sums that individual members contribute. It's a good way of learning about investing, provided the club is made up of congenial people and its membership is not too large. Members have to be congenial, or else bickering starts and the club falls apart sooner or later. I have seen some very successful investment clubs whose members worked for the same company or were members of the same bridge or golf club.

An investment club should not be too large. Once it exceeds

fifteen members, it gets unwieldy. Every member should be able to participate in the discussion and selection of securities. With twenty-five or more members this is practically impossible, and the members tend to lose interest.

How does such a club get started? Prospective members agree to get together for an organizational meeting in some home or office. An agreement is then reached as to how the club should be run, including a provision for the liquidation of the share of a member who might leave. It may be organized as a partnership, which is the usual form, or as a corporation. If a "swinging club" is to be organized with relatively large monthly contributions by members, it would probably be better to organize the club in a corporate form, because no margin trading can be done by an investment club organized as a partnership. While investment clubs are usually set up for the purpose of longer-term investing, other investment objectives may be chosen.

There is no reason why a group of more or less sophisticated investors couldn't get together to assume OTC risks (on a $20 monthly individual contribution) that they might not and should not assume in their regular investment programs. If 15 members buy 100 shares of a $3 OTC stock and it goes down the drain, the $20 tuition fee was cheap for the lesson. If it soars to $20 and is not sold and later is quoted at $1.50, there is another valuable lesson. And if it goes to $50 two years later, that is an effective illustration that there *are* sleeping beauties. Levits Furniture Corporation, a former $3 stock in the late 1960's, went to over $150 by February, 1972, after two stock splits!

At the next meeting, after the organizational meeting, the individual contributions are accepted by the treasurer (if not sooner). Some clubs add a nominal additional sum for incidental expenses. Investment possibilities are then discussed. A representative of the brokerage firm that will carry the account should be present to offer helpful investment advice for the first selection. But he should never dominate meetings and probably should be left out of future meetings so that members can learn as much as possible.

At the third and following meetings, study assignments should be given to individual members who report on facts and figures of particular companies and industries. After the individual reports are discussed, the members decide, by majority vote, which stock or other security the club will buy that month. As time goes on, holdings are reviewed, and any changes in them are also determined by a majority vote. Of course there is no reason why the club can't ask its broker for recommendations and research reports, but before acting on them, they should be thoroughly studied and discussed by the members.

The National Association of Investment Clubs publishes an extremely interesting magazine containing investment suggestions and reports on other clubs' doings.

Buying Shares in Closed-End or Open-End Investment Companies

The small investor might well consider the periodic purchase of shares in a closed-end investment company. There are over two dozen listed on the NYSE, and their shares can be purchased under an MIP plan. Besides the previously mentioned Lehman Corporation, there are the Japan Fund, with participation in fast-growing Japanese firms, American-South African, Adams Express, Madison Fund, and others.

There is no load charge with a closed-end fund. Sometimes a given fund may sell at a tremendous premium, many times the load charge of a mutual fund. In that case, forget about the closed-end fund. For example, on August 28, 1970, Overseas Securities Corporation, on the Amex, was quoted at 9¼, which was 95.1 percent above its net asset per-share value.

If you decide to buy an open-end fund, then the question to be asked is: A no-load fund, or a fund that has a sales charge? Some good no-load funds require the purchase of a minimum unit beyond the financial resources of the small investor. For example, Gibraltar Growth Fund has no sales charge, but requires a $1,000 minimum purchase; many no-loads have $500 requirements, and some go as high as $5,000 and even $15,000. Some mutual funds with sales charges also require a minimum purchase of $1,000. Other load or no-load funds have no minimum.

In Chapter 8 you will find the various services that mutual funds can give you. Does the particular no-load or load fund you are considering give them all to you? What is the fund's investment objective? Does it square with yours? What was its record in the last bear market and in the last bull market?

In the back of the monthly Standard and Poor's *Stock Guide* you will find a mutual fund summary. It will answer many of your questions very quickly. Every August, *Forbes* publishes fund performance ratings in "up" and "down" markets. Study it. The fact that both the Channing Growth and Special Funds received an A or A+ in up markets doesn't mean very much to the fellow who bought them in 1968 when both funds flunked with a big red F in "down" markets. It means Channing got its A in rising markets by taking a lot of risks.

Investing remains an art, and thus nothing one does is fool-proof. Fund people, on the whole, are a capable and dedicated lot, but they do not and cannot work miracles. If you have three MIP accounts as suggested, or if you did some dollar cost averaging on your own over the last five years or so in stocks like Echlin Manufacturing, Eckerd Drugs, or Black & Decker, you would have come out of the bear market far better than the *Forbes* Stock Fund Average. Of course, any fund also lends itself to dollar cost averaging as well as MIP on your own do-it-yourself investment program.

Trading Odd Lots

Since the do-it-yourself investment program of smaller investors usually involves odd lots, here are a few pointers about odd-lot trading. There is the already mentioned differential added to purchases or subtracted from sales.

As with round lots, all odd-lot orders go to the trading floor of the NYSE, where a regular Exchange member, a so-called associate odd-lot broker, is responsible for the execution of an order. All odd-lot buy or sell market orders are executed at a price based on the next round-lot sale—the one that takes place after the order has been received by the odd-lot house, plus or minus the differential.

Buy limit orders are executed on the first round-lot sale after receipt of the order that is below the limit by the amount of the applicable differential. If you specify, "Buy 50 XYZ at 50," the order could not be executed at 50 because with the differential added, the price to you would be 50⅛, and you specified you wanted to buy at 50 or better. A sell-long limit order would not be executed unless a sale comes along that is above the limit by the amount of the differential.

Short-sell orders come under the same rules as round-lot orders.

A buy-stop or sell-long-stop order becomes a market order when a round lot is sold at or above (in case of the sell-stop, below) the stop price. The order is filled at the price of the next round-lot sale, plus or minus the applicable differential.

You cannot give a discretionary or a not-held order.

The odd-lotter has an advantage over the round-lotter. When inquiring about the execution of his order, he is never faced with "Sorry, it couldn't be executed; there was stock ahead" because another broker had time priority, or with "Matched and lost" because two brokers were on par in the auction market, matched, and your broker lost the match. Even if only 100 shares are traded in the round-lot market, odd-lot orders for 353 shares could have been executed. The odd-lot dealer guarantees to accept all odd-lot market orders and execute them at a price based on the next effective round-lot sale, no matter what the condition of the round-lot market is when an order is received. But what happens when no effective sale occurs?

Suppose you want to buy 50 shares of XYZ ten minutes before the close of the market. But it was a dull market and no more trades are made in the stock before the gong heralds the closing for the day. What then? Enter the order as "Buy 50 XYZ at the market W.O.W."—meaning with or without a sale. If no effective round-lot sale comes along, as is the case here, the buy order is executed on the prevailing offering price. A sell order is executed on the prevailing bid price. And as long as the market is open, there is always a bid and offer for the stock. A round-lot trader cannot avail himself of a W.O.W. order.

In the round-lot market there is no guarantee that an at-the-close order will be executed. In the odd-lot market at-the-close orders are always executed on the closing bid or offer.

The small investor is most adequately and fairly treated on

the Big Board. On the Amex there are no special odd-lot brokers. The specialists execute the odd-lot orders in the stocks assigned to them. In the OTC market there are no odd lots or odd-lot differentials except in very rare cases involving less than one-hundred-share orders for stocks very difficult to find.

If you are interested in further refinements of odd-lot trading, write to Carlisle De Coppet & Co. (2 Broadway, New York, New York 10004) and ask for a copy of a bulletin entitled *The Odd-Lot Dealer System on the NYSE*. For the overwhelming majority of small investors, I suggest using market orders. You are buying for the long pull, or you want to change your holdings for a good reason; so don't be hesitant about an eighth or a fourth and miss a good opportunity to buy or sell. And don't begrudge the odd-lot house the small differential. It won't make it on every trade. If the floor member is long 65 shares of a 58¼ stock and the market turns and the stock goes down a half a point, not only has the house worked for nothing, it is actually taking a loss.

Summary

1. The economic climate over the years to come is very good for the small investor if he follows a few fundamental rules set forth here.

2. He should stick to down-to-earth, seasoned NYSE-listed stocks that are in an uptrend, such as oils, electricity, or building stocks.

3. Dollar cost averaging will always mean that the investor's average cost will be lower than the average price paid for the stock.

4. For dollar cost averaging, select a listed growth stock and forget about price. Over the long pull the results will be very gratifying.

5. If you want diversification, buy a closed-end or mutual fund or buy into diversified companies. You can dollar-cost-average all of them.

6. Stay away from monthly purchases. They cost too much. Put the money in the bank each month and buy twice a year.

7. An MIP is very economically priced if you buy on a quarterly basis. You can't buy only twice a year.

8. Anything can be done in an MIP account that can be done in a cash account, but rights cannot be exercised.

9. As a training seminar in investments, a small investment club, made up of congenial people, has much to recommend it.

10. Closed-end funds can sell at very large discounts and equally large premiums. Find out why; you might get a bargain. Stay away from them if the discount is unreasonably high. You can dollar-cost-average all funds.

11. NYSE odd-lot trading rules favor the small investors; they can do things that are denied to round-lot investors.

CHAPTER 5

The Advantages of Listed Markets

If securities markets did not exist, they would have to be invented—fast. If they were closed down, sooner or later word would leak out that on such-and-such a street corner or in such-and-such a hotel corridor individuals congregate who wish to buy or sell securities. People don't like to part with cash, their most liquid asset, unless they know in advance how they can recover it if they have to do so.

Generally speaking, the higher the degree of marketability of an investment medium, the lower the compensation that the investor demands for giving up his liquidity. The lower the degree of marketability is, the higher will be the return in terms of interest, dividends, or capital gains that will be sought before committing funds. The less the marketability of an investment, the greater the risk. When liquidation is indicated with low marketability, there is severe sacrifice of price. There are times when these guidelines do not apply. A stock may enjoy high marketability and yet carry a high yield. Why? Because the industry of which it is part is currently unpopular. Sometimes oils are unpopular; at other times, chemical stocks; at still other times, the conglomerates. But investing is not a popularity contest, so that under such conditions an investor will be handsomely repaid for independence of judgment.

Bankers also appreciate marketability. They will lend more

readily, and a greater percentage of their value, on securities that are listed on the New York Stock Exchange than on securities that are traded in the over-the-counter market.

Securities exchanges are, with the exception of rights trading, secondary markets; on their floors securities are traded that are already outstanding. The proceeds of the sales go to the individual sellers of the securities, not to corporations as issuers. Only in the primary market, in the new issues market, do the proceeds of sales go to the issuing companies. But we can't generalize. As far as liquidity, that is, marketability of shares, goes, exchanges differ greatly.

The New York Stock Exchange is a securities mass market. Its double auction market, in which buyers compete with buyers and sellers with sellers, has great depth. The American Stock Exchange has lower listing standards, and therefore the auction market tends to have less depth. This is very often disregarded by individual investors. When listing requirements are for fewer shares outstanding and fewer shareholders and earnings than on the Big Board, markets cannot be the same. But the opportunities to make and lose money (unless you know when to sell them short) are much greater, as the stories of Solitron, Syntex, Teleprompter, or Four Seasons Nursing Centers show so convincingly.

The foregoing should not be interpreted as a reflection on the Amex; it grows out of the different nature of that exchange. It is easier for corporations to be listed there; thus the Amex provides a seasoning and developing market for newer and smaller corporations. Individuals tend to buy them more than do institutions. On the Big Board, institutions accounted for about 60 percent of the public share volume during the first six months of 1971; at that time institutional trading on the Amex was less than one-third of this amount. Again, this does not mean that all stocks traded on that exchange are those of small, developing companies. Far from it. A very substantial percentage are old, well-established companies that qualify for listing on the NYSE.

A stock of only limited, regional interest, traded on a regional exchange or locally, has still less marketability, and an investor can easily be locked in a stock traded in the over-the-counter market. The 1969–1970 bear market saw bids simply evaporating in that market. It was a great boon for the NYSE and the Amex. Their listing applications increased appreciably as corporations, after their experience in a drying-up OTC market, came to value the fact that there is almost always a bid or an offer on an exchange.

Even on the Exchange or the Amex, there are days when your stock might not be traded and you will find it only under "closing bid and asked prices of stocks not traded." In 1969 Berkey Photo did not open at all one day on the Exchange because a block of seventy-five thousand shares, which an institutional investor was anxious to sell on rumors of lower earnings, could not be traded. There are stocks traded in the OTC market that enjoy as good a market as they would on the floor of any exchange.

There is really no such thing as a stock market; there are only markets for individual stocks. Rare are the days, even in a bear market, when one or more stocks don't make new highs. But despite all that, a small, new, developing investor is well advised to stick to NYSE-listed securities until such time as his capital base is broad enough to branch out into other markets.

The Advantages of a Listed Market to You

The continuous double auction market, concentrating bids and offers of all actual and potential buyers and sellers on the floor of the Exchange around the specialist, narrows the spread between bid and asked prices, makes for a more orderly market, and assures you of paying the lowest and receiving the highest prices prevailing at that time.

Your order is executed on an agency basis. Your broker, your agent, must assume at all times the responsibility of doing his best for you, the customer. For these services, up to $500,000, brokers charge a uniform rate fixed by the Exchange and known to anyone in advance. Beyond this amount, commission rates are negotiated.

All transactions are in the open. In an exchange market the investor knows the range of prices for a given security; he knows the last sale price from the ticker tape. He may ask his broker to obtain the current bid and offer, and upon that information base his decision to act. Unless sales are bunched to prevent the tape from falling behind, his own round-lot transaction will be printed on the tape. Each step in the transaction from the giving to the execution of the order is time-stamped so that all circumstances may be accurately rechecked later in case of dispute.

Things have changed in the OTC market. The computerized system called NASDAQ (for National Association of Securities Dealers Automated Quotation) has improved matters substantially in that market. A broker at his desk can now push buttons for stock prices and get the prevailing bid and offer. For the first time volume will be fed into the computer so that daily volume figures will be available for the stock. The volume figures can be misleading, however. They include only transactions of NASDAQ market-makers and could also involve double counting when these market-makers trade with each other. The securities of some 50,000 companies are traded in the OTC market. Only 2,500 stocks were included in NASDAQ when it went into operation on February 8, 1971. It was then reported that NASDAQ plans to expand its quotation system eventually to 20,000 stocks. Instantaneous information on the quotes of OTC stocks and the firms that make markets in them is important, but the instantaneous competition of buyers and sellers in *one* auction market on the floor of the Exchange is of a totally different nature.

Listed securities are the only securities, except a small group of OTC securities and the securities of federal, state, and local governments, that member organizations of the NYSE may accept as collateral in security loan transactions for margin accounts.

Local stockholders may be happy with the OTC market in their area, but the listed security protects even distant shareholders. Negotiation in the local or regional market without knowledge of prevailing prices in other OTC markets is eliminated. No matter how geographically far apart buyers and sellers are, in a listed market each, without any assistance, can easily and quickly find the highest current bid and the lowest current offer, as well as the price of the last sale. Each will know the price at which his order will have been executed, since trades are immediately made public.

Under special block marketing techniques developed by the Exchange, large stockholders can avoid being locked in. They are able to sell a block at a uniform price without too great a drop in price, or to buy it without too great a rise in price. It is, at times, very difficult to liquidate a large position in a stock in the OTC market without substantial price concessions. Ability to sell under acceptable conditions is highly important in the liquidation of estates, in large family or institutional holdings, and in the settlement of tax problems.

In the listed market the public receives maximum protection, ranging from an exchange's insistence upon prompt disclosure of all important corporate developments to supervision of trading, members, and member organizations as well as protection against counterfeit certificates. The primarily self-imposed rules of the New York and American Stock Exchanges spell PROTECTION for the investor, to a most pronounced degree. Moreover, floor transactions are not only under constant surveillance by the exchanges; the SEC, too, constantly observes trading activities. Both have their "tape watchers."

Anything out of the ordinary is looked into at once. Who is doing the buying and selling? The public? Members of the exchange? Is there any collusion? Do only a few know favorable news about the company that ought to be released by management? Management is called up and trading might be suspended until news about the company is released for all to read on the Dow-Jones broad tape. The stock exchanges know that unless material news is promptly and publicly announced, they will lose investor confidence. If that happens, they will lose business.

Factors Determining Marketability

Marketability tends to be high in the following cases:

1. The time interval required to bring buyers and sellers together is short. Orders to buy and sell come from all over the country and abroad to the floor and go to the particular spot at the trading post where the stock is traded.

2. The charges for executing public orders are reasonable. When charges are too high, buyers and sellers may stay out of the market. As a result, trading in a stock will be less active and the market value, determined by demand and supply conditions, will less likely reflect true market value.

3. Purchases and sales can be made with a minimum of price fluctuations. Take a look at yesterday's market. It is not at all unusual to read that 181,500 shares of Occidental Petroleum were traded (181,500 shares were bought and 181,500 were sold!) or 150,000 shares of Jersey Standard bought and sold, and in both instances the price changed by no more than one-fourth of a point.

4. Information on sales and bids and offers is readily and promptly available. To get the price and the name of the market makers for a security by laboriously checking the "pink sheets" of the National Quotation Bureau and then telephoning one or more firms for a quotation does not make for high marketability.

5. Investors have confidence in the integrity and experience of the individuals and institutions through whom they must work. NASDAQ and new clearing methods for stock transfer and delivery will most certainly increase investors' confidence in the OTC market.

The Exchange as Business Organization

Before doing business on the Exchange, you ought to know something about it. I always get laughs in a talk to an audience when I say that the NYSE is a nonprofit corporation. Yet the fact is that the Exchange is a voluntary nonprofit association, composed currently of 1,366 individual members. The stock exchange itself does not buy or sell securities. It has no financial interest in the price movements of securities. Its revenues are primarily derived from membership dues, service charges to members, and listing fees paid by the corporations whose securities have been admitted for trading purposes on the Exchange.

The Exchange's interest in securities is that prices are arrived at fairly, in a free, two-way auction market, and are promptly published.

The primary function of the Exchange is to put at the disposal of its members a convenient marketplace and ancillary facilities so that investors and traders may convert securities quickly and conveniently into cash, or exchange cash for securities. Exchange revenues, outside of dues and listing fees, reflect the extent to which members are using Exchange services. Revenues tend to rise or fall in accordance with general market activity just as the price of a seat does. Trading is done in accordance with strictly enforced "just and equitable principles of trade," to use the words of the original Buttonwood-Tree Brokers who founded the New York Stock Exchange in 1792 in front of what is now 68 Wall Street.

The New York Stock Exchange governs, administers, and disciplines itself, provided its rules and practices are acceptable to the SEC and its actions do not run counter to the provisions of the Securities Exchange Act of 1934.

People are sometimes surprised when they read that a seat has been sold for several hundred thousand dollars. There is nothing mysterious about that. The value of a seat or membership stems from the fact that Exchange membership is limited and a seat is salable. The only way a newcomer can obtain a seat is by buying one from another member who wishes to turn in his membership. In the over-the-counter market there is no limit on membership; hence it has no value as such. Any salable, limited membership in any organization will always have a value as long as other people want to buy one.

Just as there is a (daily) bid and offer posted for NYSE membership, the New York City taxicab industry has its market for medallions. It may have a market value of more than twenty thousand dollars, and you can buy a two-ounce medallion on about a 65-percent margin through a bank. Unless the city issues licenses for cabs freely, the only way an individual can operate a cab in New York City is through the purchase of another person's operating permit, his medallion. Making allowance for the much larger number of licensed cabs than Exchange memberships, one might well say that the market for both seats and medallions is quite brisk. How high a person will bid in either case, will depend on the income he hopes to derive from his investment.

The New York Stock Exchange is justified in saying that its members and member organizations are "governed by perhaps the most exacting code of business ethics in existence." Its rules on capital requirements, financial audits, segregation of customers' securities, in addition to the know-your-customer rule and supervision of clients' accounts, are stringently enforced. They help to safeguard the interests of the firms' clientele as well as limit the possibility of fraud against member firms (partnerships) and member corporations.

Had it not been for these rules—and granted, they should have been enforced more rigorously—the wreckage on Wall Street during the 1969–1970 bear market would have been a lot worse. On May 26, 1964, the Exchange announced that "by 1980, if present trends continue, it foresees an average daily volume of 8,000,000 shares, compared with the record high of 4,600,000 shares set last year." The release went on and said: "The Exchange Community is well along in expanding its facilities in anticipation of this growth."

No doubt it was well along in expanding its facilities for this growth, but present trends just didn't continue. Before the 1960s were out, the big volume days of 1968 had literally snowed the industry under, and the phrase "back office paper backlog" was on everybody's lips. Firms spent millions to put in computers and other electronics equipment and their cost of operations rose and then the volume collapsed and some went broke.

The recession of 1969–1970 (and some economists never admitted it was one, "theoretically speaking"), or whatever it was, affected the country relatively little. It was the security business that suffered the most, in terms of lost jobs and money. Some partners and officers of firms lost their life savings. The customers didn't lose their money or securities in bankrupt firms thanks primarily to the action of the Exchange community and later of the government. Of course, like everybody else in the industry, a lot of the customers were bleeding. In retrospect, what happened in the general bear market was a blessing because the securities industry changed itself greatly. The least imaginative and most backward industry in the land came out of its chrysalis. It has improved and is continuing to improve its operational efficiency tremendously and will now be able to give a good account of itself when the 30-, 40-, 50-, 60-, and, yes, 70-million-share trading days come along as we go toward our second trillion dollars in GNP.

It is easy to say that the convulsion that occurred in Wall Street was the result of its own reluctance to change with the times. What happened was that the nature of the business had changed so fundamentally that the typical small and thinly capitalized brokerage firm could no longer handle it. To aggravate matters, everybody wanted to build sales and little attention was given to the internal management of firms. Self-regulation did not prove, as some have charged, "a total sham." It simply broke down in vital areas under the onslaught of the twin forces of a totally unexpected large volume and the rise of the institutional investors.

From here on, Wall Street will increasingly consist of large, well-capitalized, publicly owned financial department stores providing a broad range of financial services. Government regulation of companies and markets will be more extensive. Individual investors are now insured up to fifty thousand dollars against the loss of money and/or securities left on deposit in a brokerage account; it should help much to attract more individual investors during the affluent years to come. More important is the fact that thanks to the convulsion, a series of overdue remedial measures have been taken, including the first steps toward what may eventually become one nationwide, computerized, electronic securities market network most likely built around a NYSE-Amex complex.

An Insiders' Club?

The unkindest cut of all is to say that the NYSE, or the Amex, is nothing but a club for insiders, for regular Exchange members. At one time that was true. The entire Board of Governors was made up of floor members. Today things are different.

Pending further restructuring, the thirty-three-man Board of Governors comprises not only regular members, but allied members—the general office partners of regular members or, in case of member corporations, voting shareholders. Moreover, these board members come from the New York metropolitan area as well as from all over the country. In addition, three appointed public members sit on the board who have no connection with the securities business. This is a lot more than just window dressing. They are potentially powerful individuals. Should one of them resign over a policy disagreement, he would receive more press coverage than a regular member, if he wanted it. The public may, however, raise the question whether a chairman of a big life insurance company and the presidents of an industrial and utility company are the types of board members who can really represent the public at large in this new era.

The Exchange's president is not connected with a member organization. He is a "hired hand" and serves at the pleasure of the board, a combined legislative and judicial body. It may censure, fine, suspend, or expel a member or allied member or an account executive. All penalties are final. There is no appeal to any court, nor is there an attorney present at judicial proceedings. A thirty-day suspension is more than a wrist-slapping. It can be a very costly penalty, even without a fine. The securities business is a hotly competitive business; it is also one based on integrity and reputation. Under such conditions, even a censure is a serious matter.

The Exchange does not operate through committees, with the exception of special committees set up by the board, such as one of financing a new Exchange building, and a few administrative committees. Nothing can thus be buried in committees. A full airing is given every matter pending before the complete board—another reason why public members can be very powerful personalities.

All this should help to answer the question I was asked some time ago: "Will I get a fair shake on the Exchange?" The apparatus is there, at your disposal, to assure you fair and honest treatment. But what good are all the advantages and protection of a listed market if the public does not know how to use them properly or uses them wrongly? This is particularly true of orders.

Giving an Order

An order is your instruction to the broker. Is it clear what you mean—clear to you and the account executive? Often it is not. Unless a customer fully understands the nature of the order he is giving, he will not know his liabilities or his rights or those of his broker. Misunderstandings occur between customer and broker partly because of a failure to appreciate the problems that a particular type of order may present under rapidly changing market conditions, and partly because a customer never understood the fundamental nature of his order. He didn't know what he was saying to his broker. He threw sophisticated verbiage around; the broker took it for knowledge and did not question him.

The Market Order

The great advantage of the market order is speed. In the buying or selling of an active stock, this is the best order to use. But don't rush in.

Ask your broker how the market is doing before you place a market order. In an actively traded stock, the many bids and offers coming to the floor keep the spread between them very narrow. In a "thin" market, in which there are comparatively few bids and offers or both for the stock you seek to buy or sell, the spread between bids and offers is wider and price fluctuations are more pronounced. A market order in such a case ran mean a purchase or a sale at an unexpectedly high or low price. Possibly a limit order would be better under these conditions.

Limit Orders

In limit orders the customer specifies a price limit beyond which he does not wish to buy or sell. "Buy 100 F 50" means he is willing to buy 100 shares of Ford *only* if he can buy at $50 or less. "Sell 100 F 60" means that he wants to sell *only* if he can get $60 or more. When you set a limit, you are saying to the broker: "I am *only* interested in doing business at my stated price or better. If the market drops ⅛ below, don't sell my stock. If the market rises ⅛ above my limit, don't you buy the stock for me." Yes, this is what you *are* saying!

A limit order never becomes a market order, even after the stock sells at the limit stated in the order. A limit order to buy is always placed below the prevailing market price; otherwise it would be executed at once. A limit order to sell is always placed above the market because if the market is 50 and some nitwit puts in a limit order at 48, it would be immediately executed since the price is 50 and that's better than 48. All this is in sharp contrast with the stop order.

The advantage of a limited order is that it gives the customer a chance, but no certainty, to buy a stock at less than the current market price or to sell it above that price. For trading in stocks with thin markets, subject to rather wide fluctuations, the limit order has a great deal to recommend it. Also, when a stock is making a line—that is, when it is moving over a period within three or more points up or down—the use of the limit order can be very advantageous to the trader. On the other hand, in a rapidly moving market, up or down, if you want to get into or out of the market, limit orders can become very expensive. They may never be executed.

Suppose you put in a buy limit at 50. The stock is now 52 and is hit by a selling wave, so that a sale at 50 occurs, followed by one at 50⅛, as new buying now comes in. The trade at 50 was somebody else's stock who was ahead of you in the auction market—"stock ahead" as the phrase on the floor has it. You missed the boat with your limit. The moral of the story: If you think a stock is good for a 10-point rise or you want to buy it for the long pull to double or triple your money, don't horse around with limit orders and outsmart yourself over an eighth or a quarter of a point.

Stop Orders

A stop order, to buy or sell, is an order that becomes a market order when the price of the particular security declines or rises to or beyond the price stipulated in the order. It is a memorandum to the broker on the floor to treat it as a market order when this happens. Don't call it a "stop-loss order." The NYSE uses the term "stop order" because, as will be quite evident shortly, there is no guarantee against loss in any market.

Mr. Gutkauf has bought 100 shares of Hot Oil (HO) at 50 in the belief that the company would show increased earnings and raise its dividend so that he could sell the stock at a nice profit. But he is a nervous man and thinks of the possibility that competing fuels and adverse international developments may lower the earnings. In order to protect himself against a decline in the stock's price, he enters a stop order, telling his broker to "sell (long) 100 HO 48½ stop."

Nothing will happen to the order on the floor until HO falls to 48½. Immediately after the first sale occurs at 48½, or below it if the stock does not sell at 48½ on the way down, the 100 shares will be sold at the best prevailing price, the highest bid price. In other words, the instant sale occurs at or below 48½, the member holding this stop order will act as if he held a sell market order at that moment. Most customers do not understand the operation of a stop order. They think that it will be executed at or near the stop price. While this is usually the case, the unusual conditions cause trouble and misunderstanding between the customer and the broker. On "Heart Monday," when very heavy selling took place after the report of President Eisenhower's heart attack, some customers were mad as wasps when they received reports of execution points below their stop prices. Registered representatives should be positive that clients understand the nature of a stop order.

The Buy-Stop

There are three uses for a buy-stop order: to buy stock above the market price; to limit a loss on a short position; to freeze the profit on a short position.

Let's say that in the customer's opinion, 25 is an upper resistance level for a stock. He feels that if the stock should crash through it, its upward momentum will carry it several points beyond 25. He says, "Buy 100 XYZ 25⅜ stop open." He doesn't want the stock now at the prevailing price of 24¼. He wants it after it has demonstrated sufficient demand force to carry it through and beyond the present upper resistance level. "Open" means it is a so-called open order or GTC (good till canceled), as limit and stop orders usually are.

A short seller shorts a stock at 76 because he thinks it is going to decline because of certain problems the company has. But he recognizes the possibility that the stock could rise. He is willing to call his judgment wrong if the stock rises three points. He therefore instructs his broker to enter an open buy order for him at 79. In so doing, he will limit his losses should unanticipated developments push up the price of the stock.

The courageous and sagacious Mr. Gutkauf sold Control Data (CDA) short, in 1970, at 110. The stock is now selling at 60. He has a fat $5,000 profit so far, but believes (and as matters turned out he was quite correct in this assumption) that CDA will go down farther. If so he could cover his short position at a still lower price. But having a tendency to be nervous, he wants protection for his paper profit. He tells his broker, "Buy 100 CDA 65 stop." Should the stock rise to 65, the order would be treated as a market order and at once executed. As a result, 90 percent of his profits would be maintained. The 1970 low for CDA was 28¾.

The Sell-Stop

Sell-stop orders also have three uses: to minimize a loss on a long position; to freeze a profit on a long position; and to go short below the current market price.

Mr. Gutkauf's purchase of 100 shares of Hot Oil at 50 and his entering a stop-sell order at 48½ illustrates the use of such an order to minimize a loss.

AXZ is now 87. A trader, who has watched the stock, feels 85 is a lower resistance level. Every time the stock fell, there was good buying support around the 85 level. The trader reasons that should AXZ ever sell through 85, the momentum would carry it still farther down, maybe to 80. So why not enter a sell-short-stop at 84½ and buy the stock back at 80? But things aren't quite as simple in this case. The trader could be hoist with his own petard.

No short sale can be made below the price of the last sale. It could therefore happen that his sell-short-stop was executed at the very level at which he had anticipated covering at a profit. If the stock breaks through 85 and sells down to 84½, it might continue in a series of minus tick sales, or at best occasional zero minus tick sales, until at 80 the first plus tick sale occurred. To avoid such a possibility, the trader should have entered a stop-limit order.

The Stop-Limit Order

The order would read: "Sell short 100 AXZ 84½ stop limit 84." The floor member will execute this limit order at 84 or higher, if he can do so without violating the short selling rule. But if long sales continue to force the price of the stock down, he cannot offer the short seller's order below 84. Of course, the principle of the stop-limit order can be applied to the other five situations described.

On the American Stock Exchange no stop orders can be entered for round lots; they are possible only for odd lots. But you may enter a stop-limit order provided that stop and limit price are the same. The Amex did that in order to prevent chain reactions—the execution of one stop order setting off others.

Since limit and stop orders are GTC orders, they can stay on the books for a long time, all but forgotten by you. And then there comes the day when they are executed—catching you short of cash. Remember then that there is such a thing as a margin account. Another thing you could do would be to reduce the size of your order—say, from 200 to 100 shares—without losing your position in the specialist's book.

GTC orders should be watched. Your account executive should take care of it. But I suggest you watch, too. In these matters a belt-and-suspenders approach has much to recommend it. As the Dow-Jones industrial averages go to 1,000 and way beyond, a simple technical reaction of 5 to 10 percent could mean a lot of points. There are good reasons to assume that the markets of the 1970s will be more volatile than those we have seen in the past.

The Problems with Stop Orders

Entering a stop order at the right price is a fine art. If set too far away from the market, losses on short positions can become quite large and profits on long positions quite small. One rule of thumb to follow is to set the stop price 10 percent below or above the prevailing market price. But this is about the extent of an average reaction or rally. Stop orders can be executed (and very often are!) near the low point of a reaction or near the high point of a rally. Shortly thereafter the stock bounces vigorously up the ladder, to the unhappiness of the sold-out customer, or retreats to lower levels, to the distress of the short seller.

There is no assurance that the stop order will be executed at or near the stop price. In a rapidly falling or rising market, the execution of your order may occur quite a distance away from your stop price. In the autumn of 1955, when President Eisenhower suffered a heart attack, the Dow-Jones industrial averages dropped 31.89 points in one day. On that "Heart Monday," stop-sell orders in Du Pont were executed at 210, down 20⅝ points from the day before. Du Pont did not open until thirty minutes before the close of the market, and then a bunched sale of 11,000 shares came through.

The Exchange may give you back your stop order, just when it looks like you need its protection. When lots of stop-sell orders are on the books of specialists, real trouble can develop if, as a result of bad news, sufficient market sell orders come in to trigger these orders. Like an avalanche sliding down a mountain and growing as it descends, the execution of stop-sell orders could turn a simple reaction into a minor panic. Fortunately an influx of buy orders usually turns the market. The Exchange also acts. It declares a stop-order ban in a stock. All stop orders on the books of the specialist are then canceled, and no new ones can be accepted until further notice.

When the Amex ceased accepting stop orders in round lots, its president said, "There have been recent wide-spread uses of stop orders by members of the general public who do not fully understand the nature of this type of order." The Big Board cautions: "Like any complex technique, the Stop Order must be used wisely and well—and the investor must appreciate its limitations as well as its advantages."

The Not-Held Order

Here the client must say what stock, how many shares, and whether it is a buy or sell long or short order. The order reads: "Buy 500 XYZ not held." The broker's discretion is only as to price, meaning that the firm's floor man is asked to use his own sense of timing as to the order's execution.

Not-held orders have been given by neophytes unfamiliar with the nature of such an order until knowledge was forcibly impressed upon them through an unexpectedly unfavorable price in the purchase or sale of a stock. Remember: You have asked your broker to use his own judgment. Not even the experts can predict what the market will do an hour later. The few in Wall Street upon whom I would bestow the title "expert" are the ones who most heatedly reject it. They know how often they are wrong.

Other Orders

Traders sometimes use buy or sell day orders. They remain in force until 3:30 P.M. If a day order has not been executed, it automatically expires at that time.

A fill-or-kill order (FOK)—"Buy 1,000 XYZ FOK"—can be a market or a limit order. It is to be executed in its entirety as soon as it reaches the auction market. If it can't be executed, it is canceled. Be careful here. If the order says, "Buy 1,000 XYZ immediate," then this order, market or limit, could be executed in part, with the remaining balance canceled. Tell your broker your exact intentions. Are you willing to accept a partial execution? Maybe it does not suit your plans.

An at-the-close order is a market order that is to be executed at the close or as near as possible. There is no 100-percent guarantee that it will be executed, however.

If the order is entered "at the opening," a market or limit order will be executed at the opening of the stock or not at all; any such order, or portion of it, not so executed is canceled.

Listed markets give you all kinds of advantages, privileges, and services. But you must understand their nature and, above all, make yourself understood. Not even a genie can serve you if you don't make clear what your wishes are.

Summary

1. Securities with high or good marketability carry less risk than those with low marketability.

2. A continuous double auction market gives you many advantages.

3. The NYSE is a nonprofit organization. It doesn't buy or sell securities.

4. A stock exchange seat is like a taxicab medallion—the supply of it is less than the demand for it.

5. The Exchange community is governed by perhaps the most exacting code of business ethics in existence.

6. The NYSE is not an insiders' club.

7. An order is your instruction to your broker. Be sure that you know what you're doing.

8. The best-designed device to miss the market can be the limit order.

9. A stop order is not a "stop-loss" order.

10. Stop orders have their advantages, but they are often misused.

11. A "not-held" order could cost you a lot more than a market order.

12. Fill-or-kill is not the same as an order to buy immediately.

CHAPTER 6

Are the Cards Stacked against Me

in the OTC Market?

Somebody not so long ago asked me that question. The cards could be stacked against you if you deal with a house of questionable reputation and buy a stock simply because you heard about it in the barbershop. This sprawling securities market is akin to the early American Wild West. It is colorful and exciting, and there are the good guys and the bad guys, the card sharks and the greenhorns. Hardly a week goes by that one doesn't read in *The Wall Street Journal* that some over-the-counter broker-dealer was put out of business somewhere in the country. Entrance is easy to the OTC securities business. There is no seat to buy. Capital requirements are ridiculously low for the new entrant, only $5,000.

When the SEC and the National Association of Securities Dealers close up a shop, the charges are usually violation of the capital rules (comparable to those of the New York Stock Exchange) and failure to keep adequate books. Other charges range from the distribution of unregistered securities (sometimes even members of the Exchange run afoul of this one) and violation of the antifraud provision of the federal securities statutes to the pledging of customers' securities for a dealer's own use.

Don't let the crack about the Wild West discourage you from buying stocks traded in the OTC market. Just as fortunes were made and lost in the frontier days, fortunes still await the venturesome. There are many top-notch firms in this market, and stock exchange houses often have a large OTC trading department. The rewards here can be far, far greater than in the listed market. In September, 1962, you could have bought 100 shares of Raychem Corporation at 29½. In 1968 it reached a high of $323, and in September, 1970, it was traded at 70. The company is one of the "exotic" firms; it has a new method that imparts certain qualities to plastics and other materials by radiation, making them stronger and temperature-resistant. But $323 was a ridiculous price for $3.03 worth of earnings. The stock was vastly overpriced. When people go overboard in the OTC market, they will outdo anything in the listed markets. When it is really active, it "boils," as the OTC trader says. But in a bear market, it just fades away.

High P/E stocks are not, however, traded only in the OTC market. On March 3, 1971, the New York Stock Exchange listed Electronic Data Systems Corporation at a P/E ratio of 132.8. To pay $81 for $.61 worth of earnings borders on folly, despite the business genius of Mr. H. Ross Perot. One wonders, considering all the sermons emanating from the Exchange on investing, whether the listing of stocks at such high P/E ratios constitutes a service to the investing public.

You could have done even better than Raychem with Host International, formerly Interstate Hosts. It runs restaurants, snack bars, and gift shops in airports. In September, 1962, you could have bought 1,000 shares at approximately $3.00 a share and sold them in 1969 at $45—or $45,000. Host International is now traded on the Big Board. But you could also have bought $1,000 worth of Hemisphere Fund in early 1969, and by late summer of 1970 your investment would have withered away to less than $30.

What really is this so-called over-the-counter market, sometimes referred to as the unlisted market?

The Over-the-Counter Securities Market(s)

The colorful Colonel Oliver J. Troster, whose military career stretched from chasing Pancho Villa in Mexico with General Pershing through two world wars to the Korean conflict and who, between world wars, built one of the finest wholesale OTC securities firms in the Street, said that he and F. H. Hatch, of Frederic H. Hatch and Co., the oldest OTC house in New York, invented the name. Mr. Hatch told Colonel Troster he could remember that, in his father's brokerage office right after the Civil War, government bonds were sold to people "over the counter." They were not listed on the Exchange. "Ollie" Troster continued, "That term 'over-the-counter' stuck in our minds, and in about three or four months we came up with the idea of publicizing and fastening that name to the OTC business as we know it." The two gentlemen did a good job, because the new name stuck. However, as Colonel Troster admits, it really isn't such a good name.

If you wonder where "the counter" is, you are in good company. During hearings on the Securities Exchange Act a United States Senator once asked, "Well, is there a counter some place in New York over which all you fellows gather and trade back and forth?"

An OTC transaction can be person-to-person, by mail, over teletype, telephone, any device that the electronics age puts at a trader's disposal, or any other method whereby two people get together on the price of a security—other than in the double auction market on an exchange. There is no central marketplace where brokers and dealers meet to trade securities.

Broker-Dealers

The participants in this market are called broker-dealers because they act in both capacities. But never as broker and dealer in the *same* trade. You can buy one hundred shares of American Express or Bankamerica through your regular broker and specify that you want to buy it "New York Stock Exchange Commission," and the regular Exchange commission will be charged to you. He may also quote you a net price: "I can offer the stock at one hundred forty net to you." In this case, his firm acts as a dealer and there is no commission, but he, like any other merchant, will mark up the price from his cost price.

If you are afraid he might be taking too much of a markup, insist that the stock be sold to you on NYSE commission basis. He then acts as your agent, and on his confirmation to you he must disclose the price at which he bought the stock. But don't outsmart yourself!

If you do business with a large stock exchange house that has an OTC trading department, it is at times possible for you to buy stock at the bid price. Let's say the stock is quoted 25½ bid and offered at 26. The house might have accumulated a large block at prices ranging from 24 to 25½ and may now be willing to dispose of it at the prevailing bid of 25½. People sometimes distrust such "offers." They shop around and are told everywhere that the stock is quoted 25½–26. They can even see the quote on NASDAQ (National Association of Securities Dealers Automatic Quotation). There must be something fishy if you can buy on the bid! No, it's fair and square; a merchant is trying to sell what he has on his shelf. There are always bargains around, but sometimes, as anybody in the Street will tell you, they are hard to sell. As one investor asked, "If it is as good as you say it is, why is it so cheap?" This is a tough question to answer. After all, you can't come out and call a client an idiot.

In a transaction with an OTC broker-dealer, or a stock exchange house with an OTC department, there are three possible ways to sell you Bankamerica stock. The broker-dealer can act as your broker and get it for you as an agent, for which he gets a commission. If he makes a market in the stock, he can sell it to you out of his inventory (in Wall Streetese, "position") as a dealer. Or he can take your order for one hundred shares, go out and buy them from another dealer, and sell them back to you. In both these cases he acts as a dealer; you buy net and he gets a markup as compensation.

Both American Express and the Bankamerica Corporation illustrate the fact that not all good-sized OTC companies are eager to have their securities listed on an exchange. They can meet all the requirements for listing and present as much information as listed companies, if not more. The managements of such companies will say, "The principal reason for not listing is that we have a fine market for our stock in the OTC market." Winthrop H. Smith, then managing partner of Merrill, Lynch, etc., once reminded the Board of Governors of the NYSE: "Stocks will be traded where the best markets are made for them." They don't come to the Big Board just because it is Mr. Big.

Markets Rather Than a Market

One really should not talk about *the* over-the-counter securities market. There are a number of radically different markets in this framework. It is, first of all, America's biggest stock market. Close to twenty times as many issues are traded in it as are traded on all other exchanges. It is America's biggest corporate bond market. A big bond house like Salomon Brothers might trade as many bonds in one day as are traded in the Exchange's bond room. Look at the daily report of bond trading on the NYSE. A lot of bonds are traded in very small amounts, in lots of less than twenty bonds. There are approximately one hundred of these small trades daily. The Exchange requires all member organizations to bring bond orders of less than ten bonds to the bond floor, the so-called nine-bond rule. But you can specify that your broker execute your order to buy or sell eight bonds OTC. Bond trading on the Exchange is increasing, particularly as individuals become more attracted by the prevailing high bond yields. NYSE bond trading in 1971 was almost twice the 1969 volume, an impressive $6.5 billion.

Just about all government securities and municipal bonds are traded in the OTC market. Between July 1, 1970, and June 30, 1971, dealer transactions in United States Government securities were over $32 billion—almost five times the bond volume on the Exchange. And there are only about two dozen bank and nonbank dealers in government securities. The daily volume of secondary municipal bond offerings, as shown in the *Blue List*, together with unadvertised blocks, is now close to $1 billion. During 1966 and again during 1969–1970, the secondary municipal bond market was put to a severe test in absorbing huge quantities of bonds as banks, pressed for lendable cash, sold hundreds of millions of dollars' worth of bonds. This was at a time when the whole capital market was under severe strain. These bonds were not only bought by dealers, but were redistributed by them in an orderly manner. New investors, particularly individuals, were found for the overloaded inventories. The OTC municipal bond market proved its effectiveness in these trying periods.

Most foreign securities, except for Canadian, are traded in the OTC market, usually through ADRs. Canadian banks are represented in the financial district, so that no transfer problems arise.

The open-end, mutual fund shares are also traded here, as are all new issues with the exception of newly listed securities offered through rights. The OTC market is *the* primary market. Companies that decide to go public will have to offer their shares OTC, although they may be listed soon after, as the Ford Motor Company did. Of course a market must first exist OTC for the shares.

The OTC market is a real competitor of the organized exchanges in yet another way. While a member organization of the NYSE cannot sell a listed security "off board" (outside of the auction market for the stock on the floor) without the approval of the Exchange, there is nothing to prevent a nonmember organization from buying a block of a listed stock from an institutional investor and then distributing it. Such a nonmember may make markets in listed securities, and through him you might be able, at times, to buy a listed security at the same offering price prevailing on the Exchange floor, at net—no commission.

The Money Market

In terms of dollars, the money market is the biggest sector of the OTC market. The merchandise traded there is in the form of private and public debt instruments with a maturity ranging from one day to one year. No equities are traded in the money market. The annual volume of these transactions runs high into the trillions of dollars.

A bank, corporation, institution, or individual goes into the money market to adjust a liquidity position. Anyone who is more liquid than necessary will exchange nonearning cash for an earning asset, a Treasury bill, commercial paper, or whatever the short-term debt instrument may be. When pressed for cash, he will sell such instruments.

The Federal Reserve authorities, our national money managers, also use the money market to influence, increase, or decrease the nation's money supply, which consists primarily of bank demand deposits, checking accounts, and, to a much lesser degree, currency, Federal Reserve Notes, and coins.

Negotiation

The key word in the OTC market is *negotiation*. When a broker goes to the post on the floor of the Exchange where a stock is traded and the lowest offer in the auction market is 35½, he can't say, "Look, dear fellow, I'd be happy to buy five hundred at a quarter; how about shaving your price a little?" There can be no higgling and haggling over price in the listed market. However, in the OTC market, prices are negotiated.

A trader in one house may call another for a quote. When told, he may retort, "Your offer is way out of line." He continues, as they say on Broadway, "Tell you what I'm gonna do." The inquiring trader will now make a counteroffer. But usually quotes have a tendency to be quite uniform throughout the market. If one trader's bid is higher than the others, he'll have a lot of stock dumped on him, and he finds that out very quickly. Perhaps that is what he wants, and if others want stock, they will have to match it or do better. If his offering price is lower than that of others, *he* gets the calls from buyers, not the others.

Sometimes a trader may quote a stock 30–31 "workout." This means the market in this stock is so thin that he'll have to try and see what he can do with the order. Some quotes are "firm"; others are "subject quotes," subject to confirmation. Quotes must be clearly designated as one or the other. If the quote is "firm," at least one hundred shares must be traded on that bid or offer, just as in the listed market. But good houses make better markets than that, and far larger amounts are bought or sold on a quote, just as a specialist on the floor may take far larger amounts than the hundred he must take or make available.

Narrow-Market Securities

The reason a lot of corporate securities are traded OTC is that they are not suited for the large auction markets of the NYSE or the Amex. The NYSE wants a minimum of 800,000 shares publicly held (the Amex, 300,000) and 2,000 shareholders of whom 1,800 are holders of round lots (the Amex, 900 and 600). It also wants a market value of the publicly held shares of at least $14 million; the Amex, $2 million.

In many companies officers, directors, and the families own a lot of the stock, so that the shares in the hands of the public are too few for the listed markets; in other words, the floating supply is too small to make an orderly market. This is why sometimes, when a story comes out on a successful smaller company, the stock zooms up as if jet-propelled. A lot of people want to buy, but the supply is not there. These companies also often have a small capitalization.

The danger then is that when a few individuals' repeated buying orders have driven up a stock with a small floating supply, they get locked in. The broker calls the client up and says: "Look, Fred, the stock looks terrific. Just went up another five bucks. Think of all the money you're making. Why not buy another five hundred shares?" And so he buys more. When he wants to sell his five thousand shares and take his "profit," the broker may come back asking, "To whom?" In the sharp market break in 1970, Raychem dropped by over fifty dollars in one trading session. There just were no buyers unless the price came way down. Imagine even a swinging stock like Natomas dropping that much in one day!

The OTC market is also the proving ground for unknown companies and unseasoned securities. As a company grows, becomes better known, increases its capitalization, and possibly splits the stock, more shares become available, and it may move to the Amex and, later, to the Big Board, or it may go directly there. Read *The Exchange* magazine or *The American Investor* of the Amex. In every monthly issue there is a write-up on the newly listed stocks. But Pabst Brewing Company, banks, and insurance companies must like the type of markets that are being made for their securities in the OTC, or they, as well as other "eligibles," would have moved to a listed market a long time ago.

OTC Quotations

The over-the-counter quotations carried by the major daily newspapers are not, as is the case with the daily exchange reports, statements of actual sales. They are wholesale bid and asked prices and do not include any retail markup or commission. The bids and offers you read about today were quoted yesterday by dealers to each other as of about 3:30 P.M. This has led to a lot of confusion on the part of investors.

Let's say that Wehr Corporation, a maker of ventilation equipment, is given in your newspaper as 18½ bid, 19¼ offered. You bought 100 shares of Wehr yesterday, and when you receive your confirmation, the price is given as $20. Result: You blow your stack. You are convinced that your broker has overcharged you, and all the suspicions you have harbored against the OTC market are now confirmed. But wait a minute. The quote you have in front of you was a 3:30 P.M. closing price; your shares were bought at 2:45 P.M. Markets change in that period of time. Moreover, the 19¼ asked price did not include a markup or a commission.

I repeat again: When you buy on a commission basis, the house must disclose to you the price at which the securities were bought for you. That is not done when the house acts as a dealer. The markup is not shown, and you are billed "net." But whether the firm is willing to do business with you on an NYSE commission basis is another question. On either of the stocks I cited (American Express and Bankamerica) it probably would, but on less actively traded securities it probably would not. As a general rule, trading in the OTC securities markets tends to be somewhat more costly than trading in listed markets. There is a simple reason for this: If the dealer maintains a position in a security, he takes a risk that a broker never assumes. He is entitled to compensation for this risk assumption, as any businessman is. As the old saying has it: You can never go broke taking commissions. But a lot of dealers have gone bankrupt because they held positions when the market turned against them. Sometimes a dealer incurs considerable expenses trying to locate the amount of a less actively traded stock that a customer wants to buy.

So give your broker the benefit of the doubt that you expect others to give you. As a rule of thumb, I would say that trading in the less active stocks with a reputable house might cost you a markup of up to 3 percent, or double the NYSE commission. Remember that most of the securities traded in the OTC market represent companies not eligible for listing on the NYSE or other exchanges. They cannot meet their minimum numerical listing standards. Most of the companies are small or in the developing stage, and that is where the great opportunities are for making big money. But before placing an order, you should discuss cost with your account executive. It avoids misunderstandings later.

If you do not find a security of interest to you in the daily OTC list, try the Sunday paper. Once a week there appears an over-the-counter weekly list, composed of unlisted securities less widely held than those on the daily list. Such a weekly list appears also in *The Wall Street Journal* on Mondays.

The National Quotation Bureau Summaries

The wholesale daily and weekly newspaper quotations are given out under the supervision of the National Association of Securities Dealers (NASD). Consider them a guide to the approximate range within which these securities could have been bought or sold at the closing time of each day's compilation. In addition to these newspaper quotes, there are also the so-called daily pink sheets for dealers. They contain a listing of the names and addresses, including telephone and TWX numbers, and their bids and offers of the houses that make markets in the various OTC securities. How does a trader know what firms are making the markets for securities not given by the new NASDAQ system? He consults "the sheets." A reputable house will always check the market; the trader will call at least three houses before your order is executed at the best possible price.

Where can you as an investor find an OTC security that is not given in either the daily or the weekly list? There is a monthly summary service published by the National Quotation Bureau. It is a summary of all the issues that have appeared in the daily pink sheets and it covers, in addition, thousands of names that, because of their inactivity, rarely if ever appear in the daily sheets. This monthly service is cumulative for six months. If the issue you are looking for is not in the monthly supplement, try the semiannual volume. It goes back for a period of five years, and in some cases even longer.

These summaries also give important information relative to mergers and reorganizations. They tell where the stock should be sent in the event of a liquidation pay-out. If new securities and cash were issued against it, they give the approximate value of what the investor is entitled to receive and where he should go to get it.

The summaries carry, in addition, the principal address of most of the companies listed in them; the important provisions covering conversions, redemptions, and callable features; transfer agents in case of stocks; and trustees in case of bonds.

If you live too far away from a brokerage office where you could consult these volumes, try your bank. Banks throughout the country use them in their trust departments for appraisal purposes.

There is also an NASDAQ composite stock index published daily, with industrial, insurance, and bank subindexes. In active markets it tends to outperform the Dow-Jones industrial averages.

The Cops and Fair Pricing

Under the Maloney Act of 1938, an amendment to the Securities Exchange Act of 1934, the National Association of Securities Dealers was set up and empowered to regulate the OTC securities markets in a manner comparable to the powers possessed by an exchange in regulating its markets and members. The NASD, like an exchange, can censure, fine, suspend, and expel members.

A Code of Fair Practice was drawn up whose individual rules are designed to promote and enforce just and equitable principles of trade. Violation of just and equitable principles of trade is a very serious charge and usually leads to expulsion, in the OTC market or on the NYSE. These fair practice rules are guides for OTC firms to ensure that they conduct their business on a high ethical level. The Securities and Exchange Commission, in turn, supervises the NASD cops.

When an NASD member is expelled, he is through. NASD members can only deal with nonmember broker-dealers on the same basis as with other members of the public. They are prohibited from joining with any nonmember broker-dealer in any underwriting of securities. In day-to-day trading, members may give discounts to other members that they are not permitted to give nonmembers. There is thus a strong incentive to maintain NASD membership, and that can't be done if rules are violated.

The NASD has a fair pricing policy that should be of interest to every investor. Any commission charged or any markup added is judged, if challenged, on this basic question: In the light of this particular transaction, did the customer get a fair price?

Several important factors are considered by the NASD in order to determine fairness of price. One factor is the type of security involved. Bonds merit a lower profit than stocks; they entail less risk for the dealer and tend to trade more actively than many stocks. Another factor is the availability of the security in the market and its price. The stock of the Mellon National Bank and Trust Company of Pittsburgh would thus permit a much lower markup or commission than an order for 50 shares of the First National Bank of Paducah. What was the dealer's cost of obtaining the stock, and what was the size of the order? A $1,000 order for an inactively traded mining stock might carry a fair markup of 5 percent; a $15,000 order for an actively traded stock would certainly be unfairly priced with a $750 markup. The NASD (and, if an appeal is made to the SEC, the SEC) will look at the whole pattern of the dealer's markup and whether or not he told his customers in advance what the charges would be. However, telling a customer what the charges will be and even obtaining his consent to pay them does not necessarily get a dealer past the cops. They may still nail him on an unfair price charge.

The securities business is not a public utility, entitled to a fair rate of return on its capital, any more than any other business. Suppose a firm had a lot of unreasonable expenses, such as excessive salaries to its officers and excessive commissions to its account executives or huge losses on inventory positions because the firm was speculating. It could not excuse a 40-percent markup (and there were such cases!) by pleading, "If we don't charge that much, we are operating at a loss." The only thing that counts is whether the price charged was fair and reasonably related to the current market. The NASD pricing rule is not designed to guarantee a house a profit; it is designed as protection for the customers. Quite a number of dealers were put out of business for charging and giving unfair prices. It was such practices as these that gave the OTC market a bad reputation for so long.

If you feel you were unfairly treated, discuss it first with your broker-dealer. Even with computers, honest mistakes can occur, particularly in very active markets. But be fair with him, too. I have given you enough criteria here to judge for yourselves whether the price was fair in the light of your particular transaction. Should you still feel that you were unfairly treated, it is your right to bring the matter to the attention of the NASD's district business conduct committee. The NASD is divided into thirteen regional districts, and in each there is at least one such business conduct committee. Usually the district committee itself functions as the district business conduct committee. However, when conditions demand it, the district committee might appoint a number of local business conduct committees that function then as subcommittees. The district offices currently are in Atlanta, Boston, Chicago, Cleveland, Dallas, Denver, Kansas City, Los Angeles, New Orleans, New York, Philadelphia, St. Louis, San Francisco, Seattle, and Washington, D.C. The conduct committees all have authority to examine the books of a firm and its business practices.

The Outlook

The 1970s will see a lot of new, small companies in new fields coming down the pike. Some of them will make it big for good. Others will be big just for a little while. Paste a few rules for OTC trading in your hat and look at them every time you take it off:

Deal only with reputable brokerage firms.

Before committing funds for a small, young, struggling company, try to obtain at least an annual report and an income statement. Look at it and use the tools I have put at your disposal in Chapter 15. At the time when a real growth company is cheap, its balance sheet will frighten you. Working capital is being diverted into fixed assets; accounts receivable are sold; accounts payable are large; in short, the company has hocked about everything it can lay its hands on. In such a case, forget about ratios; take 10 percent of your profits in other transactions and risk it.

Buy into an owner management that controls the business and has a high profit margin, no less than 20 percent before taxes.

Find out who makes markets in the stock. It's in the pink sheets. If the market makers are good, well-known firms, fine. If the market makers are little unknowns, stay away from the stock.

These companies have a small capitalization, and with owner management the floating supply of the stock is small. Once they move, they zoom. As the story gets around, more and more people want to buy and the supply isn't there. So up she goes by leaps and bounds. Don't forget, it works the same way on the way down.

Loral Electronics was 12 in 1959, and by June the following year the stock was 101. In 1970 it had become a listed company under the name Loral Corporation with a very uninspiring record. In early 1972 it was 6. Kalvar was 20 in 1958, and three years later it had zoomed to about 700. In 1971 it was quoted 13¼–14¼. Farrington Manufacturing Company was a $2 stock in 1958, and close to $60 two years later. In the summer of 1970 it was again a $2½ stock—with a series of deficits and an arrearage on the preferred stock. The moral of the story: Sell 'em when you can get out at what you consider to be a nice profit, and let somebody else make a few bucks. Over the long run, you will be definitely ahead of the over-the-counter game with that type of philosophy.

Above all, investigate before you shell out your hard-earned dough. On December 13, 1971, an important new SEC rule went into effect: OTC market-makers are prohibited from giving quotations on a new company's stock or on the securities of established companies that trade only sporadically *unless* they have extensive financial and other data in their files. There are still many stocks traded over the counter daily, however, about which neither market-makers nor investors know anything. That leaves lots of room for fraud. So watch it and ask for information.

Finally, don't expect the same markup or commission charge on the stock of a swinging company as the broker-dealer charges you on the purchase of a sedate and established company's stock.

Summary

1. The OTC securities market is America's biggest bond and stock market. Fortunes are made here, and those who wait too long will lose it all again.

2. If you're afraid that you will be taken, insist that you want to buy on a New York Stock Exchange commission basis. If the stock is hard to get and yoyoing around, be prepared to pay a higher commission or markup because your dealer assumes more risk and incurs greater expenses.

3. There are quite a number of stocks traded in the OTC market that are eligible for listing on the NYSE.

4. The OTC market consists of a series of securities markets.

5. The keyword is *negotiation.*

6. Quotes may be "firm," "subject," or "workout."

7. The OTC market is not an exchange market. For many of its stocks, the market is very thin because the company's capitalization is small and the floating supply is still smaller.

8. OTC quotations are not reports on actual sales. They merely indicate a range within which business could have been done, at a certain hour.

9. Trading in the OTC market tends to cost more than trading in listed markets.

10. If you think that the price you were charged wasn't fair, discuss it with your broker. He knows you can always complain to the NASD's business conduct committee—and you should.

11. If you can't find anything on the company, look for the summaries of the National Quotation Bureau.

12. The fairness of the markup or commission is determined in the light of the transaction and the prevailing market.

CHAPTER 7

Which Fund Should It Be?

The question of which fund to buy involves two different basic aspects.

First, the type of fund to be chosen must fit the investment objective of the buyer. Second, within a particular type of fund a selection of a specific fund must then be made. This second choice will be made on a basis of the costs and the rights given to shareholders under the contract and on the past performance of that management. This is not an easy task today. The asset value of open-end investment companies, mutual funds, decreased from about $53 billion in May, 1969, to $38.5 billion at the end of June, 1970. Redemptions over this period were $3.9 billion. Closed-end fund assets also showed substantial declines. By the end of April, 1971, mutual fund assets were back to the $55-billion level.

By getting out of a fund early in 1969, the investor did far better than by staying with even the best of funds through this period, particularly if he invested his money in short-term federal agency notes.

What happened to the professional money managers? Why didn't they sell their stocks and go into short-term private or public debt instruments? They couldn't do it for many reasons. A lot of funds have to keep under their charters a certain percentage of their assets in common stocks. Moreover, there is here a very ticklish question: How can you charge 8½ percent to manage somebody's money when you put it all into cash equivalents? The investor doesn't need management for that; he can do that by himself. Some funds, however, did have very large cash positions. Imagine also what would have happened to the stock market had all funds liquidated their stock portfolios! A crisis would have developed that would have made 1929 look like a technical reaction by comparison.

Both the Windsor Fund and the Channing Special Fund performed marvelously in the previous bull market. In the bear market both showed substantial losses. Windsor was down 29 percent; Channing, over 66 percent.

This illustrates the problem of selecting a fund; it also shows the difficulty of properly defining an investment company. For example, should we define an investment company as an investment medium that by its very nature is condemned to ride a bear market all the way down? Maybe so.

An investment company can be broadly defined as a corporation or, in some cases, a business trust that funnels the funds of individual investors into one single investment account. The dollars of the investors are converted by the fund's management into securities that are then placed into a basket, and every investor receives a certificate showing his proportionate and undivided interest. If the fund is $10 million, which would be much too small today, and he put in $100,000, he would have a 1-percent undivided interest in the fund's net assets. If his investment is only $1,000, he would own 0.01 percent of the net value. This shows that large and small investors alike can obtain diversification and professional management for the continuous supervision of the assets. No wonder funds caught on. In the ten-year period 1959–1968, the open-end investment companies more than tripled their assets—from $15.8 billion to $52.7 billion. The life insurance companies, even during their biggest growth years, only doubled their assets every ten years. No wonder so many of them entered the fund business when their growth rate was slowing down.

The Investment Company Act of 1940 says, ". . . investment companies are divided into three principal classes." They are (1) face-amount certificate companies, (2) unit investment trusts, and (3) management companies.

The Face-Amount Certificate Company

It guarantees to the purchaser a fixed sum, the face amount of the certificate upon its maturity, which is usually in ten years. The difference between the investor's periodic payments (or a single payment) and its maturity value is, of course, compound interest.

If we disregard the insurance feature, this is comparable to an endowment policy that also guarantees a fixed amount at the end of a given period. Under the 1940 act, the reserves to be held against the outstanding certificates must be "in cash or qualified investments." "Qualified investments" are defined as "investments of a kind which life insurance companies are permitted to invest in or hold. . . ." For a long time to come, way past the 1970s, interest rates will stay high, far higher than what used to be considered normal in the 1950s or the mid-sixties, so that more attractive investment outlets will be available to all investors who wish to purchase debt instruments. As with all debt instruments, there is no chance for capital gains with a face certificate. And with a great economic expansion staring us in the face, investors are still out for capital gains.

The Unit Investment Trust

The Investment Company Act says, "Unit investment trust means an investment company which (A) is organized under a trust indenture, contract of custodianship or agency, or similar instruments, (B) does not have a board of directors, and (C) issues only redeemable securities, each of which represents an undivided interest in a unit of specified securities; but does not include a voting trust."

This classification fits the Municipal Investment Trust Funds discussed in Chapter 14. Here is a so-called fixed trust that invests, in this case, "in a unit of specified securities," to wit, municipal bonds. The MITs are issued under a custodianship; a bank or trust company has physical possession of this fixed list of municipal securities, and they cannot be changed. The sponsor-managers cannot change this list except to sell a security that threatens to go bad. The proceeds cannot be reinvested at the discretion of management; they must be distributed pro rata to the shareholders. There is therefore no annual management fee.

Instead of municipal securities, fixed trusts could, of course, be organized to invest in a list of corporate and government securities. In view of the managerial debacle of so many mutual funds in the recent big bad bear market, we might see a new increase in fixed trusts, unmanaged investment companies, which invest in a fixed list of common shares.

Fixed trusts, from a legal point of view, also include the so-called contractual plan company. Here the investor makes a unilateral contract with the plan company that he will invest, say, ten thousand dollars over a period of ten years. The plan company, in turn, invests the periodic payments in a fund under its complete control. When considering the purchase of a contractual plan—and there is a lot that can be said for them—you must under law receive two prospectuses—one of the plan company, and the other of the underlying fund. Since the plan company has full managerial powers, from a practical point of view it makes more sense to discuss "contractuals" in connection with open-end fully managed investment companies, that is, the mutuals.

The Management Investment Company

We quote the 1940 act again: "Management company means any investment company other than a face-amount certificate company or a unit investment trust." A management investment company has discretionary powers to manage the fund as it sees fit—subject to the investment objectives as stated in the prospectus or charter. There are two types: the open-end investment company, or mutual fund, and the closed-end company.

The Closed-End Investment Company

A closed-end investment company has, at any one time, a fixed amount of shares outstanding just as any other corporation.

It may, of course, issue additional shares, but they will be distributed through an investment banking group. It is under no contractual obligation to redeem its shares. As any other company's shares, they can only be bought in the secondary market, wherever that may be—on an exchange or in the over-the-counter securities market. If the investor needs his money, he must sell in the secondary market.

The price of the closed-end investment company's shares is determined by the demand for and the supply of the investment company's shares. When many people want to buy them, they will sell at a premium over their net asset value; when many investors want to sell them, the price will be at a discount from net asset value. This is in sharp contrast to the price determination of mutual fund shares. Their prices depend on the demand for and the supply of the securities that a fund has in its portfolio. The mutual fund shares will always sell at net asset value plus whatever, if any, sales charge a fund has. You will never buy a mutual fund share at a discount from net asset value. It would be against the law, because the new shareholders, who bought at a discount, would take money away from the old shareholders.

Among the pioneer closed-end funds are Lehman Corporation and Tri-Continental. They have ridden out many a storm and are listed on the Big Board. There are about two dozen more that are traded on the NYSE. The Niagara Share Corporation is among them; it has done quite well in both "up" as well as "down" markets, and is therefore some kind of rarity among all funds. If you can buy it at a discount from net asset value, it might be a good idea for you to do so. Central Securities, on the Amex, is more of a swinger. It has done very, very well in bull markets, but very, very badly in bear markets. The question then always arises: Can you take such a risk? Suppose you have to liquidate in a bad market?

In the wild and woolly days of yesteryear, quite a number of closed-end investment companies had considerable leverage in their financial structure. They had bonds and/or preferred stock outstanding. As long as the fund earned more than the total interest and preferred dividend charges, things just couldn't be more lovely. Just think, a fund with a portfolio of $10 million has 50 percent bonds and preferred stock outstanding. A 10-percent rise in the value of the portfolio would cause a 20-percent increase in the net asset value of the common shares, because bond and preferred shareholders are only entitled to the face value of the bonds or shares plus a small call premium. A 10-percent decline would, of course, have the same effect—on the downside. Leverage causes both the net asset value and income for the common stock to fluctuate widely. I need not stress the fact that during the Great Depression these leveraged funds were really hanging on the ropes. For this reason almost all the closed-end companies have either retired their senior securities or increased the amount of senior securities in their portfolios in order to offset the leverage in their capitalization.

The Dual Purpose Fund

In early 1967 a new type of leveraged closed-end investment company made its appearance: the dual purpose investment company. When the Gemini Fund came out, it issued 1,650,000 capital shares, now listed on the NYSE, and an equal amount of income shares.

The income shares are entitled to all income earned on the capital furnished by both classes of stock. The capital share-holders are entitled to all capital appreciation from the capital furnished by both classes of stock. They will receive no dividends or capital-gains distribution as long as the income shares are outstanding. All income shares are to be redeemed at $11 (they were originally sold at $12) on December 31, 1984. The minimum cumulative dividend on the income shares is about 4.7 percent. The selection for the Gemini's portfolio, which is typical of the dual vest funds, is made with a view of potential growth of both capital and income. When 1984 rolls around and the income shares are paid off, Gemini will probably be changed into an open-end fund.

The Gemini income shares have done quite well, with about an 8-percent dividend return in 1971. Other dual purpose funds have done even better. Income and capital shares (the shares are on the NYSE) paid 9.6 percent. The income shares of American DualVest Fund are also doing very well, with a return of 10 percent. In this case both the common and the preferred stock (which is what income shares are) are listed on the Big Board. I have a very strong feeling that account executives don't understand these dual vest plans. For example, American DualVest preferred was selling for $13.50 in early 1972, with a dividend given as $1.07.

But if leverage works for the income shares, won't it work equally well for the capital shares? The investor in capital shares will receive in 1984 whatever capital gains have been achieved on an initial investment of $2 over 15 years for every $1 paid in by him when the corporation was started. This is why I insist that brokers don't understand these new securities. They cannot be compared to conventional securities for income and capital appreciation. They forget that, given time, stocks with growing earnings will produce both—greater income and capital gains.

Suppose the Dow-Jones industrial averages, if we still retain the silly things in 1984, rise over the next 15 years by 50 percent. This is very conservative when you figure that the DJIA were 442.72 in 1955, and GNP was then $398 billion. So assuming just a 50-percent rise in the averages by 1984, figure out what these leveraged capital shares will be worth!

Scudder Duo-Vest capital shares were quoted on the NYSE in February, 1972, at 8¾. They came out originally at $9.15! In 1982, when the income shares will be redeemed at $9.15 or converted into capital shares at whatever the net asset value of the shares will be then, GNP will be close to $2 trillion. Do you want to guess again what their value will be? At 8¾ this is discounting future values at a ridiculous percentage. These dual vest capital shares will outdo the DJIA performance by a wide margin; they have to, for they are leveraged. Buy some and put them away for the kids' education.

The Open-End Company

The open-end companies, the mutuals, are usually organized as corporations, but a handful of them were set up as common-law trusts. All offer their shares to the public continuously and stand ready to redeem them at any time at the bid price, that is, the net asset value that is computed daily after the close of the market. There is no leverage in their financial structure, but they may provide leverage through the purchase of shares in leveraged companies.

Mutual fund shares are usually offered through an underwriter, also called distributor, wholesaler, or sponsor, who buys the shares from the fund at net asset value and resells them to the public through a group of dealers. The public offering price, the asked price, is the net asset value plus a sales charge. For the smallest amount of purchase it varies between 7½ and 8.8 percent. As the amount purchased increases, the sales charge declines substantially. Out of an 8-percent sales charge on a $10,000 purchase, the dealer, your brokerage firm, usually retains 6½ percent, part of which goes, of course, to the salesman. Out of the other 1½ percent the sponsor pays the expenses of promoting the fund, such as sales literature and advertising. The fund must always receive the net asset value of the shares sold.

Some funds have their own sales organizations, notably the newly established funds of the life insurance companies. Shares in no-load funds are purchased directly from the fund. They are usually associated with an investment advisory organization that receives as its compensation an investment management fee. Lionel D. Edie and Co. was an investment counselor that sold two no-load funds. Now it is part of Merrill Lynch, Pierce, Fenner & Smith. Bache & Co., Inc., the second largest financial department store in the securities industry, started its own Bayrock Fund. It was a luscious business for a profit-starved Wall Street in 1970: an 8½-percent load charge or whatever the charge is, an investment advisory fee, and commissions for executing the fund's buy and sell orders. It almost looks as if all this is a little too much and harbors a conflict of interest. You can bet your last dollar the SEC will be watching. It should. But if firms can bring out Municipal Investment Trust Funds, why not a stock fund?

Over the years a series of open-end funds have developed that are rather sharply differentiated by their investment objectives. They are general-purpose diversified common-stock funds, balanced funds, growth funds, income funds, specialty funds, the United States Government Securities Fund, hedge funds, and exchange funds.

The General-Purpose Diversified Common-Stock Fund

These funds, as illustrated by the Affiliated Fund, also known as "the conscience of the mutual fund industry," are the largest group in the mutual fund industry. Their general investment objective is long-term growth of capital and income. As a rule, a large percentage of their assets is invested at all times in good-quality common stocks or securities convertible into them. The remainder of the assets are in cash and short-term public or private notes such as Treasury bills, government agency notes, or commercial paper.

The Balanced Fund

These funds invest in high-grade bonds, and preferred and common stocks. The prospectus may stipulate that they be bought in a certain ratio, or the directors may have complete discretion. Group Securities Balanced Fund would be an example here. It is, as are balanced funds in general, most conservatively run, far better protected in "down" markets than other funds, but not likely to show a lot of appreciation in "up" markets.

The investment objective of this type of fund is to produce reasonable current income with protection of the principal over the long pull. But what is meant by "protection of the principal"? To keep it intact in terms of dollars, or in terms of purchasing power? There is a whale of a difference between the two.

The Growth Fund

The investment objective here is growth at the sacrifice of current income. These funds concentrate on companies that plow back their earnings and are leveraged. Often the stocks of smaller, developing companies are purchased. They carry a higher risk than the general-purpose diversified common-stock funds and are more volatile. This is best illustrated by the Enterprise Fund, a hot fund that built almost to one billion dollars in assets, primarily by buying into smaller companies. It had a stellar performance as long as the market went up, and a catastrophic one when it came down.

The Income Fund

While these funds resemble balanced funds, they carry a higher risk. They sacrifice quality in order to obtain higher income than the more conservatively managed balanced funds are capable of producing. The Channing Income Fund seems to have done rather well, no matter what market trends were.

The Specialty Fund

This category is a catchall for different types of "specialties." The industry specialized funds may invest in a single industry or related industries such as the Chemical Fund, which has done very well. It invests not only in chemical companies, but also in the oils. Other specialty funds would be in electronics, insurance, oceanography or ocean technology, and other areas. There are also those that specialize in foreign securities such as Canadian, Western European, or Japanese.

The U.S. Government Securities Fund

In 1970 the mutual fund for investing in United States Government securities was set up. Fattened with Treasury interest payments of nearly 8 percent, it paid at the end of its first 6-month period $.36 on each $10 share, or an annual rate of 7.2 percent. Of course, prospects for growth are not too great.

Arthur Lipper Corporation, a firm that keeps tabs on the mutual fund industry, as do Arthur Wiesenberger and *Forbes*, said that 459 out of 464 mutual funds closed the first half of 1970 with a lower per-share net asset value than on January 1, 1970. The average decline was 25.7 percent. The government securities fund, however, increased its assets by 3.75 percent, the result of lower interest rates. It heads the list of the five funds that managed to post small gains.

The minimum investment is $250, which should enable smaller investors to come back into the government securities market. They were driven out when the minimum purchase of Treasury bills was boosted to $10,000. Here is your chance to get more than you could on government savings bonds or in a savings deposit at the bank. You can buy into this new fund through a payroll savings plan. If there are sizable deductions in the interest rate ahead over the next few years, this fund is not bad at all as a haven for savings. But then it becomes as speculative as other funds, except that here you speculate on interest rate changes.

The Hedge Fund

These funds—such as the Hedge Fund of America, started in 1968, and the Hubschman Fund, started two years earlier—are high-risk investments. They do about everything. They buy some stocks and sell others short, hopefully expecting to make capital gains no matter whether the market is going up or down. They might even buy or sell (that is, write) options.

The Exchange Fund

At the beginning of the last decade, another type of fund was established, the exchange fund or swap fund. Suppose an investor had bought 200 shares of Jersey Standard at 50 back in the late 1940s. By 1960, through two splits, he would have owned 1,200 shares at about 60. This gave him a capital gain of $62,000 and a tax bill of $15,500. In an exchange fund, such as one of the series of Empire Fund, he could have exchanged his 1,200 shares of Jersey for Empire Fund shares without having to pay a tax. His capital base was thus kept intact, so that he could have made larger future gains than he would have if his capital had been reduced by $15,500. The tax liability would be settled when the fund shares were sold.

The Congress has now outlawed this type of tax-free exchange fund. I mention them here because—who knows?—they may come back some day, and you ought to know about them. The exchange funds did not make a continuous offering of their shares in exchange for a list of other securities, but there was always another one coming out, such as with the MITs. But they must be considered mutual funds because their securities are redeemable at net asset value. Quite a number of them are, of course, still in existence with some $750 million in assets.

Advantages of Mutual Funds for the Investor

Funds give *diversification,* and that reduces the risk factor. Many investors kid themselves when they think that just picking and choosing different stocks adds up to diversification. It may just add up to an investment mess. This is where *professional management* comes in—for selection and continuous portfolio supervision.

Just as a bond is whatever the indenture says it is, a mutual fund is whatever the prospectus says it is. You *must* read it if you contemplate buying a fund. The load charge ranges from a legal maximum of 9 percent to zero with the no-load funds. A lot of them charge 8½ percent up to $25,000. Affiliated Fund has an initial charge of 7½ percent; Istel Fund, 3 percent. All mutual funds give *100-percent liquidity;* they will redeem the shares on any business day. What other rights and privileges does a fund give you? The prospectus will tell you.

Does the fund you intend buying give you a *conversion privilege?* This could be very valuable to you. As you approach retirement, you can afford to take much less risk than before. You should change from a growth to a common stock or perhaps a balanced fund. Does this particular fund give you the right to convert from one fund into another in the same family without a load charge? If you own securities outright and you sell them and reinvest the proceeds, you have two commissions to pay. There is 2 percent right here. In either case you must pay capital-gains taxes if there are gains.

Do you have the *right of accumulation?* This allows you as you purchase additional shares to consider the current value of the shares you already own. The applicable sales charge is determined by adding together your current purchase plus the value of all previously accumulated shares. This can reduce your sales charge appreciably when you accumulate shares.

What about the privilege of using your fund accumulation, before or after conversion to a more suitable fund, as a *with-*

drawal plan? While this is not a scientific liquidation of an estate (as would be the case with an annuity), it can give you everything the annuity gives plus a lot more. An annuity pays you as long as you live, and if it is a survivorship annuity, it pays someone else. But the fixed annuity is exposed to the inflation-induced erosion of purchasing power, and the few variable annuities have very bad performance records. I suggest that you set up a 6-percent withdrawal plan a year before retirement and let one year's earnings, derived from dividends and capital gains distributions, accumulate as a contingency reserve. A good fund earns consistently considerably more from both sources than 6 percent, so that it is quite common to have a 6-percent annual withdrawal, and after ten or twenty years the "annuitant's" fund is considerably larger than it was before the retirement payments began.

If you are a younger person, by all means start *a voluntary accumulation plan with decreasing term life insurance.* Agree that you will buy, say, $10,000 worth of a given fund's shares over a ten-year period, but buy the shares on the pay-as-you-go plan with decreasing term life insurance. The insurance, being group insurance, is very cheap and you protect your family. If an investor dies after having made payments for five years, he would have $5,000 plus dividends and capital-gains distributions reinvested plus whatever appreciation the shares showed, and $5,000, the proceeds of the life insurance policy, will also be invested in fund shares. In other words, the contract is guaranteed to be completed. The widow and children will probably be able to live quite comfortably on Social Security and any proceeds from life insurance that the deceased might have had in the business or by himself. Ten years later the $10,000-plus in the mutual fund could easily be $20,000 or $25,000. Reread this paragraph in the light of what I said in Chapter 2 in regard to financial planning. It will pay you.

Funds lend themselves beautifully to *dollar cost averaging,* under which your average cost of the shares will *always* be less than the average price paid for the shares. Think of the bargains that somebody bought in 1969 and 1970 who regularly invested $100 a month in a fund. When the price was low, he bought many more shares than when the price was high.

Under the Self-Employed Individuals Tax Retirement Act, more commonly known as the *Keogh Act,* mutual funds are specified as one of the four permissible methods of investing. A lot of people have tax deductions under this act but don't take them.

A professor who gets an additional ten thousand dollars a year from consultant work can deduct 10 percent of this and put it into a mutual fund *provided* the firm that hires him does not make any withholding-tax deductions. The fact that he is covered by Teacher's Insurance and Annuities Association and College Retirement Equities Fund makes no difference. The fact that an individual is covered by one pension arrangement does not disqualify him from setting up a Keogh plan for himself from other income.

Here is not only a $1,000 annual tax deduction (it might be as high as $2,500), but any income or capital gains in his Keogh plan is not taxed to him until he retires. This means he has a larger capital base on which to build. Many people eligible for a Keogh plan either don't know anything about it or don't do anything about it, foolish as it seems.

Another way to whittle down the sales load is through a *letter of intent.* Suppose you have bought $25,000 worth of a given fund's shares today. Sign a statement that you will buy another $25,000, or whatever the amount is, over the next 13 months if funds are coming in to you over this period. You will at once receive the lower sales charge applicable to $50,000. You have three months to make up your mind to sign such a letter. But if you come along in the fourth and all-of-a-sudden think of it, you have missed your chance. If the money doesn't come in and you can't invest the other $25,000, no damage is done. You will simply pay the higher charge applicable to $25,000. Some of the shares are held by the bank, which is the fund's custodian, in escrow to provide for an adjustment in the load charge that must be made if the additional purchase is not made.

Under the heading of *convenience,* I can mention several important items:

Have you ever sat down on April 14 to make out your tax return and found that neither you nor your wife could figure out what was income from your securities and what were short-term or long-term capital gains? Most funds make it easy for you. They will mail you at the end of each year a Treasury form showing what was received as income and what was a short-term or long-term capital-gains distribution.

A busy man or woman is not continually plagued by investment decisions that must be made. In case of death of the investor, there is no break in investment management and supervision.

Instead of a lot of stock certificates, there is only one, so that physical security is much less of a problem.

Why should older people bother with dividend checks? Why be obliged to go to the bank in all kinds of weather to deposit dividend checks or have a surly daughter-in-law drive Mother to the bank when she ought to take Junior to the dentist? Sell your securities and buy a good withdrawal plan. Life can be so much simpler and happier.

Taxation

Under the so-called conduit theory, dividends and capital gains may flow through the fund to the shareholder without the fund assuming any tax liability. Most mutual funds distribute 100 percent of their net income in order to avoid paying taxes. If you were to buy fund shares today and if, one month from now, you received a long-term capital-gains distribution, it would be a long-term gain to you. You could hold shares for five years, but if the distribution was a short-term capital gain to the fund, it is a short-term gain for you.

But now look at tax matters in the light of the 1970s. Most funds today have tax credits. They sold securities at losses. As a result, many funds can sell securities to offset new capital gains against their losses without distributing the proceeds of the sale, and can then reinvest them because no tax liability was incurred. The shareholders benefit because they pay no tax either. The fund can carry long-term capital losses forward for five years and offset future gains against them. Instead of having these new capital gains distributed, so that the investing taxpayer pays the tax and reinvests a smaller amount, the fund can now build up the net asset value of the old shares without incurring any tax liability to the shareholders until such time as the tax credit carried forward is exhausted. The disaster area of the go-go funds offers here intriguing possibilities, if they perform well from here on and make capital gains.

These tax aspects will also increase a fund manager's portfolio flexibility. He can now sell stocks with large capital gains, since he has tax offsets. The stock market should reflect this by increased trading volumes.

Criteria to Judge Mutual Funds

What is the *expense ratio*—the ratio of total expenses to the average net assets for the period? Naturally ratios of large funds tend to be a lot lower than ratios of smaller funds.

What is the *income ratio*—the percentage of the fund's income absorbed by expenses? But don't compare an income with a growth fund!

How much is paid out in *management fees?* Usually 0.5 percent of the fund's total assets or less. During the bull market of the late 1960s, a number of fund managers said they wanted to get paid on a sliding scale depending on their performance. Some were modest; others, like some hedge funds, had no ceiling. Now with bad markets in 1970, the bright boys don't think so much of performance fees any more. But there can be a sensible arrangement to give incentive to a fund's management *if* there is a reasonable ceiling.

Check the *sales charge,* particularly the break points. At what point is the charge reduced and by how much? Can dividends be reinvested at net asset value? Some funds permit it; usually capital-gains distributions are reinvested at net asset value.

One measure of *performance,* which includes both dividend income and capital gains, can be obtained by taking the net asset value at the end of the period, adding both income and capital-gains distributions, and then comparing the total with the net asset value at the beginning of the period.

You can also look in the annual volume on *Investment Companies,* published by Arthur Wiesenberger and Company. You will find investment objectives, management, and past performance for both closed-end and open-end funds.

Contractual Plans

Finally, let's consider the much-maligned contractual plans. They have a "front-end load." Suppose an investor contracts to buy $10,000 in shares of the underlying fund of the plan company on a periodic payment basis. To help enforce the plan, up to 50 percent of the first year's payments is used to pay part of the sales charge applicable to the entire program. This, of course, reduces the sales load for the payments in future years. But if the plan has been sold badly and is terminated after two years, the investor takes a beating. It is this feature that gave the plan the name "penalty plan" and caused so much criticism. Nevertheless there are redeeming features of the plan that are usually not mentioned.

It carries cheap decreasing life term insurance to guarantee the completion of the program. If a payment is not made for more than one month, the insurance lapses and the plan becomes simply another voluntary accumulation plan.

All dividends can be reinvested at net asset value.

The shareholder has the right to withdraw a portion of his holdings at any time and put the money back later, when he can, at net asset value.

Contractual plans with life insurance cannot be sold in a number of states. Perhaps there should be an adjustment made in the rather high initial sales charge. But the fact that the completion rate of contractual plans is very high speaks for the program. The companies must be doing something right.

Summary

1. Investment companies range from face-amount certificate companies to fixed trusts and fully managed companies.

2. The managed company can be open-end or closed-end. The closed-end companies can be listed or unlisted.

3. The dual purpose funds are misunderstood. There is *value* in the capital shares.

4. Sales charges go from zero to 9 percent.

5. The income fund is not the same as a balanced fund, nor is a general-purpose diversified common-stock fund the same as a growth fund.

6. Specialty funds come in many hues.

7. Be careful of hedge funds. Can you assume the risk?

8. The advantages of mutual funds are many, a lot more than just diversification, professional management, and liquidity. Don't overlook your eligibility for a Keogh plan.

9. Read the prospectus. A fund is whatever the prospectus says it is.

10. Voluntary accumulation plans, as well as contractuals, with decreasing term life insurance, deserve a good look from younger people, those who are in the accumulative stage of life.

11. Funds with large tax credits may make attractive investments for the future.

12. A withdrawal plan can be set up so that it compares most favorably with an annuity.

CHAPTER 8

The New Issues Market

There is no reason why you shouldn't venture into the new issues market if the purchase of the securities squares with your investment objective. But first of all let's agree on terminology.

The "new issues market" has two quite different meanings. It may refer to new corporate or public securities distributed through the primary securities market or it may mean newly marketed issues of companies that have just gone public and are selling stock for the first time.

The sale of bonds by established companies makes up 80–90 percent of all new issues. In 1970 almost $39 billion of new issues were sold, of which over $30 billion were bonds. In 1969, the previous record year, $26.7 billion of new securities were sold, of which $18.3 billion were bonds. Dividends, unlike bond interest, are not a tax-deductible expenditure, so preferred stock sales amounted to about $1.4 billion in 1970 and $682 million in 1969. Most of these senior equities were utility preferreds. The question of tax deductibility is not as significant to utilities since they are entitled to earn a fair rate of return on their capital value. Common stocks reached an all-time record of $7.7 billion in 1969 and just under $7 billion in 1970. When common stocks are selling at a high P/E ratio, corporations are much more inclined to raise new money through them than when P/E ratios are low. Raising new money by selling stocks at low P/E ratios means more shares will have to be sold to bring in the needed capital, and the dilution of the equity will thus be relatively high.

Buying the securities of established companies in the primary market is really not very different from buying them in the secondary market except that you buy them on a net (dealer) basis rather than on an agency (commission) basis. Watch out for package deals. For example, a company may offer bonds with warrants. The question is, How long will the bonds sell with the warrants, and at what point do they sell without them? It could be very disturbing to an investor, who intended to keep his warrants and sell the bonds, to be told that regular delivery includes the warrants. There is no uniform time period in which a bond may sell with warrants.

New Stock Issues

Problems for the unwary investor arise in that sector of the new issues market in which the common stocks of companies that have just gone public are sold.

Wall Street always seems to contract a new disease. At one time electronic stocks will go through the roof and nobody wants oil stocks; another time, nobody wants to buy chemical stocks as airline stocks fly into the wild blue yonder.

Then there is the new issues fever that grabs investors. An epidemic of that type swept through their ranks during 1961–1962 and again in 1969. Look at what can happen. The Scientific Control Corporation, which designs and makes small digital computers, was one of the hottest performers in the 1968 OTC market, reaching a high of 68½. In November, 1969, it filed a petition under Chapter 11 of the Bankruptcy Act for an arrangement with its unsecured creditors. Four Seasons Nursing Homes was another hot item. It made quite a few paper millionaires, but that company also wound up in bankruptcy court. While the risks here are high, so are the rewards. When Comsat came out, it sold at $20 a share; before long it went to $70.

Some ground rules on new issues: First, do your securities

business with a large house with a strong capital position and an excellent reputation for dealing fairly with its clients. You have a right to ask for a financial statement before opening an account or any time thereafter. A good house will mail you its annual statement.

Second, play fair with your broker and don't engage in fancy tricks. Morton Shulman, M.D., in his widely read book *Anyone Can Make a Million,* tells his readers that they should do "free riding." Very often there is a one- to two-week time lag between the client's purchase of a new issue and the stated payment date. A "hot" issue may come out at $10 per share, and before the week or even the day is out it may reach $25. Of course, you can have a free ride until settlement date. But remember, you cannot sell a security before you have paid for it, and to buy new issues simply for a quick speculative ride (Dr. Shulman says that if the new issue sells at or below the issue price the same or the next day, sell it "immediately") is most unfair to the issuer and to the broker. The originating house is trying to make a fair market in the stock and is risking its capital. The company needs funds and wants shareholders. If you try to "free ride" on any occasion, your account may be put on a "cash on the barrelhead before your order is executed" basis, or worse, the house may refuse to do any business with you and turn your name in as a disreputable character, a warning to other brokers. One does not, in the age of the computer, play fast and loose with one's credit. If you keep your account, whether cash or margin, properly, when the time comes for special consideration, you will get it. If something special comes out, your broker will call you rather than the cute character.

Third, stay away from the more colorful fringe of the underwriting business. Once you have bought a new issue, an unforeseen emergency might compel you to sell it. But who makes the "aftermarket," the market after the issue has come out? How good is the market? One small fringe underwriter brought out an issue and then closed his office for several weeks "for vacation." Suppose you have 500 shares and the market that a small house makes is only good for 100 shares, which is all a dealer is required to take on his prevailing bid and make available on his prevailing offer. Suppose he quotes the market

8 to 8¼. How far down will the bid be by the time you get rid of the last 100 shares? It could easily be down 2 or more points. During the 1969–1970 bear market, a lot of bids disappeared completely. Such fringe underwriters don't only operate in New York; they are all over the country. The story of Connecticut-based Tellier and Company during the uranium fever in the 1950s is told in Hillel Black's *The Watchdogs of Wall Street*. Tellier bought the shares of Consolidated Uranium Mines, Inc., at $.01 and sold them as high as $1.87 per share, with the most glowing statements that the stock would go to 20. Quite a number of questionable underwriters have been put out of business by the SEC and the NASD, but there are some still around. For future information on this matter read your *Wall Street Journal*. A good, strong house will make good markets, good for a lot more than the required 100 shares. That means a new issue has good sponsorship, and that counts a lot with knowledgeable investors.

Fourth, read the prospectus. Don't ever buy without having received a prospectus. If you were given a preliminary, so-called red-herring prospectus, you must also be given the permanent prospectus when it appears. Every prospectus states, "These securities have not been approved or disapproved by the Securities and Exchange Commission nor has the Commission passed upon the accuracy or adequacy of this prospectus. Any representation to the contrary is a criminal offense." The SEC tries to give investors all information necessary to make an investment decision. But if the prospectus tells you that the cost of floating an issue is 20 or more cents on the dollar, when do you think the company will be able to pay a dividend? Many issues come out that are highly speculative, not to say "junk." The prospectus says so. As long as no fraudulent act has been committed, companies cannot be kept off the market. After all, this country was built on speculation and will continue to grow on it. A new company may have something to offer the public even though the financial statements in the prospectus are frightening. Check the originating house. Good securities houses have a list of dealers with whom they will not do business. Listen to your broker when he refuses to accept your order for a stock. He has good reasons.

The traditional "full-disclosure" approach to prevent fraudulent new issue promotions has not been an unqualified success. Far from it. One small company, whose stock went from $2 to

$7.50 and from there to zero, had stated in its prospectus that 60 percent of the proceeds of the issue would be used for past-due accounts payable, repayment of loans, back wages and back rents, and other debts. All that could be said after reading the prospectus was that somebody must have discovered a method to delay inevitable bankruptcy.

But I repeat, don't buy small new issues without reading the prospectus thoroughly. Be wary of the whisper: "Right now, it will be traded in the OTC market, but before long it is going to be listed on the Exchange." However, there are stocks that over the years, as the company develops and prospers, do appreciate anywhere from 100 percent to 1,000 percent.

Problem Areas in the New Issues Market

When a small company wants to go public, it may encounter great difficulties finding a good underwriter. In 1969 one of the strong houses raised its minimum requirements for companies that it would consider for public offering, to $7.5 million annual sales, a track record of 5 years with an annual income after taxes of $300,000, a net worth of $2 million, and the public offering to be not less than $2 million. Other large houses have similar high standards.

What then is to happen when a company needs $750,000 or $1 million? Will these companies be pushed to the periphery of underwriting? A good after-market for new securities is very important for a company. However, many small companies go public far too early in their corporate career. Owners are enticed by a fringe underwriter to do so, or they see an active new issues market. If book value is $7 and the name catches on, the stock might trade at $20 a share before long. Perhaps, some owners figure, we can unload some stock in a secondary offering and get rich quickly. Quite a number of them did when the new issues market was a-boilin'.

The securities industry shuns its social responsibility when it sets high requirements for accepting new underwritings. Smaller companies are also entitled to good investment banking services. A plan should be worked out under which a group of strong, reputable houses would jointly own an investment banking firm that accepts lower-priced speculative issues and thus would give these companies access to the capital funds market on better terms than they now get. It would also give the investor a fairer shake.

An inherent conflict of interest is often involved that, apparently, is never decided in favor of the smaller investor. The underwriter finds something out about a company that indicates future financial difficulties. Even the best houses are tempted to advise large institutional investors to get out of such an issue before the situation becomes public knowledge. The small investor is left to pick up the pieces. Ask your broker if his research recommendations go to the big (institutional) clients first, or if everybody gets them at the same time. A good house won't give preferential treatment.

The underwriter is on the spot when his research people come out with a sell recommendation, or, worse, a sell-short recommendation for a stock the underwriter brought out originally. He feels under obligation to "his" company, and he is concerned that word might get around that his organization is recommending the sale of the stock of a corporate client. Will he get new underwriting business? Management doesn't like sell recommendations for its stock. If a house does not recommend the stock it underwrote, get out. You probably won't be told specifically to sell it.

Ask your broker how he feels about a specific stock that his house brought out and in which it is making markets. If he says, "We're still bullish on it," and then a few months later the company goes into receivership, you have the basis of a lawsuit. Material facts were withheld from you, and the court will be on your side.

New Issue Pricing Policies

You can go on the assumption that a responsible underwriter underprices an issue, perhaps by as much as 20 percent. There are a number of reasons for doing so.

He isn't sure what the public's evaluation will be of the new company's past earnings and its discounted future earnings. Always discount future earnings, since one dollar received next year or in the future isn't worth one dollar today. The evaluation is complicated by the fact that it is a completely unseasoned issue.

In view of this, the originating, managing underwriter of the issue knows that the next issue will have a much better chance to be successful (meaning it will be sold out quickly and the after-market price will rise). That type of offering results in happy future customers for the underwriter. It also makes the other company shareholders happy, those who have not yet sold their stock. Insiders, directors, officers, and large stockholders might find themselves quite rich—at least on paper. Just think, a stock is put on the market at 12 in the morning, and that afternoon it is traded in the OTC market at 27 bid.

If the issue "goes out of the window" or is oversubscribed, the underwriter is very happy. He has made his profit, the difference between the price to the public and the proceeds to the company minus his expenses. It saves him money because the capital of even the large underwriting houses is quite small for the amount of underwritings undertaken, and they must borrow money unless their capital can be turned over quickly by successful underwriting deals. Despite the aura of aloof grandeur in which investment bankers love to wrap themselves, they are really like any other merchant, out to make a buck. If capital is limited, any merchant wants a rapid turnover of his inventory, whether in groceries or in securities.

The prospectus of any (new) issue says that "in connection with this offering, the underwriter may . . . effect transactions that stabilize or maintain the market price of the securities at a level above that which might otherwise prevail in the open market. Such stabilizing, if commenced, may be discontinued at any time." This is, of course, a form of manipulation. The price of the security is something other than pure demand and supply market forces would make it. Society sanctions it, during the period of distribution only, because the process of capital formation requires it. How can the nation's stock of capital goods be increased if the securities can't be sold whose proceeds enable corporations to expand their plant facilities? And how can the newly issued securities be sold by the underwriters at the offering price if the market price is lower? They can't.

Investment bankers don't "pull the plug" and let an issue

find its own level after distribution because they are a bunch of thieves. Society needs the investment banker, and it therefore allows the stabilizing operations carried on by the managing underwriter. If the issue sells slowly, it ties up the underwriters' capital. The more successful an issue is, the less such stabilizing transactions are necessary.

So here you have it: The underwriter(s) underprice the issue in order to make it successful and save time and money for themselves. But a successful issue is also good for the company. It means the investor has a sweet taste in his mouth, and when the company needs to come again to the market for more capital, it will be almost assured of a favorable reception. However, there is another aspect: Let's say that an underwriter brings out another stock issue for a company that had gone public not so long ago. The price for the old shares in the over-the-counter market is quoted at 20 bid and 20½ offered. He wants to bring the new issue out at 19. If he underprices the issue by the usual percentage, a full evaluation of the stock would be around 23½. In order to assure the success of the new flotation, he asks two of the important market makers to sell the stock short. In order to keep them from losing their shirts, he promises these other dealers to deliver to them stock out of his compensation at the offering price. In many cases underwriters receive a part of their fee in stock, and/or they are given options by the corporate issuer to buy a large number of shares at a price near, or even below, the original offering price. Once again, it is the best of all possible worlds.

The market-makers are assured of not taking a risk, since stock will be made available to them at 19, the offering price, and—who knows?—maybe they can stabilize the price at 20. In that case, they will make $100 on every 100 shares they sell short at 20, because they can cover themselves at 19. Investors who want to buy stock in the market, since they won't be able to get any from the underwriter, get it cheaper than would otherwise be the case. The issue comes out and is a success. It shoots up to 23, and everybody is happy—the company, the new and old shareholders, the originating underwriter, and the market makers in the secondary market.

Statistical studies support the statement that buyers of new stock issues enjoy a higher *short-run* return on the average than is possible to obtain either in the listed or the over-the-counter market.

Once the new issues market gets to be really active again, check what happened after a week, on the first Friday after offering. How many issues during that week shot right away to a premium? How many showed decreases? And how many registered no change? Out of 100 new issues, the following would be more or less typical: 51 show increases; 26 issues, decreases; and perhaps 23 register no change. Probably a good half, up to 60 percent, will do better than the NASDAQ OTC index or the Dow-Jones industrial averages. But in view of the peculiar composition of these two unweighted indices, we can't be too sure just exactly what that really means.

The studies become most interesting four weeks after offering the issue. While probably the overall average percent change is higher than the levels shown by the NASDAQ and the DJIA indices, it tends to be below the average percent price change that existed on the first Friday after offering. So if you want to make a quick buck, and you don't mind possible consequences, sell the newly issued stock you bought on the first Friday, assuming it sells at that time at a premium.

If you sell, however, after one week, you are going to have great trouble having another chance at another future offering. For the account executive will lose his commission for having sold the stock improperly, and if he has a lot of clients like you, he may never again be included in any future issues that his house brings out. You are supposed to hold these new issues for a while. Don't let me mislead you by what I predict might be the case in four weeks. Take the investors who bought Culligan, Inc., now an NYSE-listed issue, when it first came out and who held it; they did very well indeed.

In a rising stock market, and the 1970s will bring at least as much of a rise in securities prices as the 1960s, a lot more of these new issues will register increases than decreases. But the declining issues tend to show much steeper declines than the more seasoned issues. In other words, there is greater risk involved in investing in new issues than in seasoned securities. If you can assume the risk, put part of your funds, or possibly of your profits, into these new issues and buy them regularly from the house with which you do business. Hold them for a while. A good issue in rising security markets will reward you handsomely, far better than the returns available in the general market.

Going Public

Family-owned businesses go public as the owners grow old. Otherwise the heirs would face quite a federal tax problem if they were forced suddenly to raise cash by selling stock without a ready market for it. The changes in the federal estate tax laws now require that heirs pay within nine months of death, instead of fifteen. This creates a need for faster liquidity of an estate. Moreover, if shares have been sold or given to key employees for their incentive, as they get older and want to raise cash they will have difficulties selling them at a good price when no ready market is available.

When a company's management arrives at this crucial stage in life, two ways are open to it to establish a public market for its shares:

1. A quite popular way of going public is to merge with a company whose stock is already publicly traded. But is it to be a merger that will swallow up the company, or can a so-called reverse merger be worked out, an exchange of stock that would give control of a much larger concern? Such a deal has several advantages: Stock of another company received in a merger exchange wouldn't normally be taxed until it was sold; if the original owner-managers wanted to remain active in a public company in which a family had a substantial stock interest, they could do so, because both together would probably have effective control; and finally, there would be no underwriting fees and expenses connected with an SEC registration, which is mandatory when unregistered stock is distributed to the public.

2. If such a "reverse merger" cannot be effected, there is only one other way to go public with the owner-managers retaining control. They could sell a portion of their stock to the public while keeping enough shares to guarantee them effective control. But this can be rather expensive. The underwriter's fee probably comes to 8 percent. There will be bills from attorneys

and public accountants in connection with the SEC registration statement and the required prospectus. Worst of all, in such a secondary distribution of stock by selling shareholders, practically the entire proceeds would be taxed 25 percent. Still, it might be preferable to a merger with a publicly owned company that would take complete control over the business.

Brokers Going Public

A number of brokerage houses in the securities business have already gone public. Others are waiting in the wings for a chance to get a good price for their stock. The collapse of so many firms during the 1969–1970 bear market has probably set back most of these plans for quite a spell. The public now has had a dramatic illustration of the severe cyclical character of the securities business. And since the stock market is the focal point at which people's hopes, dreams, fears, and greed meet, we shall continue to see unwarranted optimism change into equally unwarranted pessimism. During the 1969–1970 bear market, the industry lost more firms through mergers, dissolutions, and liquidations than disappeared during the Great Depression from 1929 to the end of the 1930s.

No one should buy stock in a big house (I like to call Merrill Lynch, Bache, duPont Glore Forgan, Walston, and others "financial department stores") unless a complete breakdown of income is given. How much of the earnings come from underwriting, trading, or the commission business? No one ever went broke taking a commission, but firms can take whopping losses when they make markets in securities or trade them, because positions will invariably be taken. A house could also have a nice profit on its investment banking activities for eleven months, but one bad, unsuccessful underwriting deal could substantially reduce it or even wipe it out altogether. There might even be an insurance or real estate department involved.

What would substantially help the sale of stock in these financial department stores would be a change in our tax laws under which securities houses would be permitted tax credits for setting up loss reserves comparable to those set up by the insurance companies and the commercial banks. Dr. Leon T. Kendall, the president of the Association of Stock Exchange Firms, has suggested such a procedure in order to increase forcibly the capital funds of the firms.

Securities firms will have to go public in order to raise the capital that they will need in the days ahead when 30 million shares are traded on the NYSE and such volume will be regarded as a quiet day. Naturally, the officers and account executives who have bought stock in their firms at book value will lick their chops when the stock is offered to the public at a multiple thereof. Every owner in a business that has gone public shares this glowing feeling and should not begrudge Uncle Sam the $1 out of his $4 on the profit he takes when he sells some or all of his stock.

Stock in financial department stores, in view of the tremendous growth potential, should hold out good opportunities for gains to the investor. What P/E ratio will be paid for it should depend on the disclosure of earnings through departmentalized summation and the more effective regulatory roles that the exchanges, the SEC, and the NASD can assume. Certainly, quite a number of firms that bit the dust in 1969 and 1970 would still be around today if these agencies had been more vigorous and farsighted in the regulation of their members' finances and, particularly, their operational capacities.

In the past, business always increased too suddenly and too fast for an industry geared to a lower volume. When I project the 30-, 40-, 50-, 60-, and even more million-share days on the Exchange that the 1970s will surely bring, then I wonder whether self-regulation, as we have known it in the past, can prevent another 1969–1970 fiasco. When public money becomes involved in a Securities Investor Protection Corporation (SIPC), perhaps an outside, public supervisory and examining agency should be set up. After all, the state banking association, a voluntary nonprofit association, does not supervise and examine the banks in a state, though it assumes some supervisory functions. Yet the exchanges and the NASD, other voluntary nonprofit associations, assume such functions. With 35 million investors projected and with securities houses going public, I think the old system is no longer good enough, and a public supervisory and examining agency other than the SEC is definitely indicated.

Secondaries

A "secondary" involves the distribution to the public of stock in a company that is already public and whose stock is already traded in a listed market or in the over-the-counter market. The sellers here are shareholders, and the shares are already outstanding. The proceeds of this "secondary" sale do not go to the company, as is the case with a new issue in the primary market, but to the selling stockholders.

The managing underwriter will announce, after the close of the Exchange market, the price of the secondary issue and the discount that participating firms will receive. You will buy net; there is no commission. If the stock is unregistered stock sold by insiders, it must be registered with the SEC, and you must be given a prospectus before the stock can be legally sold to the public. If the stock was accumulated by an estate in the regular market, it could be sold without going into registration first—unless it was accumulated by a person in control relationship to the company. In that case, the already registered stock might have become "tainted" and the SEC might require another registration.

The important question for you is this: Why is this secondary offering made? Does somebody need money to pay estate taxes, or does somebody just need the money to buy a big cruiser, a house, or something else? Or does this mean somebody knows something, and that is why the stock is offered?

If "smart money" thinks stock prices are too high and therefore wants to distribute its large holdings while the public still has an appetite for common stocks, then a rising volume of secondary offerings of such nature will foreshadow a decline in the market. If that is the case, then profitable short sales are possible in these stocks. Look around for confirming signals of your suspicion. For example, what does the market's breadth index say? Did the secondary occur right after an important downside breakout from a major support level on the stock's or the market's chart?

When the public is attracted by a rising stock market, with lots of volume, activities, and stories, it doesn't pay any attention to secondary offerings or count them. It doesn't ask why somebody would want to sell a big wad of an auto stock if the industry predicts record auto sales for next year.

Sometimes a "piggyback" secondary is made. The company needs some money, and investment letter shareholders sell stock at the same time. It is a device under which the selling shareholders save the expenses in connection with a registration. Sometimes they accept the stock under an investment letter, agreeing that it will not be sold for a number of years. The company, in turn, obligates itself to register the stock for the shareholders at the end of such a period and absorb the expenses.

Exchange Distributions and Acquisitions

A large individual or institutional shareholder may want to sell fifty thousand shares. The regular auction market on the floor of the Exchange cannot absorb the block without beating down its price, and the NYSE gives its permission for an exchange distribution. Your firm will then try to generate offsetting buy orders and cross them on the floor of the Exchange with the sell order at the prevailing market price. Of course, a good house will only do that if it thinks enough of the stock as an investment. This is a good opportunity for you to buy net, without paying any commission, because the seller pays two commissions. Don't be suspicious when your broker calls you up and says, "Here is your chance to buy XYZ on the floor of the Exchange at the current price net." If you buy 200 shares, you could easily save $100 in commissions.

An exchange acquisition is the obverse of this procedure. A large buyer wants a block and your broker will say, "Look, you have nice profits in ABC; maybe we ought to take them and get into something more promising. Here is a chance to sell net at the current exchange market price." Once again you have a chance to save a nice piece of change.

Another possibility to trade net would be in a special offer or special bid. Here somebody wants to sell or buy a very large block of stock, and the entire Exchange community is invited to participate, since the regular auction market can't possibly take that much stock. The investor, under such a procedure, may buy at a price somewhat below the prevailing best offer on the floor, and the seller might get a price slightly above the best bid on the floor. The saving is then compounded: no commission and a better price.

Summary

1. Be careful buying new, unseasoned issues from a small, fringe underwriter.

2. Don't try to "free ride." Your account may be restricted to a cash with the order basis.

3. What kind of an after-market will the originating underwriter make for the stock? Will any other house trade the stock?

4. Small companies have difficulties finding underwriters with lots of capital and a big distributing capacity. Some of them are pressured into going public too early. Big houses want large underwritings to keep all their branches happy by allocating stock to them for their clients.

5. If your broker doesn't have a buy recommendation for stock he once underwrote, maybe you ought to sell the stock. Houses don't like to issue a "sell" for stocks they brought out; managements don't like it either.

6. New issues tend to be undervalued.

7. There is, as a rule, more money to be made in good new issues that are held over a period of time than in listed securities.

8. A "reverse merger" might be a good way to have your cake and eat it too. You are still actively engaged in business, but you are now "public."

9. When brokers go public, insist on a breakdown of the "store's" earnings.

10. When buying stock in a financial department store, remember it is a cyclical business—with its pronounced ups and equally pronounced downs. Who watches the store? Only an industry group or an outside public agency.

11. Secondaries could be "sell" signals, and if you have a strong heart, "sell short" signals.

12. Exchange distributions and acquisitions, special bids and offers give you an opportunity to trade net at prevailing prices as quoted on the floor of the NYSE. You save all commission charges because somebody else has to pay two.

CHAPTER 9

What about Warrants?

Should you buy warrants? Yes—if you like leverage. The greater the spread is between the price of the warrant and the stock, the greater will be the degree of leverage. If a warrant sells for $4 with the right to buy stock at $16 and the stock sells for $20, a doubling in the price of the stock will mean a 600-percent rate of return for the warrant holder. Should the stock go to $40, the warrant would have to sell for at least $24, because $16 plus a warrant will buy one share of stock. The warrant will most likely sell for more than $24, because in a bull market warrants tend to command a premium.

Leverage is, of course, quite as pronounced on the down side. Suppose the stock goes from $40 to $30, a 25-percent decline. At $30 the value of a warrant would be $14, about a 40-percent decline. Leverage can be compounded if warrants traded on exchanges are bought on margin. Warrants traded in the OTC market are not eligible for margin.

Suppose a company sells bonds with detachable warrants. In that case a warrant is another way of participation in the future prosperity of the company; it is a form of equity kicker. This is quite distinct from a convertible bond. When the bond is converted, the investor loses his bond. In the case of a bond and a detachable warrant, he may sell or exercise his warrant and still retain the bond. This could be very advantageous when the bond was bought in a depressed market with a high yield and the company does not pay a cash dividend, or pays a very low one. Sometimes warrants are issued in connection with a preferred stock in lieu of making the preferred convertible.

The Nature of Warrants

A warrant, then, gives the holder the right to purchase one or more shares, or fraction of shares, of the issuer's stock at a future time and at a stipulated price. The option is exercisable at the discretion of the holder by submitting the contractual price to the company. The option price may be the same during the entire period the warrants run, or, as with convertible securities, it may be scaled upward. A warrant thus provides the company with funds, in contrast with the exercise of the conversion privilege, which does not increase the company's capital. The financing with warrants is very logical when a continuous demand for additional funds exists.

Warrants are a call on the company's stock. Usually they have a time limit, but a few warrants are perpetual. The Allegheny Corporation's warrants give their holders the right to buy Allegheny common from the company at $3.75 a share at any time. The Tri-Continental Corporation's warrants entitle the holder to 3.03 shares of common stock at $22.60 a share, also in perpetuity.

The warrant holder does not have a direct equity in the company; he has no claim against the assets of the company. Warrants have no voting rights. They do not share directly in profits, nor do they pay dividends.

How Warrants Are Issued

Warrants may be given with bonds or preferred stock in order to enhance their salability by providing an equity kicker. When issued in connection with a new bond, good delivery may mean bond *and* warrant, perhaps up to a period of six months after issue. Ask your account executive to explain exactly how the bonds are traded, WW (with the warrants) or WO (without the warrants), in case you wish to sell your bond and hold on to the warrants. An investor may sell his bond only to discover that he unwittingly sold both.

Warrants may also be given in reorganizations with or without the new common stock. In 1940 the Radio-Keith-Orpheum Company was reorganized. The old shareholders received one-sixth of a share of new common stock for each old share. In order to soften the blow, they were also given for each old share a warrant, good to buy one share in the reorganized company at $15.

Two years later RKO stock was still selling for 2½ a share. The chances that the stock would ever sell above $15 seemed remote, so that the warrants were quoted at ⅟₁₆, at 6¼ cents a warrant. Yet in 1946 these warrants were selling at $13. A $100 investment in 1,500 warrants in 1942 would have been worth almost $20,000 in 1946. In 1948 the Hoffman Radio warrants were selling for $.05. In 1950 they were selling for $25. Those interested in stimulating interest in warrants have never forgotten these and a few other cases. But with few exceptions, warrants are highly speculative. I wouldn't want to call the AT&T warrants highly speculative, but then the chance of gain is very much more limited than with a highly volatile stock.

The classic example is the warrants of the American Foreign Power Corporation. Warrants for over 7 million shares of common stock were issued in connection with a preferred stock issue. In 1929 the warrants reached $175 with an indicated market value for the total issue of $1 billion. When the company was recapitalized in 1952, the warrants were completely eliminated and made valueless. The fellow who coined the phrase *sic transit gloria mundi* must have been an unhappy investor.

During the 1960s warrants were frequently used by the then popular "conglomerates" in their acquisitions and mergers. It earned these securities the name "funny money" as more and more of these papers were sprinkled over the landscape. The Fuqua Industries, a Georgia-based conglomerate, announced on March 6, 1969, that under a new dividend policy, stockholders would receive, instead of cash, one warrant for each 20 shares of common stock owned, entitling them to buy Fuqua stock at $50 from July 1, 1970, to July 1, 1977, and then at $55 through

December 31, 1980. The highest price of Fuqua common was $47, in 1969, and in the summer of 1970 the stock could have been bought for $8. Needless to say, that type of dividend policy was discontinued. But this shows what can happen to the darlings of yesterday when they become the bums of today.

As so often before, Wall Street was again overdoing it in 1970. First, a completely unrealistic price was put on the conglomerates on the up side. Then, on the down side, the price was just as unrealistic. In 1970 Walter Kidde was selling at $15, down from a high of $87 in 1968; Litton was at 15⅜, down from a high of $120. Investors who retained their sanity could have bought these stocks in 1970 and sold them in 1971 at a 100-percent profit, taxable as long-term gains.

The Ling TV warrants fluctuated during these years between 2½ and 6⅜. The company's fives due in 1988 were selling in early 1970 for less than $160 a $1,000 bond. A friend called me from Texas and said, "Look, I know the company has enough money to pay the interest at least this year and possibly next. So we get a hundred dollars in interest. Surely, if it should come to a fundamental corporate reorganization, the bonds should get at least sixty dollars." In 1971 the bonds traded as high as $570. I should have listened, but then, B-rated bonds just don't appeal to me. Standard and Poor's says, "Bonds rated as low as B are speculative. Payment of interest cannot be assured under difficult economic conditions." Ling TV could have toppled over the edge, in which case the warrants would have become worthless. In such conditions, two questions seem to arise: One, how much risk are you willing or able to assume? The other, how strong is your stomach?

The 1970s may yet see a different use of warrants by less "swinging" companies. Corporations have discovered that they can control the exercise of the option, which so far has been regarded as a drawback to bond-warrant financing. They knew they could always force conversion by calling bonds for redemption, but in the case of warrants, when would they be exercised? When would the cash for the stock come in? In driblets? Warrants have tended to remain outstanding for longer periods than convertible security options.

Some people now reason: Warrants are superior to convertible bonds from a cash-flow standpoint, since in addition to the initial funds from selling the bond-warrant package, they will bring in more cash later, and furthermore, the time of this can be controlled. The minute the debentures sell without the warrants, they will go to a discount from par, because the bond with the warrant was sold at a lower interest rate than a comparable ordinary straight bond. This is, after all, one reason why the company gives an equity kicker with the bond, to reduce the coupon on the bond. Suppose a couple of years from issue, the bonds sell for $900, at a 10-percent discount from par. The company could now come out and induce, not to say force, the exercise of the option by announcing that it will accept the debentures at par in payment for the stock. As the debt is wiped out and equity substituted, management could then sell a new debt issue and obtain the cash that way.

The Wilson warrants (a meat-packer and an LTV subsidiary) make an interesting example here. They are good until 1978 and entitle the holders to turn in one warrant plus $16.62 in cash to obtain one share of stock. The Wilson debentures, the 6½'s of 1988, may be used *at par* instead of cash. Since these bonds sell at a considerable discount from par, the $16.62 cash payment required would thus be considerably reduced by using these bonds at full face value.

Management might also be given the power to lower the exercise price on the warrants for a limited period of time, thus encouraging exercise of the option. Here then is a chance for equity financing, whenever management deems it appropriate, without any worries about (and costs of) an SEC registration, short-term market conditions, or an underwriting fee. Corporate ingenuity will find new ways of financing, and investors will find new opportunities for making money. The days are certainly over when the use of warrants was considered to detract from the prestige of the company's financial standing or to give the company a bad image.

Discretionary pricing of warrants will, however, present another problem: How can the specialist on the floor of an exchange make a market in the warrants or in the stock with such flexibility? Will exchanges list warrants that can be "flushed out" by management? In the age of the computer, a lot of questions tend to be answered. Perhaps this one will be.

The Market for Warrants

Up to 1970, when the AT&T warrants made their appearance, warrants were not traded on the New York Stock Exchange. The Exchange did not list them with an expiration date of more than ninety days from issue. A spokesman for the Big Board said, "There is always the chance that warrants become valueless, and why list a security whose value may one day be zero? We have enough trouble as it is!" The new listing requirements for warrants are quite stiff, so that the overwhelming majority of listed warrants will no doubt continue to be traded on the American Stock Exchange. Roughly speaking, forty issues of warrants were traded there in 1970, about half of them exercisable in stocks traded on the New York Stock Exchange. In 1971 twelve warrants were listed on the Exchange.

Market Behavior

When the stock rises, the price of the warrant must also rise since it is a call on the associated stock. If the holder has a right to buy XYZ stock at $10 and the stock sells currently for $20, he will not sell his warrant for less than $10, because that would be his immediate profit if he gave the warrant plus $10 to the company in exchange for a share of stock that could be sold at once for $20. If the warrant owner feels that the stock is on the way up, he might not sell the warrant for less than $15. The difference between the $10 current market value and the $15 market price is called the premium.

A warrant is worth the market price of the stock, minus the option price, minus a discount to compensate for the fact that warrants do not receive dividends—plus or minus an allowance for the chance of appreciation or depreciation of the stock. Arbitrageurs will keep the warrant price from falling below the market price, less the option price, of the stock.

The observation that the price of a warrant and its associated stock rise and fall in unison, though not necessarily at the same rate, needs qualification. Situations might arise that could cause the prices of warrant and stock to move in opposite directions. The declaration of an increase in a cash dividend will encourage a rise in the stock, but will make the warrant price go down. The warrant owner not only does not receive dividends, but his future share in the equity of the company will be reduced as a result of the increased pay-out. If the dividend is in the form of a stock dividend, he had better enjoy the protection of a properly drawn antidilution clause.

Earnings may be retained, a policy characteristic of growth companies. In this case, the price of the common may drop or level off, but the price of the warrant tends to rise. Regardless of the circumstances affecting the common's price, even should it rise at a time when the warrants approach expiration, the price of the warrants will fall. Other deviations from the average behavior of prices between the warrant and its associated stock (they tend to move up or down in unison) may be due to the stock's volatility, short selling, or margin trading. Fluctuations in the warrant's price will, of course, be more pronounced, up or down, than the common stock's price because of the inherent leverage.

If a warrant is due to expire within eighteen months or so and the associated stock is selling considerably below the option price, that warrant might be an excellent candidate for a short sale. In a study of a number of listed warrants, prices were compared eighteen months and two months before expiration. The prices dropped on an average of 46 percent. Short selling these warrants would have given the trader an appealing 46-percent profit. You can make such a speculation more or less foolproof if you buy the stock or a call on the stock when the warrants are sold short.

A warrant with an option price of $20 for the stock sells currently for $5, the market price of the stock being $10. We now sell 200 warrants short for $1,000 or on 55-percent margin for $550. We simultaneously buy 200 shares of stock at $10 for $2,000. As the warrant approaches maturity, the stock goes to $20; the warrant, to $2. Our profit on the long stock will be $2,000; our profit on the short warrants, $600. A $2,600 return on an investment of $2,550 is not bad! The warrant can only rise if the stock goes up, and there is a tendency for the warrant's price to be depressed as it approaches maturity.

Things to Keep in Mind When Buying Warrants

The date of expiration. As a rule, warrants should not be bought with an unexpired life of less than four or five years. When the related stock sells appreciably below the option price, short-term warrants have a tendency to be overpriced.

The Atlantic Richfield warrants (on the Amex under Cities Service warrants) entitle holders to purchase one share of common at $110. They expire September 1, 1972. In December, 1971, the stock was in the 60's on the NYSE. The warrants were trading between $3 and $4 and had been trading as high as $11⅞ that year. The high of the stock was $78¼. This is a good illustration that short-term warrants tend to be overpriced. If you are tempted to sell such warrants short, however, read the following carefully.

The American Stock Exchange will notify brokers a month before the warrants expire that they will be delisted in two weeks. Brokers, in turn, will advise account executives who have clients short in these warrants that they will be delisted two weeks before expiration date. If a short position is not covered prior to delisting, the trader's broker will go out into the over-the-counter market, where the warrants are now traded for the remaining days, and cover the short positions. He will buy clients in on the basis of the oldest short position first. This could be very expensive, for the traders in the OTC market are waiting with loaded guns for the stupid bears.

What is your protection against dilution? As with an unprotected convertible security, the common stock could be severely diluted through stock dividends. Will the option price of your warrant be automatically and instantaneously adjusted, or are there loopholes in the antidilution clause? *Stay away from callable warrants.*

The leverage factor should be at least 2 to 1 and for a good speculation stick to warrants whose associated stock is volatile and whose company has good or hot prospects for the future. Even if the "prospects" are based on rumors, the trading in such warrants might be very profitable.

In periods of market uncertainty, the investor may sell his stock, take his profits, and then reinvest a portion of the proceeds of the sale in warrants. This will decrease his vulnerability to loss and yet provide him with an opportunity to make good gains should the market continue to rise. The important point is that now his commitment is considerably reduced. He may also wish to compare the price for the warrants with that for a call option.

Because of their *inherent leverage,* warrants can *magnify gains.* They usually present an opportunity to participate in a market rise of the associated stock without the commitment of large sums of money. In 1957 General Tire and Rubber warrants dropped to a low of $4.50. By 1959 they had risen to $206. In 1962 United Air Lines warrants could be bought at $4.25. By 1966 they had risen to $126. In 1942 Tri-Continental warrants were $.03. In 1968 the price was $70.25. But Hilton Hotels warrants had at one time dropped from 17⅜ to 3⅛; Martin-Marietta warrants, from 46¼ to 14⅝; McLean Industries, from $120 to $16. Will history repeat itself? No, but like causes tend to have like effects.

Volatility on the down side can be just as great as on the up side. If you follow the pointers given here, you can substantially improve the odds that you will come out nicely ahead of the game. But if you can't be bothered with devoting a little of your time to studying warrants, your chances are worse than in Black Jack. I suggest you try that if you want to gamble. It goes faster.

The Nature of Subscription Warrants, or Rights

In contrast to warrants, rights are *short-term warrants,* usually running for a period of three weeks or somewhat less. The rights, or *subscription* warrants, entitle the holder to subscribe to new stock of the company at a price *below the prevailing market price.*

Each share outstanding has one right. If for each 20 shares of old stock one new share is issued, a shareholder with 110 shares would receive 1 full-share subscription warrant giving him the right to subscribe to 5 shares of the new stock at the subscription price. He might also receive a fractional-share subscription warrant entitling him to 10/20 of a share. He may sell the 10 rights or buy an additional 10 rights in the market to enable him to subscribe to 1 additional full share. A company may, however, give any holder of warrants evidencing less than 20 rights the privilege of subscribing to 1 full share. Holders in excess of 20, but not divisible by 20, may also be given the privilege of subscribing to 1 more full share. In that case, subscription is on a first-come-first-served basis.

The Trading of Rights

Subscription warrants are first traded on a "when-issued" (WI) basis. Once the warrants are mailed out by the company, they are traded "regular way." Usually a day after mailing, the stock goes "ex rights," meaning that beginning with that day the purchaser of the stock will no longer receive the rights with it. The price of the stock will be reduced by the value of the right. Prior to that time, the stock sells "cum rights" or with the "rights on." Trading in rights stops at noon on the day when the rights to subscribe expire.

Your broker, however, requires you to give him instructions to sell or exercise rights not later than noon, New York time, the day *before* the rights expire. If you want to sell rights, they must be in New York by that time.

Rights Offering or Direct Sale?

New common stock can be offered to the public through the use of transferable rights given to stockholders of record, entitling them to subscribe to the new stock in proportion to their current holdings at a discount from the prevailing market price or through a direct sale to the public at or near the prevailing price of the old stock. The former method is called preemptive buying or, more commonly, a rights offering; the latter is usually called a cash offering or a direct sale. What determines whether I as stockholder will receive rights? That depends.

Some companies must, under the corporate law of the state in which they were incorporated, offer all new issues of common stock and of securities directly or indirectly convertible or ex-changeable for (or carrying warrants or rights to purchase or subscribe for) common stock to their existing stockholders through rights. Other corporations are not so required under state law, but may have such a provision in their charters. If a company is not compelled under legal or charter provision to offer the new stock to its current owners, management may then make a rights *or* a cash offering.

In those cases where management has full discretion, it is easy to say that "stockholder interest should always be con-sidered" when answering the question of rights or cash offering. In practice the decision is a difficult one, for there is no cate-gorical answer to the question. What method, from the stand-point of benefits accruing to the existing stockholders, is pref-erable will depend on a number of factors, notably the type of business that is involved. For example, electric utilities, whose stock is selling at a good premium over book value, should seriously consider a cash offering in place of a rights offering.

Reasons for Issuing Rights

The traditional arguments for granting subscription rights rest primarily on two points: (1) The owners should be per-mitted to share in a new stock issue in order to preserve their proportionate share in the voting control of the corporation, and (2) the preemptive right will preserve their equity in the surplus, retained earnings, when the new stock is offered at less than market value. Let's take a good look at these arguments.

Voting power can hardly play a role in companies in which no one even approaches the ownership necessary for control. Large stockholders are usually heavy sellers of rights. Execution of their rights might upset the balance in the portfolios. It could also jeopardize marketability, which they wish to maintain, since the auction market on the Exchange might not absorb the new larger block. Funds required for the exercise of the rights might not be available or could be employed more profit-ably elsewhere. Under certain conditions legal restrictions also limit the investment in one company. Large investors are simply, as a rule, not interested in maintaining their proportionate voting strength. Nor is the small investor who executes his rights or perhaps even borrows to do so.

The other argument for a rights offering is based on the ability of the current stockholders to retain their proportionate interest in the equity of the company. Suppose that the stock has a par value of $50 and an accumulated surplus of $30 per share, as shown below. For simplicity's sake, let's assume book and market value for the stock coincide.

Assets		*Liabilities*	
Total Assets	$1,000,000	Current Liabilities	$200,000
		Capital stock, par $50, 10,000 shares outstanding	500,000
		Surplus	300,000
		Total Liabilities	$1,000,000

A new issue of 2,000 shares offered at $65 will increase assets (cash) by $130,000 and shares outstanding to 12,000. Formerly the surplus per share was $30 ($300,000:10,000). Now it amounts to only $25 per share ($300,000:12,000). The new shareholders have paid $65 for a stock worth $80 in the market, and the old stockholders have had their investment reduced from $80 to $77.50, in terms of book and market value. The equity is now $930,000 (capital stock plus surplus); divided by 12,000 shares, this comes to $77.50. If we apply the formula given below, the theoretical value of a right as long as the stock sells cum rights comes to $2.50.

A sale of the new stock to holders of record, so the argument runs, will keep their investment intact; a sale to outsiders will transfer to them property rights of the old stockholders. If this is the case, then any funds realized from the sale of rights are not windfall profits; they are a return of part of the investment.

The tax laws seem to recognize this. No taxable income is received by a holder of the common stock upon the receipt of the warrant or its exercise. If he sells the rights, then the question whether the income or capital-gains tax laws apply is decided by the length of time that the stockholder has held his shares prior to the receipt of the warrant and whether he apportions a cost basis to his rights. Suppose the investor paid $40 for the stock four months ago and he decides now to sell his rights. Assume that the rights sold for $1.25. Rather than declaring the sum realized as income, he can write the cost of his stock down to $38.75. When he sells the stock at a profit later on, he will, of course, show a larger profit by doing so, but now the $1.25 per share is taxed as long-term gain.

The tax laws are seemingly more realistic than the textbooks that assume that a dilution of the equity will unfailingly occur. Dilution is not inevitable, as IBM financing shows. When sales increase rapidly, any dilution caused by a new issue will almost certainly be more than counterbalanced by the expanding sales and income within the year of issue.

Other arguments, besides retaining proportionate voting right and equity, are also debatable. For example, current stockholders constitute the most ready reservoir of new equity money available to the company, but the record shows large stockholders sell their rights. In the absence of a rights offering, many stockholders will not be aware of the stock sale, but account executives would call their attention to it. Moreover, stockholders simply like rights, and it is therefore a matter of good stockholder relations to give them what they so ardently desire. But what happens then to management's profession that "stockholder interest should always be considered"? No, the question of rights or cash offering can be much better answered.

When a company is engaged in a new and rapidly expanding business, which holds forth the promise of becoming very profitable, the rights offering is unquestionably of advantage to the stockholders. Similarly, if by reason of temporary adverse factors, the market price of the stock is depressed to a figure below the book value per share, stockholders should be given the right of first refusal when new stock is sold, in order to be able to protect themselves against the dilution of their investment that will occur in such a case.

The IBM Saga

In 1957 IBM offered 1 new share for 10 old ones. The 1,050,000 shares offered at $220 per share was a lot of stock for a new industrial issue. During the subscription period, the market price for the stock ranged from $288 to $337; the rights, from $6.57 to $10. Only 2,035 shares, or 0.2 percent of the shares offered, were unsubscribed when the subscription period ended.

Was there a dilution of the earnings? No. The book value was actually "diluted upward," to $49 a share from $32.90, on March 31, 1957. IBM, because of the new issue, was able to accelerate its growth; it could not have done so through retention of earnings alone. The question whether a new stock offering will dilute the value of the currently outstanding stock cannot be glibly answered by pointing to the decline in the market price of the stock when it goes "ex rights." A careful analysis should be made of the contribution that the new funds will make, as compared with the company's growth based on the funds previously behind each share.

The Case against Rights

The circumstances that would ordinarily make it preferable to sell new common stock on a rights basis do not apply to electric utilities when the stock is selling at a considerable premium above book value and when earnings are restricted by regulatory authority to no more than a fair and reasonable return on capital invested.

For simplicity's sake, let's say a utility with 900 shares of stock outstanding, with a book value of $10, is earning $1 per share—10 percent. Growth now demands that management must raise new capital. The market price of the stock is $18, and 100 additional shares are sold to the public on a best-price basis of $17 per share. What happened to the original owners?

Instead of having $9,000 of capital divided among 900 shares, the company now has $10,700 of capital divided among 1,000 shares. The per-share investment of the original shareholders, the per-share book value of their stock, has increased from $10 to $10.70 without their putting a single additional penny into the business. The per-share earnings have increased from $1.00 to $1.07, because the company now earns 10 percent on $10,700 rather than on $9,000. The shareholder obtains a 7-per-

cent increase in his earned return without adding to his investment. A rights offering here just doesn't make much sense.

The Determination of the Value of a Right

An industrial stock is 67½ prior to the announcement of the
new issue. The news is now out and the "pre-offering pressure"
pushes the stock to 66, because investors withhold their purchases in anticipation of a lower price for the stock once the
effect of the additional supply, the result of the rights offering,
is felt. The subscription price is set at $55. Any shareholder of
record with 10 shares will be able to subscribe to 1 new share
at $55. Prior to the mailing of the warrants, the stock will be
traded "cum rights," so that in order to ascertain the theoretical
value of a right prior to the "ex right" trading day, an allowance
must be made for 1 right. To do this a "plus 1" is added to the
offering ratio in the denominator of the rights formula. It reads:

$$V = \frac{M-S}{N+1} \quad \text{OR} \quad \text{Value of a right is} \frac{\$66-\$55}{10+1} \text{ OR } \frac{\$11}{11} \text{ OR } \$1$$

(Here M is the market price of the old stock and S is the
offering price, the subscription price for the new stock; N is the
number of rights required to buy 1 new share.)

When the stock sells "ex rights," we need no longer add the
"plus 1" to the offering ratio, but the stock will sell down by
about $1, the value of a right. Arbitrageurs are usually in the
market to maintain a proper value relationship between the
rights and the stock. Whether rights, in a given case, are worth
more at the beginning, middle, or end of the subscription period
cannot be answered. It depends on the price of the stock, and
who can forecast that?

The Size of the Discount

Despite the concern of management with the value of the
rights, many companies want the subscription price quite close
to the market price. But a small discount gives a small value to

the rights, so that investors might simply disregard the whole business; more important, a small discount creates a large risk of the market price falling below the subscription price and making the offering into a failure. Why buy stock at a higher price than it can be bought in the market? A reason for a small discount is management's desire to maintain the same dividend rate and earnings per share. Many managements are reluctant to sell common stock below the book value of their outstanding shares. As I have said, being able to sell stock above book value can be very important in a company's earnings growth.

Should You Exercise Your Rights?

You have various alternatives. Which do you want to choose? If you like the company and think its growth rate is good, and the stock is not overpriced in the market, then subscribe by executing the subscription form on the warrant and send it with a check to the company's subscription agent. He won't charge a service fee; your broker most likely will.

If you want to buy additional rights to increase your holding, you can do so, or you may execute only a portion of the rights and then sell the remainder on a when-issued or regular-way basis. You can sell all your rights, on whatever basis you choose.

Whatever you do, don't let the rights lapse without doing anything. Unsophisticated shareholders have thrown away a great deal of money in a rights offering. In a previous AT&T rights offering of 11,172,000 shares, $895,000 was lost by stockholders who neglected either to exercise or sell their rights.

Summary

1. If you like leverage and can afford the risk, by all means buy warrants. But follow the rules laid down here.

2. Leverage works both ways—up and down.

3. Be familiar with the option price. Is it the same throughout the period, stepped up, or flexible?

4. The stock price may not always lead the warrant price. They may go in opposite directions.

5. There could be money in selling short-term warrants short. But watch the expiration date. If you are afraid, buy the stock too.

6. When will the warrants expire that you want to buy? Stay away from short-term warrants.

7. Are you properly protected against a dilution of the equity through splits, and particularly stock dividends?

8. When the market is high, maybe you should sell out, take your profits, and buy warrants to reduce your financial exposure.

9. Warrants run for a long time; they give you the right to buy stock above the market price prevailing at issue. Subscription warrants, or rights, are short-term warrants; they give you the right to buy stock below the market price at issue.

10. A rights offering does not result in an inevitable dilution of the equity.

11. Your company should give you the preemptive right to subscribe to new stock if it is a good growth company or if the market price for the shares is temporarily depressed. If management doesn't give it, it isn't being fair with you. An electric company might do you a big favor by not giving you this right.

12. Whatever you do with your rights, don't let them lapse without doing anything. You could throw quite a few dollars away. But if you wait too long to sell them and the market goes down, they might make a fine wall decoration for your bar.

CHAPTER 10

Options for Investment, Speculation,

Protection, and Income

Too many investors pass up security options because they don't know anything about them or they somehow identify them with wild speculation, not to say gambling devices. When I told a trustee on the investment committee of a large university that his institution should write options to increase its income from its portfolio, he was visibly shocked that I should propose such a "wild idea." But insurance companies, mutual funds, some member organizations of the New York Stock Exchange, trusts, even unions are writing them—in addition to a number of sophisticated individuals.

Some people confuse options with hedging, which is the counterbalancing of a sale or purchase of one commodity or security by a purchase or sale of another for the purpose of protection. For instance, I have 1,000 shares of ABC in my box on which I have a profit. This profit can be protected by selling short against the box. No matter what happens, by so doing I have put it on ice. Should the stock rise, the value of my long stock improves, but what I gain here, I lose on the short position. Should the stock drop, what I lose on my shares in the box, I make up on the short sale. In other words, the hedger takes an identical position on the buy and sell sides of the market so that no price change, up or down, can bring him a loss or a gain. It is like a person betting an equal amount of money on both teams in a ball game. The hedger has no option. He has made two complete trades. The holder of an option exercises it only if it is to his advantage to do so.

Options are as old as commerce. Phoenician and Roman merchants sold what would today be called options on the goods aboard their vessels enroute from and to foreign markets. The modern security option had its origin in the 1630s in Holland. During the tulip bulb craze, when one rare bulb would sell for as much as 200 or 250 pounds sterling, options were widely used. When a businessman shipped tulip bulbs from Holland, in order to protect himself against their loss on the high seas, he would take an option from a grower for the purchase of a certain amount of tulip bulbs at a specified price. If the cargo was lost, he could take up the option and replace his tulips. If the tulips arrived safely, the exporter would simply let the option expire. By 1634 the market for these bulbs was highly organized, and the stock exchanges of Amsterdam, Leyden, Rotterdam, and others had made space available for the trading in tulip bulb options; two years later they were publicly sold on the London Exchange.

In the United States we haven't gone quite that far—yet. Options are not traded on any exchanges. The Chicago Board of Trade, the world's largest mart for trading commodity futures, said in December, 1969, that it was pushing ahead with plans to set up a central marketplace for stock options. The SEC gave its tentative approval in the fall of 1971. The board's next step will be the setting up of an affiliate securities exchange, probably dubbed the Chicago Board of Options. Trading will most likely not start before 1973. When it does, it will be on a small scale: call options in twenty to fifty widely held, actively traded stocks. After a "pilot period" the board plans to expand the list and begin trading of put options. What a revitalized NYSE-Amex complex will do remains another question. Now that warrants are traded on the Exchange, maybe option-trading will be next.

Throughout our country's history, options have been popular financial devices. The railroad builders used options on land when planning their routes. Oil and natural gas leases contain option clauses. The management of a baseball club takes out an option on a player. The late Mr. Bernard Baruch tells in his autobiography how the Guggenheims were able to checkmate the Rockefeller interests on the west coast through the purchase of options on mining and smelting companies. Just about every large business in existence today has used or is using options in one way or another. You probably have used an option on a piece of real property. So why should it then be surprising to find options to buy and sell securities? It shouldn't. They are one of the stock market's time-honored trading devices.

Options are fascinating gadgets. They can increase income from a portfolio to 30 percent or more a year. They can protect your profits on a long position far better than a hedge, because an option not only freezes your profit but gives you another chance to cash in on a further rise in the price of your stock. If you are short and the stock is down, an option will give the same protection on the profit plus a chance of making more if the stock declines still further. Above all, your maximum loss potential is always known in advance. You can't possibly lose more than the price of the option.

You want to shoot at an unlimited profit at a limited risk? Let me start by enumerating the different types of options and their many uses. Then I shall show you that you too can write options, and I'll discuss some extremely interesting tax aspects.

Several different types of security options have evolved. They are call and put options, straddles and spreads, strips and straps, and special options.

The Call Option

A call is a contract that gives the holder the right to buy stock, to "call" it, over a stated period of time from the maker, sometimes called the writer or seller, of the option at a previously agreed price. An option presents a choice of action to the holder: He can buy the stock from the maker of the option at any time during its life and put it into his portfolio; he can resell a valuable option; he can call the stock and simultaneously sell the shares; he can even trade against the call; or if it suits his purpose, he can simply forget about the whole thing.

The Put Option

A "put" is a contract that gives its holder the right to sell stock, "put" it, over a stated period of time, to the maker of the option at a previously agreed price.

In options the so-called striking price is the price at which the option can be exercised; it is generally the market price of the stock prevailing at the time the option is bought. Option contracts are usually written in units of 100 shares for periods of 30, 60, or 90 days, 6 months and 10 days, and occasionally for 1 year. The SEC mentions in its 1961 *Report on Put and Call Options* a small number of options that were written for a year plus 1 or 2 months. Sometimes even longer periods were covered, for example, 2½ years; such options are, however, specially arranged and are not regularly sold in the option market. Probably as much as three-fifths of all trading is done in the 6-month-and-10-day options. As we shall see later, the possibility of tax savings is the main reason for the 6-month-and-10-day period.

Options are ordinarily written for 100 shares or multiples thereof on listed common stocks, the bulk of which are traded on the New York Stock Exchange. Rarely is an option sold for 50 shares, and even more rarely for odd amounts. A small percentage of options covers warrants and preferred stocks; only occasionally is an option on bonds encountered. Options on OTC securities are now also increasingly available.

The Straddle

The straddle is a combination option, consisting of a separate put and call option, giving the holder the right both to buy and to sell over a stated period of time 100 shares of a certain stock at a fixed price, generally the price prevailing in the market at the time the option is written. It tends to be less expensive than buying the call and put separately.

The Spread

The spread is similar to the straddle; it too is a combination of a separate put and call option under which the holder has the right, at his discretion, to sell the maker of the contract a stated number of shares at the previously agreed price before the option's expiration date and also the right to buy from him the stated number of shares at the same price before the same expiration date. The spread differs from the straddle in that the put is exercisable at a number of points below the price at which the call portion may be executed. The spread has been largely replaced by the straddle.

Strips and Straps

A strip is a straddle with an extra put; it is a call on 100 and a put on 200 shares. A strap is the reverse; it is a straddle with an extra call so that the holder has the right to buy 200 shares of the stock and sell 100 shares to the maker of the option at a specified price over a stated period of time.

Special Options

Put and call options advertised by a put and call dealer in the daily newspapers are known as "special options." These are options that he has acquired for one reason or another. A writer might have sold him a straddle for $600, with the put remaining unsold. The dealer might be able to sell it for $350 if the market does not rise; if it does, the put would become valueless.

The put and call dealer carries an inventory that he offers through the special options to the public and on which he hopes to make a profit.

Reasons for Buying Options

There are four general reasons for buying put and call options or a combination of them:

1. Speculation on a small amount of capital under conditions of a limited potential loss and an unlimited potential gain.

2. Protection of a long or short position at the start of the commitment or during the commitment.

3. Riskless in-and-out trading against an option.

4. The achieving of tax savings.

Speculation on a Small Amount of Capital

Many investors like options because they get more for their money than by buying stocks outright or even on margin. They also appreciate the fact that an option limits the amount of loss without limiting the chance of making money. Here is high leverage because a small premium can control thousands of dollars worth of a stock.

Let's say that a 3-month call on ABC at 68½ costs a little less than $600. If the price after 2 months goes to 80½, the speculator will have made 100 percent on his investment— $1,200 minus the $600 the call cost him.

The successful trader could now resell this valuable option, which has still one month to run, to a put and call broker-dealer, or he could contact his regular broker, whose house has an option department, and ask him to find a buyer for his option. He could also instruct his broker to exercise the call and simultaneously sell the shares. But to do this, he must put up 25 percent of the value of the optioned shares or $2,000, whichever is greater, because the New York Stock Exchange says selling an option or calling and selling the stock is the equivalent of a day trade, and the margin for a day trade is 25 percent.

Should ABC go to $51, our speculator would forget the whole thing and his loss would be $600. Had he bought the stock outright or on margin, his loss would be $1,750.

Another use of a call would be when the investor has bought all the stock he cares to buy, but he is still very bullish on it and would like to own additional shares without unbalancing his portfolio. The purchase of a call will give him control over more stock without diverting a disproportionate amount of funds.

Still another use of a call is to average after a break in the price of the stock. We bought 100 ABC at $80, and the stock is now $50. For $500 we buy, at this point, a 6-month call at 50. Later the stock goes to 70 and we sell out. Result: We have a $500 profit instead of the $1,000 loss we would have had if we had sold the 100 shares bought originally at 80. As it was, we could call another 100 shares at 50 and sell that out at a $2,000 profit. That gives us a $1,000 gain minus the $500 for the call.

Protection—At the Start of the Commitment

A trader buys 200 shares of stock at 50 in the assumption that the stock will go to 75. Not wishing to expose his capital to the risk of the stock going down to 30, he buys two put options at 50 for 90 days. It guarantees him that no matter how far the stock may decline, he can deliver 200 shares at 50 to the maker of the option at any time within 90 days. The trader will thus not become a panicky seller during a price decline, because he knows he can dispose of the stock at 50 over the life of the option. We all know from bitter experience how a stock can easily drop 10 or more points and weeks later go up 20 or more points. An individual long on the stock may become nervous and sell his shares, after he has watched them decline day after day, at the low point of a market reaction to a temporarily over-bought condition only to see the stock come back after a few weeks. The put premium is in the category of an insurance premium. This type of "insurance" is often more important than coverage on the family car, because a commitment in a stock tends to be a much larger part of an individual's assets. He can be wiped out if he isn't careful.

Just as a put can be used by the buyer of a security to protect his investment, so can two calls be bought to protect a short sale of 200 shares at 50 at the start of the commitment. Should the trader's judgment turn out to be wrong and should the stock advance 25 points, he can cover the short sale by calling the stock at the call price of 50. Instead of being forced to cover his short position at a $4,000 loss (and perhaps at a wrong time!), the call contract enables him to buy in at the approximate price at which he sold the stock short—50 minus the call premium.

Protection—During Commitment

Over the last few years electronic stocks have recorded tremendous advances, presenting the investor time after time with a dilemma: Should he hold the stock further, chancing the loss of some or all of his profits in case of a market reversal, or should he sell out, depriving himself of additional gains if investors continue to bid up the price of the stock? Rather than entering a stop order, which could cause the client to lose the stock in a technical reaction at or near the low point only to watch it make a new high thereafter, a put contract can be bought. The accumulated profit is thus protected throughout the put, and at the same time he is still able to take advantage of any further advances in the price of the stock.

The customer could also have sold his stock and purchased a call at the same price. Should the stock then continue to rise, the terms of the call option would allow him to recapture the stock sold earlier. I prefer selling and buying a call, because the sale will release cash and enables me to take advantage of another opportunity. I have exchanged a gun with only one barrel for a gun with two!

Let's say the stock was bought at 40 and now sells at 80. A 6-month call costs $800, so that my net profit, in case the stock goes down, was $4,000 − $800 = $3,200. With a put and the stock down to 60, the profit would be the same. The use of neither call nor put will change my profit should the market go down. But with the sale-plus-call combination, I have a greater chance to make money. Always try to get the maximum mileage out of your dollars. *Leverage*—that is the name of the game.

A number of years ago one of my students had inherited a little money and we decided to buy Texas Instruments at 26. When the stock reached 121, he decided to sell out, not wishing to buy an insurance policy in the form of an option. The stock continued to rise and eventually more than doubled. It is not very wise to wave aside an option under such conditions, for no one knows how high is high or how far the stock could decline from the high. It makes no sense to assume risks when one doesn't have to. The price for the insurance is a small one to pay.

A large profit on a short position can be similarly protected by the purchase of a call option. Suppose someone had sold Brunswick short at 70. The acquisition of a call option at 50 would have protected the not inconsiderable profit in the latter part of 1961. Yet at the same time the option would have enabled the trader to add to it as the stock continued to decline. Here again the stop order is a questionable tool. It might buy the short seller in at or near the high point of a rally, after which the stock may resume its downward trend—as Brunswick did.

Riskless In-and-Out Trading against an Option

The holder of a put or call option may buy and sell the stock as many times as he wishes during the life of the option. The put-and-call dealer himself buys options and trades against them. Why not take a page out of his book? As long as the purchase price of the stock remains below the contract price in case of a put, and above the market price in the case of a call, the trader will not assume any risk.

A trader has bought 100 shares at 80, margins them, and simultaneously buys a put option at 80 to protect himself against loss should the stock decline. The stock now goes to 88, at which point he sells the 100 shares. Now he is really in business, because the option, his insurance, costs him nothing. When the stock declines to 75, he can buy another 100 shares, knowing that he can put them to the maker of the option at 80. Should the stock go again to 85, he can sell the long stock, and if it drops back to 75, buy another 100 shares knowing that he can still put them to the option maker at 80. Sometimes stocks trade within a range for quite a spell, so that this type of riskless trading can be profitable fun.

Another trader sells the stock short, on margin, at 80 and buys a call at 80 to protect himself against a rise in the stock. It declines to 73, and he decides to buy 100 shares as cover against his short sale. Here again he now has his option for free. The option price has been recovered. When the stock rises to

80 or above, he can sell short another 100 shares without assuming any risk, since he can call 100 shares at 80 from the maker of the option while it runs.

Stocks at times make a "line," a sidewise movement during which they will fluctuate within an upper and a lower resistance level. In view of the continuously changing business climate and investor confidence, the "line" is simply a period of delay in adjusting to underlying values. Eventually the stock will register an up-side or a down-side breakout. The longer it has made a line, the more substantial the change in the market price tends to be when the breakout occurs. Then the judgment of the buyer of the call or put option is vindicated, and he makes substantial profits. Waiting for the breakout is no reason for being inactive. If it does not take place prior to the expiration of the option, inquire whether the writer of the option would consider an extension for an additional premium. If the answer is no, another option can be purchased. As long as the stock continues to make a line, trading against the option can continue—without risk.

The Achieving of Tax Savings

There are no stock transfer taxes on put options. The same taxes that are levied by New York State, and the SEC, on any sale of stock must be paid, however, by the buyer of a call option at the time the contract is written.

The informed investor can save many a tax dollar if he knows his options. Consider this example. Five hundred shares of Natomas were bought in May, 1970, at 15. By the end of August, the stock had gone to 34. The paper profit was $9,500. Alas! it is a short-term gain; waiting until November, when the gain would be taxed as long-term, is very risky, for who knows what a swinger like NOM will do over the next three months? Let's shoot for a long-term capital gain through a put option. If NOM continues to go up, a tidy long-term capital gain would be registered in November. If the stock goes down, I still have a long-term gain when I "put" my stock in November at 34.

Whatever you do, don't exercise a call at 50 and simultaneously sell the stock at 75 in the market if the call option has been held for more than 6 months and a day. Your profit then would be considered a short-term gain, taxed at the steeply progressive federal income tax rates. In this case the thing to do is to sell the option back to the put-and-call broker-dealer. The option is a physical asset that you have held for over 6 months and thus entitles you to long-term capital-gains tax treatment.

A short seller is never eligible for long-term capital-gains tax treatment, no matter how long he has maintained the short position. However, if he purchases a put option for 6 months and 10 days on a stock selling at 90 and after 6 months the stock is at 65, he may sell his put option back to his put and call dealer and the profit will be a long-term capital gain. That is the only way a long-term capital gain can be made on a short sale.

Before I take up the writing of options, a few questions remain to be answered.

What Happens to Dividends and Rights?

Cash dividends paid during the life of a call are credited to the holder of the option, reducing his premium. In the case of a put, they are charged against him. If a stock dividend or a stock split occurs, the holder of the call will receive from the writer of the option the additional or new shares when he exercises the option. The holder of the put option must deliver them to the maker of the option.

Stock rights used to be very confusing, because they would fluctuate in price before they expired. The owner of a call would like to reduce his call by the highest price at which the rights were sold during the subscription period, and the maker of the call would like him to reduce it by the lowest price at which the rights sold. In order to simplify matters, the Put and Call Brokers and Dealers Association ruled that when a stock goes ex-rights, then the first sale of the rights on the exchange, usually the New York or the American Stock Exchange, shall be deducted from the price of the call or be charged against the put option outstanding.

Is It an Ironclad Contract?

Suppose I have a call at 25 and the stock is now 50. Can I be sure I shall always get my stock at 25 when I want it? Can it be always put at 50 when the stock is 25? Answer: Yes. All options must be endorsed or guaranteed by a member organization of the New York Stock Exchange. This guarantee, plus the use of a standardized option form, makes options acceptable anyplace as a fully negotiable instrument.

What Determines the Cost of Options?

The premiums charged for options are determined by many factors. In a very active market, they cost more than in a sluggish market. In a rising market, the demand for calls will be stronger than the demand for puts; calls will therefore sell for more than puts. In a declining market, the reverse will be true. In addition to demand and supply factors, one must consider the length of time the option runs and the price of the stock. The longer the option, the higher the price of the stock, and the more expensive will be the option. Premiums for options written on very volatile stocks are usually higher than those on less volatile stocks. The higher option price is a reflection of the greater demand for options on highly volatile stocks and the greater likelihood that they will be exercised.

The Writing of Options

The brochure of a big put and call broker-dealer says, "Anyone can write options." I disagree. Option writing is for you *if* you can have the proper attitude. If you sell a call at 50 for $500 on 100 shares of ABC and the stock rises to 75, making you regret having lost your stock and possible profits, don't write options. If you sell a put at 50, the stock goes to 40 and is put to you, and you are unhappy over it, don't write options. Option writing is not for the individual who thinks of doubling or tripling his money. It is for people who want to increase their income.

The Percentage-Minded Individual

Writing options is for the percentage-minded individual or institution that understands the nature of the option business. By writing calls or puts, depending on the length of the period, a yield of anywhere between 20 and 30 percent is quite possible. Of course, if you write straddles, you can do even better.

An individual sells a 90-day straddle on 100 ABC at $50 for $700 against a long position. His annual rate of return, assuming he does this 4 times a year, would be:

$$\frac{\$700 \times 4}{\$5,000 \ (\text{the cost of the shares})} \times 100$$

OR

$$\frac{\$2,800 \ (\text{annual income})}{\$5,000} \ \text{or } 56\%$$

This is a gross figure; the commissions and transfer taxes possibly incurred could reduce this to 53 percent. Many an in-and-out trader won't make that in the market.

So if you meet the test of percentage-mindedness, all you need to be in the option-writing business is to have listed stocks in your portfolio and/or the cash with which to buy them if required and a margin account with a member organization of the New York Stock Exchange that endorses options and has an option department. If it doesn't have a good option department, you can of course go to a put-and-call broker-dealer. You can find their ads for special options daily in newspapers such as *The New York Times* or *The Wall Street Journal,* and they also advertise to buy options (such as "Straddles Wanted") on a list of securities.

Exercise of Options

What is the chance that the options I write will be exercised? As I said before, if exercising options bothers you, don't write them. As a question provoked purely by theoretical interest, I shall deign to answer it. It is really impossible to answer except in a rather vague manner. First of all, statistics do not exist for individuals, only for groups. Just because a mortality table says 45-year-old men have a life expectancy of 29.39 years doesn't mean that you couldn't live to 103 or be killed tomorrow by a car crossing Wall Street. If a study shows 50 percent of options exercised, this doesn't mean only one out of each two options you write will be exercised. Maybe none of your options will be exercised because they were bought by hoggish people who sit on their options to the last day, hoping to make more and watching a previous profit fade away.

Second, any time period chosen for study is arbitrarily selected. Who knows how representative it is of the past or the future? Options bought for protection will not be exercised if the stock can be sold or bought more advantageously in the market. Options against which trades have been made will not be exercised if the market price of the stock is above the put price. No one knows how many such options were in the period selected.

With these qualifications in mind, you can now read the SEC *Report on Put and Call Options*, which states that during the period June, 1959, through January, 1960, 42 percent of all the options included in the study were exercised—43 percent of the call options and 40 percent of the put options. Of course, not all these options were exercised at a profit; some of them were exercised to minimize a loss. Estimates previously given for the percentage of options exercised have been much lower. Even the SEC itself must have had doubts about its figures, for it says in the report that "the high rate of options exercised, as found in the present study, apparently reflects exceptional fluctuations in the market during the period covered by the study."

The Investor, Too, Writes Options

Options can also be written profitably by investors who wish to acquire stocks. Two investors, A and B, want to buy shares in various companies totaling $100,000. Investor A buys his securities in the market, and B writes 90-day put options for which he receives $5,000 in premiums.

The market breaks and A shows a loss on his portfolio. Investor B has all the stocks delivered to him, but he has reduced his cost of these securities by $5,000. If the market rises, A would show a profit on his stocks, but B would still have $105,000 uninvested. He would not have profited by the higher price of the securities, but he is free to sell additional put options on the same list or another list of stocks. Perhaps now he wants to make a change in his list of stocks. If B does that in 90-day periods for a year, his return is 20 percent. To that we should add the additional return he might receive from investing the $100,000 in Treasury bills, plus the fact that the average capital investment over a year would be $110,000 ($20,000 in premiums divided by two), so that he can buy additional shares on which to get premiums or the higher-priced shares will bring higher premiums. If that is done, B's total return for the year will be appreciatively better than 20 percent. Over a period of time, B should do better than A.

Another investor, several years ago, had bought 200 shares of a cargo airlines company stock at $8 a share and sold two 6-month calls against them for $600. When the options expired, the stock was still at $8, so that they were not executed. He had paid $1,600 for the stock and received $600 in call premiums, so that now the stock was costing him only $1,000, or $5 a share. If he sold 2 more calls, he would have written his stock down to $2 a share. The stock would either have been called or not. Suppose the next two calls were exercised at $8. He then would sell the two 100-share lots that had cost him $400 for $1,600, or at a profit of 400 percent.

Margin Requirements for Writers of Options

When a call is *not* written against an existing long position or a put against an existing short position, the New York Stock Exchange requires that the minimum margin an endorsing firm must demand from writers of options is 30 percent of the market value of the stock in a call and 25 percent of the market value of the stock in a put. In case of the endorsement of a straddle, strip, or strap, the margin required is the one of the put or call, whichever is greater. Of course, if you have the stock in your margin account or write a put against a short position, no margin needs to be put up.

The 25- or 30-percent margin must be maintained throughout the life of the option. If an individual sells a call on 100 shares at 50 and does not have the stock, he must deposit $1,500 with the endorsing firm—30 percent of $5,000. Should the stock go to 60, the option writer has a $1,000 loss, because if the stock is called at 50, he now has to buy it in at 60. His equity is now reduced to $500. To bring it up to $1,800 (30 percent of $6,000) he must deposit an additional $1,300. The writer is here in the same position as a short seller when the stock goes against him.

These margin requirements constitute tremendous leverage for the option writer—with all its risks and rewards. Suppose he owned 200 shares of ABC, selling currently at 50. He could sell them and use the $10,000 as equity against 6 calls. But don't gamble on the ability to sell options against the 30-percent margin (25 percent in case of puts). You must always be in a position to cover your option(s) when the market goes against you. A put should never be written unless the maker of the option is prepared to own the stock. If its investment quality does not suit his investment objectives, the option should not be written. As a general rule, options should not be written on stocks unfamiliar to the writer.

If the option writer does not know his stocks, he almost surely will waver in his market judgment and tactics, and he could be whipsawed. An individual sells a call on long stock that begins to go down. He thinks it is going lower, and he sells the shares. The following week the market has a strong rally. Now he really worries about his uncovered call, and he repurchases the stock. Final act: A week later the rally reverses itself and the stock keeps on going down, down, down.

Tax Advantages for Option Writers

Our tax laws give the writer of options special advantages. A premium of $500 received for an exercised call at 50 is treated as an increase in the price of stock the writer must sell to the holder of the option. He is selling the stock not at 50, but at 55. If the stock has been held longer than 6 months, the $500 income is treated as long-term capital gain.

A premium of $500 received for an exercised put at 50 is treated as a reduction in the price of the stock the holder of the option has put to the writer. When the stock is sold later at 60, a capital-gains tax must be paid on $1,500, since the cost price of the stock was 45. The tax would depend, of course, on the holding period.

If put or call options are not exercised, the premiums received are treated as ordinary income.

The greatest tax advantage is for the writer of straddles. A $1,000 premium received for such a combination option must be allocated (acceptably) 45 percent to the put side and 55 percent to the call side. The premium for any exercised side is treated just as described above for a call or put. The premium for an unexercised put or call of a straddle is considered a short-term gain.

The fact that taxes on option-writing income can be deferred until the exercise or the expiration of the option period also presents an opportunity. For the larger untaxed capital can be used during such a time.

If there is any value in an option, it should be exercised. When a call is bought at 50 for $400 and the stock on the eve of the option's expiration is only 52, the option should be exercised so that at least half of the option price can be recouped. The remaining $200 can be used as a short-term capital loss to offset a capital gain.

Summary

1. Learn about options. It can be very profitable for you —as buyer or seller.

2. Trading in options is not gambling, nor is it hedging.

3. Options are not traded in an exchange market, but in a special over-the-counter market. Perhaps it will pay you to do a little window-shopping before making commitments.

4. The striking price of options, with the exception of

spreads, is the market price of stocks at the time the option is bought.

5. Options permit speculation on small capital with limited risk and unlimited chance of making profits.

6. Options are ideal for protection at the start of or during a commitment.

7. You can engage in riskless in-and-out trading against options.

8. The sophisticated investor can use options to make long-term instead of short-term capital gains.

9. Don't worry—you have an ironclad contract.

10. Option writing is only for the percentage-minded.

11. It might be much better to accumulate stocks via puts than to buy them in the market.

12. There are special tax advantages for option writers, especially the writers of straddles. They also get the largest premiums and tend to sell stocks after a rise and buy them when they are depressed—a very sound investment procedure.

CHAPTER 11

The Pleasures of Convertible Securities

Many former buyers of straight bonds, including institutional investors such as insurance companies, now want to share in a company's future prosperity. They insist on an equity kicker with their bonds or preferred stock. One way of getting it is through the purchase of convertible securities. The protective feature of a bond or senior equity, coupled with the right to share profits with the owners, brings these "converts" about as close to having one's cake and eating it as is possible. Corporations, in turn, have their own reasons for issuing such securities, so that one need not wonder why so many convertible securities come into the market.

There are many good reasons why investors ought to consider buying convertible bonds and preferred stocks during a period of good economic growth.

If a $1,000 bond is convertible into 25 shares of stock ($40 per share) and the stock goes to $60, the bond will sell for at least $1,500 since the 25 shares will be worth that amount. If it doesn't reach that selling price, arbitrageurs will buy the bond and sell the stock; this tends to raise the price of the bond and lower that of the stock. Most likely the price of the bond will be somewhat above $1,500 because the bondholder has a call on the stock over an extended period of time. To buy a call on 100 shares would cost several hundred dollars, and the time period in which to call the stock would be much shorter.

Buying a convertible security is a good way to share the goodies of a firm without assuming the same degree of risk as the common shareholders. A convertible bondholder or preferred shareholder comes before the owners in the line of claimants if the company gets into financial trouble. Not all convertible securities are converted. If they are bought just on the basis of investment value, you enjoy the status of creditor or preferred owner, and the conversion privilege, when, as, and if it becomes valuable, is extra sauce on your meat and potatoes. How good a bondholder's portion will be depends on the indenture or terms of the bond. A preferred stockholder's position depends on the stock's contractual provisions.

Sharing the fruits of the owners without assuming their risk can be even sweeter when the common stock pays no cash dividend, or a low one, and the convertible bonds carry a much higher yield. American Airlines shares were selling at 19½ and paying an 80-cent dividend in the summer of 1970, a yield that was a shade better than 4 percent. The convertible 5¼ shares due in 1991 were selling for 76, $760 for a $1,000 bond, giving a yield of almost 7¼ percent. Moreover, the conversion price of $30.75 was practically identical with the stock's depressed 1970 high. Despite the problems of the air transport industry, this was a good deal. By December, 1971, the bonds were selling at a premium, at 140; the stock, at 41¾.

Another reason for buying convertible bonds instead of stock is that it is much cheaper for the investor. Three $1,000 American Airlines bonds of convertible 5¼ shares are roughly the equivalent of 100 shares, 97.56 shares to be exact. The commission is $5 a bond; the commission on 100 shares at $20 is $27, without the surcharge. So there is a saving in buying and selling bonds.

For the more venturesome, convertible bonds have still another attraction: They can be bought on a margin (or down payment) of 50 percent in contrast with 55 percent on stocks. You can thus buy twice as many bonds on margin as for cash. Five thousand dollars can buy $10,000 worth of convertible bonds, but only about $9,000 worth of stock. Convertible preferred stocks carry the same margin requirements as common shares. Convertible bonds thus provide greater leverage than stocks.

Finally, while convertible bonds have no upper ceiling, they provide greater protection in a "down" market than stock. The higher the stock rises, the higher the price of the convertible bond will go. Suppose the stock goes from $40 to $20 a share. What then? The convertible bond cannot possibly decline to $500—unless you buy into a corporation whose credit rating is so low that you should have never done it in the first place. The bond will not go below $700 or $750 because of its investment merits as a bond. A 5½-percent bond selling at 70 with a maturity of 20 years would sell at a *yield to maturity* of about 8¼ percent. Fifty-five dollars (the annual yield) plus $15 (divide the discount of $300 by the 20 years to maturity to get the annual accumulation of the discount) means $70, which is then divided by the average value of the investment over the 20 years, or $850, to give a yield of 8¼ percent, disregarding any conversion privilege. When the conversion price is $30.75 and the market price $20, the privilege isn't worth anything, or at best very little.

When the market goes up, convertible securities rise with the stock. When both the market and interest rates go down, the convertible securities as income-producing investments will go up. When both stock and bond markets decline, convertible securities will not decline as much as the stock.

How would you have fared, disregarding commissions and interest paid on margin accounts, had you invested $13,000 in American Airlines stock and an equivalent amount in bonds in the summer of 1970? Assuming you are venturesome and bought the securities on margin:

1,000 shares at 20	$20,000	65% margin	$13,000

OR

343 bonds at 76	$26,068	50% margin	$13,000

In both cases, by December of 1971 there would be a nice, long-term capital gain. You sold:

1,000 shares at 42	$42,000
Repayment to broker—the loan of	7,000
Proceeds from sale	$35,000
Original investment	13,000
STOCK PROFIT	$22,000

OR

343 bonds at 140	$48,020
Repayment to broker—the loan of	13,000
Proceeds from sale	$35,020
Original investment	13,000
BOND PROFIT	$22,020

Financially, you would have done about equally well in either case, disregarding bond interest and dividends. The bond route was a lot less risky. Why take risks if you don't have to?

The Nature of Convertible Securities

Convertible securities are bonds, quite often subordinated debentures, and preferred stocks that may be exchanged for the common stock of the issuer at the option of the holder, subject to conditions previously agreed to. At times the conversion may be into securities of another company. For example, the Owens Illinois Glass Company 4-percent preferred stock was not exchangeable for the company's own stock but was convertible into that of an affiliate, the Owens-Corning Fiberglass Corporation. Now and then there is a bond that is convertible into preferred stock, which is then usually made participating. Unless this is done, there would be little incentive for the bondholders to give up a first lien bond for a junior lien stock if they improve their yield by only a measly 1 percent or so.

Since dividends on preferred stock, in contrast to bond interest, are not tax-deductible for the company, it is not surprising that relatively few convertible preferred stocks come to the market. The purpose of convertible issues, other than making an issue more appealing to the investor, is to raise equity capital for the company at a more advantageous market price than would be possible without the conversion feature.

A convertible debenture, subordinated to any funded debt the company has at the time of issue or will have during the life of the bond, gives the company elbow room to do debt financing should the need arise. Stocks can't always be sold, because if the P/E ratio is too low, it would be akin to giving the company away. But a first mortgage or debenture bond can always be sold, and subordination of the converts permits management to do it. The result of this broad subordination is a relatively low bond rating.

Check the back of Standard and Poor's *Bond Guide* to find a list of convertible bonds. There are over 600, and you won't be able to find 20 issues rated A or AA. These apparently low ratings reflect, in many cases, the looseness of the indenture provisions rather than the current credit rating of the companies. Many an investor fails to appreciate this distinction, so that at times some of these low-rated convertibles may be bought at bargain prices.

In the summer of 1970 prices of most convertible bonds were low, offering high yields. In that bear market, stocks were selling far from their conversion prices, so that the bonds were selling on their investment merit. A BB-rated bond, says Standard and Poor's, has earned charges "on average by a fair margin, but in poor periods deficit operations are possible." Those who could afford the risk could have bought a bond yielding 10 to 11 percent and held it for a few years until the conversion price became worthwhile. The Wharton School's econometric model projects a GNP of $1.8 trillion for 1980, in 1980 prices, as contrasted with a GNP of $932 billion in 1969. These long-range forecasts have been surprisingly accurate! Reason dictates that this goal cannot be reached during the last two or three years of the 1970s. It has to be done more evenly. Therefore a 10- to 11-percent yield now and a rising stock market later as expansion proceeds will bring even better capital gains as conversion prices and market prices come together. The potential rewards seem well worth the risk.

A caveat, however: Look at the annual report of the company you want to buy. Assets should exceed the par value of the bonds by a good margin, and the company should have an established earnings record. If the corporation is listed on the Big Board, you need not worry, for one of the requirements for New York Stock Exchange listing is an established earnings record.

Conversion Price or Ratio

The right of conversion may be exercisable throughout the entire life of the bond, or it may be limited to "on or before" or "on or after" a certain date. The conversion price, or ratio, may be constant throughout the life of the bond or may be stepped up later. For example, American Machine and Foundry (now AMF, Inc.) shares at 4¼ due in 1981 had a conversion price of $54.88 until March 1, 1971; thereafter it jumped to $59.19. There are two reasons for the step-up. It tends to force conversion so that the bonded debt will be wiped off the company's books, enabling it to do new debt financing. Also, the higher conversion price will reduce the degree of dilution in the equity of other shareholders as fewer shares are issued per bond at the higher price.

Since the varied hues of the investment world are only exceeded by those of the fashion world, it is not surprising to find all kinds of investment contracts. There are even preferred stocks that are convertible at a stepped-down ratio if the investor keeps them long enough. The later they are converted, the greater the number of common shares the investor receives for his preferred stock. But it could be a case of the fine print taking away what the large print gives you if the antidilution clause is loosely drawn. Don't ever, ever buy a convertible security unless you read and understand the conversion clause and the antidilution clause.

Generally, when bonds are converted, no adjustments are made in respect to dividends accrued on the stock to be received or in respect to interest accrued on the bonds. One of the notable exceptions to this is AT&T, which makes such adjustments. If a company makes no interest-dividend adjustment and the conversion is properly timed, it is possible to collect both the semi-annual interest and a quarterly dividend.

In the case of uneven conversion, where bonds do not convert into an even number of shares, company policies differ. The prospectus of the convertible subordinated debentures of the Bunker-Ramo Corporation due in 1995 says the company "will not issue fractional shares of common stock but will pay a cash adjustment therefor." Other companies permit the investor to pay cash in order to obtain one full share. More rarely, even conversion is required, in which case the investor loses part of his bond. The company might issue warrants for the fraction that could be sold or in connection with other warrants be used to acquire an additional share.

Protection against Dilution

The owners of a convertible security, as do the owners of warrants, want to be protected against a dilution of the equity. Otherwise the conversion privilege could become more or less meaningless. Suppose a $1,000 bond is convertible into 25 shares of stock and the stock rises to $60. At that point the conversion privilege is quite valuable, because 25 shares of stock now sell for $1,500. But suppose the board of directors, which has sole jurisdiction in this matter, declares a sizable stock dividend or proposes a stock split. The resulting dilution of the equity, the increased number of shares now outstanding, could bring the market price of the stock below the conversion price of $40. If the conversion price was $70 per share or 14.28 shares per $1,000 bond and a 2-for-1 split-up is declared, the conversion price should be immediately adjusted to $35 a share or 28.56 shares per bond.

There are bond indentures that permit payments of stock dividends, in one case up to 5 percent a year, for a number of years without requiring an adjustment in the conversion price. This is definitely a restrictive provision for the bondholder of which he should be aware when considering the purchase of a convertible security. There are companies, sometimes with a fine growth potential, that do not pay cash dividends, only stock dividends. If a convertible bond or preferred stock is not protected against such dilution, the investors can easily be "induced" to convert their securities into common stock at the expense of income.

Remember, then, no convertible security should be bought unless there is a properly drawn antidilution clause providing for instantaneous adjustment in the conversion price or ratio in case of splits or stock dividends. Executive stock options can be disregarded, because the amount of dilution is minimal. In case of a newly issued convertible bond, there is always a section in the prospectus on conversion rights under the heading "Description of Debentures." Read it. The manuals of Moody's Investor Service or the *Corporate Record* of Standard and Poor's will give information on antidilution provisions for outstanding securities.

Callability

Convertible securities are convertible at the option of the investor, but they are also callable at the option of the company. It can "force" the conversion. This sounds worse than it is. As a rule, a company will not call the security unless it sells considerably above par because the stock is selling above the conversion price. At least one month's notice must be given when bonds are called. If the premium on the bond is quite small, a decline in the stock could make conversion unprofitable. The company finds itself then in the embarrassing position where it must pay off the bondholders, having called the issue for redemption. In view of such a contingency, a senior issue is rarely called unless the call price is substantially below the market price.

Since convertible securities are sold to raise equity, the investor can't blame management if it calls the issue and forces conversion. Upon call, the investor can sell the bond or preferred stock and take his long-term capital gain or surrender it for the company's common shares. If he owns a bearer bond and overlooks the call date, quite a bundle of money could go down the drain. Convertible bonds should be held in registered form although quite a number of companies make them available to less sophisticated investors in bearer form.

Can a management abuse the call privilege and call the issue when it begins to be valuable or on the eve of some very favorable developments for the company? Yes. But it does not pay to play dirty financial pool. Any management that is so short-sighted as to engage in questionable financial practices will have great difficulty finding a reputable investment banker to participate in the underwriting of that company's next issue. The Street and the investor have long memories.

A basic rule in buying convertible securities is to know who the originating underwriter is and who the members of the underwriting group are. A large investment banking firm, a member of the New York Stock Exchange, a firm like Morgan Stanley and Co. or the First Boston Corporation, is a pretty good guarantee against unfair treatment. The most precious asset an investment banker has is his reputation, and he will not jeopardize it by sponsoring the securities of companies that engage in shady financial practices. No investment banker wants to acquire the reputation that he peddles junk.

In the event of a merger, convertible securities are usually called for redemption. When Chance Vought Aircraft Company merged with Ling-Temco Electronics Company, it called the entire remaining issue of the 5¼-percent subordinated convertible debentures issued four years before.

When Does the Investor Convert?

The investor will convert under the following three conditions:

1. Dividends on the common stock will bring him a higher income than interest payments on the bond or the dividend payments on the preferred stock. If the income differential is sufficiently persuasive, he will assume the additional risk of a common stockholder.

2. The conversion privilege expires or the bond is about to mature, and the stock is selling above the conversion price. If this is not so, the bondholder or the owner of the preferred stock will either keep his investment or take repayment at par in cash upon maturity or at call.

3. The company forces conversion by calling its convertible securities. If the conversion price is below the market price, the investor will of course convert rather than accept repayment of the principal sum. If he sells the securities, he becomes subject to the capital-gains tax. Conversion will postpone the taxable gain indefinitely. When conversion equals buying the common stock at a very high P/E ratio, it would probably be better to sell the senior security rather than convert it and pay the tax. Not wanting to pay a tax, if there is no other good reason, is a poor reason for keeping an investment. In a portfolio with a planned bond-stock ratio, conversion will change it. This may require a compensating adjustment through the sale of another common stock and subsequent reinvestment of the proceeds.

The Arbitrageur

A great deal of conversion occurs through the action of arbitrageurs. Without them conversion would be a far more difficult task than it is. If we rule out merger arbitrage, then arbitrage is riskless and quite correctly defined as "the simultaneous purchase and sale of equivalents." The arbitrageur buys in the cheap market and sells in the dear market. In so doing, he is bringing markets closer together. That is his contribution.

If the price of a convertible security in relation to the common stock into which it is convertible is out of line, the arbitrageur might sell the stock, buy the convertible security immediately, tender it for conversion, and deliver later on the shares against the sale of the stock. If a bond convertible into 25 shares sells for $1,000 and the stock sells at $26, 40 shares of the stock could be sold at $1,040. The bond bought at $1,000 will give the arbitrageur the stock for delivery against the sale. The description is oversimplified here, for there are brokerage fees, transfer taxes, a Securities and Exchange Commission fee, interest charges if the transaction is made on borrowed money, even the possibility of an interest payment on the bond or a dividend payment on the stock. There might be a charge for borrowing the stock because the New York Stock Exchange requires delivery of stock sold on the fifth business day and the arbitrageur can't meet this date because it will take time for the conversion.

As a rule, arbitrage transactions are for the professional, because he pays a lower commission rate as a member of the Exchange or has the inside market as a professional trader in the over-the-counter market. But now and then an exception occurs. For example, the Studebaker-Packard merger, in 1954, stipulated an exchange of 7½ shares of Packard for one of Studebaker. Packard sold then at 3⅜ and Studebaker at about 20. An arbitrageur could thus sell 750 shares of Packard at about $2,500 and buy 100 Studebaker for delivery against the Packard sale. He would make about $500 in this transaction, enough to pay regular commissions and have a tidy profit. Watch out for merger arbitrage; the merger might not go through, and you could buy into a lawsuit.

Don't think that when a company calls a convertible security, it calls the whole issue for redemption. The major part of the issue has probably been converted through the action of professional arbitrageurs over several years. Thus earnings per share reported "on a fully diluted basis, as reported in accordance with Accounting Principles Board opinion" can be rather meaningless. Suppose a company issues $25 million of convertible debentures. What is the meaning of earnings reported as if the debentures had been converted? Little, if over the years gradual conversion takes place via arbitrage transactions and the company continues to improve its earnings.

Price Behavior of Convertible Securities

The market price of a good-grade CV (convertible) bond or preferred stock will be affected by changes in interest rates, just as any low-risk bond, if it sells at or near par and the stock is below conversion price. If the bond carries a rating of CCC or CC, it is an outright speculation, carries a high credit risk, and the changes in the (mis)fortunes of the company will determine the market price. Once the stock is above the conversion rate, then the convertible security will behave like the stock. Quite often a convertible security will sell above conversion parity because the investor is willing to pay something for having a call on the stock. In contrast with a six-month option, he has a far greater time span working for him.

Converts are not super-securities, although they are often presented as giving the investor "a floor but no ceiling" and as permitting "speculation with safety." Corporations, at times, look upon them with an "all this and heaven too" attitude. Not all convertible securities are converted. If conversion does not take place, the company will have two strikes against it: It is now saddled with debt, and nonconversion leaves a long-lingering bad taste in the mouth of the investor. The company's stock will be affected. If a straight preferred is sold, both problems are avoided. This is one good reason why a company may issue preferred stock. If converts are properly used as a finance or investment medium, everything said about them can be true. But there are many pitfalls for the unwary traveler on this road, as was well illustrated in 1966 and 1970.

Convertible securities began in 1966 at high prices in many cases. As the monetary authorities continued to tighten credit, interest rates rose and convertibles declined in price below their original investment value, below the prices they should have brought as straight bonds or preferreds. Later that year, stock prices declined under the impact of the credit crunch, and the convertibles were hit again. What was supposed to be a floor-and-no-ceiling security turned out to be a twice vulnerable security, vulnerable both as a fixed-income investment and as an equity investment. And look how battered the convertible securities were in 1970! Low stock prices and historically high interest rates really socked it to them!

The floor-but-no-ceiling argument is true *if* the convertible security is of good quality as a bond or preferred and has been bought close to par. In that case the low interest rates usually encountered in the declining phase of the business cycle will push bond and preferred prices above par. During prosperity periods, the rise in common stocks will carry the converts along as high as the stocks will go into which they are convertible. But watch out for rising long-term interest rates, which might foreshadow a decline in the stock market. In that case the place of refuge is in short-term notes. Run and wait for a better day! Great fortunes have been made in convertible securities and will be made in this decade when they are bought right. Moreover, you can always double your pleasure by buying them on a 50-percent margin.

Why Convertible Securities Come to the Market

The companies that issue convertible securities reach from one end of the financial spectrum to the other—from the seasoned issues of long-established firms with good earnings records to highly speculative ones, from the AA-rated security of an electric company to the CC- or CCC-rated bond of a marginal-equipment-leasing or computer-leasing company. Why are they issued?

A new company might be unable to sell its bonds unless it gives the lender, possibly a venture capital company, a chance to share in the future profits. If the debt of the company is large in relation to the equity, as it so often is with evolving companies, the lender assumes what is in fact the risk of an owner. He has more at risk than the owner. Normal people are unwilling to do this without proper compensation. Otherwise his loan is a heads-you-lose-and-tails-I-win proposition. If the business succeeds, the lender receives nothing but the stipulated interest and, eventually, the principal back. If it fails with a high debt ratio he loses more than the owners. For this reason, lenders want a part of the action. There are a few small business investment companies around that have a lot of goodies, warrants, options, and convertible notes and bonds in their portfolios. With the expansion in the 1970s, some ought to pay off handsomely.

The hiring cost of new money will be lower than with a straight bond or preferred issue. In return for the privilege of sharing future profits, the company expects the investor to take the securities at a lower yield. When money is very tight, companies prefer to sell convertible issues in order to bring the rate down. During the late 1960s, a lot of fine companies, such as General Electric, Eastman Kodak, Honeywell, and others, set up international finance companies in Western Europe as subsidiaries through which they marketed dollar bonds convertible into the common stock of the parent companies. This had two advantages for the companies involved: lower interest rates than straight bonds would have required, reinforced by the fact that interest rates in Western Europe were lower than in the United States. This was really killing two birds with one stone! But it gives Europeans a chance for what should be a very profitable investment. With the development of a Western European Common Market consisting of more than the original six countries, the foundation will be laid for more Europeans owning American shares and for more Americans owning European shares— once the interest-equalization tax has been laid to rest.

The unsecured subordinated debenture, if the indenture is

loosely drawn, does not impair the borrowing power of the issuer. Without the convertible feature, a subordinated debenture, particularly one that is subordinated to any debt the company has at issue or will have during the life of the issue, either could not be sold at all or would have to carry an embarrassingly, forbiddingly high rate of interest.

When convertible securities are sold, the equity is not diluted until the money has become productive. The proceeds of an immediate sale of stock will not at once raise the earnings of the company, so that the current earnings are highly diluted, having to be divided among a larger number of shares. Tax-deductible interest charges do not have the same impact.

If new common stock were sold for cash, the offering price would be about market price. Should the shares be offered to stockholders under a so-called rights offering, the price, as described in Chapter 10, would be at a discount, away from the market. When a convertible preferred stock is sold, the conversion price might be 15 percent above the prevailing market, and in case of a convertible bond, even more. The issuer thus sells equity above the market price.

Growth companies, those that grow faster than their industries and/or the national economy, have a particular incentive for issuing convertible bonds. If they were to sell more shares, they would have to be sold at a very low price, management knowing (hoping) that it will be a multiple thereof a few years hence as the company comes to the market with new products that will boost sales and profits. The convertibility feature brings down the coupon rate (the cost to the company), and the interest cost is tax-deductible. But I want to warn you: The balance sheet of such a growth company at an early stage of its life is enough to frighten anybody. Every place you look, there is *debt*. But debt spelled backwards says *opportunity* and *leverage*. At any rate, in such a case, forget about the meaning of investment value, the value of a bond excluding the conversion privilege, as a tool for the appraising of such a security's quality. For subquality bonds, other yardsticks will have to be used. Take a look at what the company intends to do, what is the market potential for it, and, above all, how good its management is.

When management feels that, temporarily, the price of the stock is abnormally low, the convertible bond or preferred stock is again a marvelous idea for the owners of the company as well as for the prospective owners of the convertible securities to be issued. Keep your eyes open! There is gold in them thar convertibles.

A Baker's Dozen of Convertible Bonds to Consider

Apco Oil Convertible Subordinated Debentures	5s	1988 – B
Becton Dickinson	5s	1989 – BBB
Burroughs Corporation	4⅝s	1994 – BBB
First National City Bank Convertible Capital Notes	4s	1990 – NR
Georgia-Pacific Corporation Convertible Subordinate Debentures	5¼s	1994 – BB
Kerr-McGee Corporation	3¾s	1992 – BB
S. S. Kresge Company	5s	1995 – BBB
Pennzoil United	5½s	1996 – BB
Philip Morris	6s	1994 – BBB
Ritter Pfaudler, now Sybron Corporation	4½s	1980 – BBB
Seaboard World Airlines	5s	1986 – BB
Sinclair Oil Corporation, now Atlantic Richfield	4⅜s	1986 – A
U.S. Financial Corporation	5½s	1991 – NR

(NR means that the securities, for one reason or another, were not rated.)

Summary

1. If you want a piece of the action, to share the goodies of the future, buy a convertible security. It comes as close to having one's cake and eating it too as is possible in this life.

2. Buy on 50-percent margin and double your pleasure—if you can assume the risk that goes with leverage.

3. The convertible security will often yield more than the stock into which it is convertible.

4. Convertibles have no upper ceiling, and they won't drop as far as the stock will.

5. Don't let a low rating on a convertible bond fool you. Evaluate it.

6. Take a good look at the company's balance sheet. What protection do assets give you? Or should you put your money on management?

7. Make sure what conversion rights you have.

8. Check the antidilution clause carefully.

9. Don't convert, unless you have to, unless the yield on the stock is higher than on the convertible bond or preferred stock.

10. Leave arbitrage transactions to the professional, but keep your eyes open. Occasionally even you can do it.

11. In developing tight money markets, it might be better to sell the convertibles, no matter where they sell, above or below the conversion price, and seek refuge in short-term notes.

12. There are good reasons for management to sell convertible securities—and equally good reasons for you to buy them.

Part III

What Bonds?

CHAPTER 12

Should I Buy Corporate Bonds?

Reasons for Buying Corporate Bonds

If you believe that we have found the key to ever-rising standards of prosperity and affluence coupled with at least continued mild inflation, don't include corporate bonds in your portfolio for *long-term investment.* As fixed-income obligations, they carry no protection against any further erosion of the purchasing power of money. If you believe, however, that we shall still encounter occasional dips, recessions, and bear markets for stocks, then as a person dependent on income from your portfolio, you should include some high-grade corporate bonds in it. This is particularly true if the bonds are judiciously bought during periods of high interest rates and a depressed bond market.

Bonds also make *good trading vehicles.* If low-coupon, deep-discount bonds are bought when our Federal Reserve authorities are switching from a tight to a less tight or an easy money policy, the investor-trader must gain. An increased money supply will bring down interest rates, and under the laws of financial physics, lower interest rates spell higher bond prices. It's as simple as that. The AT&T 2¾ bonds due in 1980 could have been bought as low as $600 a bond in 1969 and sold for over $740 in early 1972—and that was an AAA-rated bond!

From time to time the bond market also offers opportunities to buy temporarily undervalued bonds and sell overvalued bonds. Sometimes little demand exists for a particular type bond or maturity, and its price will thus be abnormally low. At other times, the reverse is the case. A trader will do well buying something when it isn't wanted and selling it when the demand for it grows stronger.

There will always come a day in a rip-roaring bull market when common stocks are grossly overvalued. In Wall Street, market tops and bottoms will always constitute exaggerations, for securities markets are where a lot of people's greed, fear, hope, and panic meet. The years 1957, 1966, or 1969–1970 make interesting reading in this respect. A switch from common stocks into bonds in the spring of 1957 would have been very profitable by late fall of that year. Then the bonds could have been sold at a modest profit, because an easier monetary policy had brought down interest rates. The stocks sold in May could have been repurchased at a substantial discount, in many cases 30–40 percent, from the late May or early June prices. The investor who sold his common stocks in early 1970 and bought bonds with the proceeds did well. On account of both a declining stock and bond market, he had to sell his bonds in the early summer of 1970 with a small loss, but the money from his bonds would have bought him about 130 or 140 or more shares for every 100 shares he held in January. This was a very profitable stock-bond-stock switch despite a declining bond market.

Finally, the *commission* or markup on bonds is *much less* than on stocks. Roughly speaking, the commission on 10 bonds ($10,000) is about half the charge on 200 shares of stock selling at $50.

But the investor must understand what he is doing. A great many account executives are not particularly well versed in bonds; many consider themselves stock brokers and do not wish to give the bond market much time for study. There are all kinds of corporate bonds; their titles can be very misleading. The pitfalls for the unwary are many. So let us now discuss *things to watch out for when buying corporate bonds.*

Coupon and Registered Bonds

A bond is nothing but a long-term promissory note. The face, par, or principal value of the bond may be $1,000 or more or less than this amount. Under the promise-to-pay clause, printed on the face of the bond, the corporate debtor may issue coupon or bearer bonds and/or registered bonds. With the former, title is transferred simply by hand-to-hand delivery, as the security has no named owner. In this respect it is, like currency, a sought-after object of all thieves. But the transfer of title to a registered bond is effective only upon the owner's endorsement; it involves the cancellation of the old bond and the issue of another bond to the new owner.

There are other differences between bearer and registered bonds. On the dates mentioned in the payment clause, April 1 and October 1 or whatever the semi-annual interest date stipulated, the bearer bondholder clips the interest coupons due, which are attached to the bond, and takes them to his bank for deposit just as he would checks. But coupons are pesky little things that can easily be lost. Be careful not to cut off or into coupons not yet due, and do not write on the face of the bond: "Property of [your name]." In both these cases the bond would no longer be accepted by a broker as "good delivery" and would be unsalable for the time being. The registered bondholder receives his semi-annual interest payments by check.

Any individual desiring a monthly interest income could distribute his investment funds among bond issues with different semi-annual payment dates so as to receive an interest payment, by check or coupon, every month of the year. The same could of course be done with dividend checks by selecting companies with different monthly dividend payment dates.

Besides being stolen or lost, there are even more convincing reasons why investors should hold their bonds in registered rather than coupon (bearer) form. Each year many dollars are lost because corporations call bonds for redemption, refunding, or sinking fund, amortization, purposes. When a bond is called for payment, interest payments stop. The company can notify the registered owner, but no one knows who the bearer-owners are. Sometimes bondholders will not clip coupons because they think this is a good form of compulsory savings for them. If they do not cash in due coupons, they won't spend the money. Then comes the day when the coupons are deposited at the bank and they are told, "Sorry, but these coupons are no good. The bond was called a year ago."

For these and other reasons, about three-quarters of all bonds issued today are in registered form. But relax. If you must— for a convincing reason, I hope—have your bonds in bearer form, it can be arranged quite easily. Corporations give with the registered bond the privilege of one free exchange; that is, the bondholder may exchange the registered bond at any time for a bearer bond free of charge.

Call Protection and Call Premium

During periods of tight money, and consequently high interest rates, bonds are made noncallable (NC) for five or ten years, and more rarely, even longer for *refunding purposes*. The company thus obligates itself not to call the bonds for payment when interest rates are down and to pay them off with the proceeds of new bonds with a lower coupon. By such refunding operations, the investor has his comfortable high-yield-bond rug yanked right out from under him. But bonds, particularly lower-quality bonds, are quite often callable for *sinking fund purposes* in order to assure payment by maturity. A company issues $50 million in bonds due in 1986, with no annual sinking fund payments. Suppose 1986 is a bad year for the company, the industry, or the national economy, and it just does not have the $50 million to pay the issue off. The choice for the bondholders would be: Extend the maturity of the bonds, or let the company go through the wringer of bankruptcy. Annual amortization payments eliminate that risk. With a high-quality bond, such gradual repayment over the life of the bond is of less importance.

At times there is a postponed sinking fund; there are no annual amortization payments required for a period of three or five years. Of course, this again spells call protection for the bondholder, but with a lower-quality bond this can present him with another problem. Such annual amortization payments come after taxes; bond interest comes before taxes, since it is a cost of doing business. To meet $500,000 sinking fund payments means the company must have $1 million before taxes, and the longer the postponement is, the larger the payments tend to be. In a business recession, this could prove embarrassing as accounts receivable payments slow down and bank credit is less readily available. Call protection against refunding and sinking fund purposes is nice, but the investor in these cases is well advised to stick to high-quality bonds.

Bonds are also callable for *redemption,* to pay them off. The investor should always find out what his call protection is and against what. Refunding? Sinking fund payments? Redemption? When bonds are callable, he should ask, "What is the *call premium?*" What is the compensation paid to him by the company for losing his bond? The call premium is on a decreasing scale. The sooner after issue a bond is called, the higher will be the premium; the later it's called, the lower the premium. Since amortization protects the bondholder, the call premium for sinking fund purposes is less than the call premium for redemption or refunding.

The 9¾-percent first mortgage bonds of the General Telephone Company of California, issued in 1970 and due in 2000, are protected against refunding until June, 1975. But they may be redeemed on 30 days' notice at any time. If they are redeemed in 1972, the bondholder will receive $1,000 per bond plus $98.90 as compensation for losing his bond; this is, of course, in addition to the interest payments. If they're redeemed in 1984, the call premium is only $53. By 1996 it will shrink to $10.60.

In view of the danger of loss, theft, and interest stoppage when called, the ownership of registered bonds is preferable to that of bearer bonds. Registered bondholders will be notified when their bonds are called.

Types of Corporate Bonds

Buying bonds is like buying a new car. What make or model shall I have? What color or upholstery? What optional extras?

Like cars, there are many bond "models." The principal types of corporate bonds ordinarily issued are mortgage bonds, equipment bonds, collateral trust bonds, debenture bonds, income bonds, and subordinated debenture bonds.

Mortgage Bonds

Mortgage bonds are secured by a lien on the corporation's real property. It may be a first, second, or further-removed mortgage, but since the designation of a mortgage bond as anything except "first" does not sound well to investors' ears, the term "general" mortgage is used. This conveys no meaning whatsoever as to the priority of the lien. Only a study of the bond covenant or the prospectus in case of a newly issued security will reveal that.

Some railroad bonds are an intricate maze of senior and junior obligations, secured by various types of mortgages on the different properties of a railroad. A *divisional lien bond* may have a first mortgage on one piece of property, a second on another, and a third mortgage on still another property, if indeed the chain stops there. How good such a bond is depends less on the priority of the lien than on the type of property forming the security. How essential is it for the operation of the railroad? How valuable could it be to a real estate developer?

Do not attach too much significance to the word "first." Yes, first mortgage bondholders have first claim on the company's earnings and on real property if the company should be liquidated. But how good is such protection if the company's junior bonds go into default and their owners throw the company into receivership and reorganization?

The bond contract of an electric company's first mortgage bond issue is usually in the form of an *open-end contract with an after-acquired property clause*. Under it, the utility can issue successive series of bonds called *series bonds* as the need for funds arises. All series bonds issued under the same open-end mortgage enjoy equal priority. Their interest rates will differ because money rates vary with demand and supply conditions, as does the price for any commodity. The after-acquired clause assures the bondholders that the corporation will bring under the mortgage all properties acquired or constructed with the proceeds of the new series of bonds. The issue of additional bonds is usually limited to an amount not in excess of 60 percent of the acquisition costs of *unencumbered* property additions.

The leasehold mortgage bond, another form of mortgage bond, usually carries a higher interest rate than a first mortgage bond, because it is actually a junior bond. It is issued in connection with the construction of commercial buildings erected on leased land. The rental income from the edifice will be available to pay operating expenses, ground rent, and bond interest and amortization. The risk here arises from the prior claim of the lessor. If the landlord is not paid, he may repossess the land with the building on it. Leasehold mortgages are today sold directly to institutional investors. Some years ago, such bonds were sold publicly, and they may well be again, particularly if they are sold as "stabilized bonds," that is, bonds protected against inflation by tying long-term rental contracts to an index of prices, sales, or possibly, in the case of hotels or motels, to gross income.

Equipment Bonds

Besides real property as security, a corporation may use such chattels as locomotives and cars, busses and trucks, airplanes, or more general equipment. Publicly distributed *equipment trust certificates* are primarily issued by railroads. As a group, these securities enjoy a high credit rating and excellent market standing. Their record, even during the 1930s, is most impressive. Even railroads in bankruptcy continued paying interest and principal on their equipment obligations.

Such equipment trust certificates are usually issued in *serial* form with maturities ranging from one to fifteen years. Each year a part of the bonds matures. They are thus referred to as *serial* bonds, a term not to be confused with the *series* bonds issued under an open-end mortgage. Serial maturities enable investors to purchase the specific maturity they desire. If they buy a 1984 maturity, they can rest at ease; their bonds will not be paid before 1984. This is about the only way to be completely protected against a premature call and retirement of bonds. Under the so-called Philadelphia or equipment lease plan, the railroad usually pays 20 percent to the manufacturer of the equipment, and a bank will pay the remaining 80 percent. An investment banking group will sell the securities to the public and turn the proceeds over to the bank, reimbursing it. The bank, as trustee, takes title to the easily movable and legally easily repossessable property. The bonds will mature more rapidly than the cars and engines depreciate, so that the underlying security for them tends to increase rather than diminish. The railroad's annual payments for the use of the equipment are sufficient to pay interest and the annual serial maturities. When the last annual maturity is met, title to the equipment will pass to the railroad. One confusing aspect is that the interest payments on these "bonds" are called dividends, and the coupons are referred to as dividend warrants, because these obligations are not really bonds but certificates of beneficial interest.

Equipment obligations issued by air transport companies or industrial firms do not enjoy a high credit rating similar to those issued by railroads. Here the title to the equipment is held by the corporate borrower. Moreover, the second-hand resale value of industrial machinery is problematical, and in the case of airlines the equipment financed represents an extremely high percentage of the value of all the assets of the issuer.

Collateral Trust Bonds

Collateral trust bonds are secured by a lien on securities deposited with a corporate trustee. The collateral may be bonds, notes, or stocks. The issuing corporation has the privilege of substituting securities of equal value, which may be of significance in case a finance company is involved. Any interest or dividend payments on the collateral go to the issuer. Pledged stock may be voted by him.

For the bonds to be salable at issue, the market value of the deposited securities collateral must be at least 30 percent larger than the face value of the bonds. The additional margin is insisted upon as protection for the creditors should the issuing corporation default and the collateral be sold in an unfavorable market to pay off the bondholders.

Debenture Bonds

Debenture bonds, or "debentures" for short, are corporate *unsecured* long-term promissory notes. No property of any type is specifically pledged. The underlying security is the total of all the unpledged assets of the company, a status the debenture holders share with all other general creditors. But if the issuer agrees not to issue any prior debt, the debentures become, in fact, the senior debt. The American Telephone and Telegraph Company will surely never issue first mortgage bonds. The bond indenture for such an issue would be about the size of the Manhattan telephone book! The company's debentures have a top credit rating because there is and will be nothing ahead of them.

The secured bond used to be the darling of the investing public. However, investors now appreciate the fact that, particularly as far as industrial bonds are concerned, the mortgage bond is obsolete. After all is said and done, only earnings give value to a security. With the exception of railroad equipment bonds, property often has little value in a forced sale. It is either too specialized, or it is a drug on the market. If business is bad, what can the creditors do with a company except reorganize it or sell the equipment for scrap? No one will want to enter the industry, so that the market for second-hand plants and equipment is nonexistent. Nor will scrap value be very much under such conditions.

Subordinated Debenture Bonds

In this case the issue may be subordinated to all debt maturing later than twelve months in existence at the time of the issue of the bonds or to any such debt the company may incur during the life of the bonds. This is buying a pig in a poke! When subordinated debentures are bought, it is of the utmost importance that *the degree of subordination* be ascertained.

The subordination agreement provides that in the event of bankruptcy, liquidation, or reorganization, the senior bondholders shall be entitled to full payment of principal and interest due *before* the subordinated bondholders receive anything. In the event of default of the company's subordinated debt, all outstanding senior debt issues will become immediately due and the holders of the senior bonds will again be entitled to full payment of principal and interest before the subordinated bondholders receive a dime. This, of course, assumes that funds are available to pay off the senior debt. As we have seen in the case of convertible subordinated debt, the degree of subordination is of far less importance.

Income Bonds

Interest payments on the types of straight bonds discussed so far must be met as they fall due. Failure to pay them would be an act of default. But interest payments on income bonds may be missed without bringing the consequences of default. Interest here need *only* be *paid when it is earned* by the corporate debtor or to the extent that it is earned. Perusal of the debt covenant is of the utmost importance here. Accounting is an inexact science at best, so that a company may earn the bond interest under one set of accounting procedures and not earn it under a different accounting setup.

Usually the interest is cumulative for three or four years, after which the cumulative feature becomes inoperative. The security is legally still a bond. There is here a definite promise to repay the principal when it falls due, but the maturity date is often very far off. Income bonds shade into preferred stock on which the dividend payment need not be made if management should decide to pass it. They are superior to the company's preferred stock in that they have a prior claim to earnings and assets. In the past they were often issued in railroad reorganizations as *adjustment bonds* with very long maturities, extending way into the next century. Very often they were made convertible into the common stock of the issuer at the option of the bondholder. Sometimes they were dressed up as "general mortgage convertible income bonds." During the 1950s a number of companies, industrials as well as rails, called in their preferred stock and replaced it with long-term income bonds. Through such an exchange a company's preferred dividend payments that were not tax-deductible became so as bond interest. Without any additional increase in earnings, the company could thus report an increase in its per-share earnings because of the tax savings. But the company's debt was larger, possibly limiting its capacity to do new debt financing in the future. Investors apparently did not care for this type of bond. The subordinated debenture, often convertible, has taken the place of the income bond sold earlier as a substitute for preferred stock. However, finance, like fashion, has its fads. Who knows what will come next?

This hybrid security has other peculiarities. The income bond is always issued as a registered bond with interest payable annually, as much of it as there is. Since no one knows whether any interest will be paid until the company's books are closed for the fiscal year, the issue of coupons would make no sense.

Bond Quotations

Bonds are quoted on exchanges in percentages of par value. Corporate bond prices are usually given in fractions, in eighths; maturities of less than one year may be quoted in terms of thirty-seconds. A bond quoted at 100⅞ has a price of $1,008.75 for the $1,000 bond certificate. A –½ indicated in the net change column would mean the bond went down by $5 yesterday. But in the case of straight bonds the purchaser would have to pay also the interest which has accrued since the last interest payment date. It is said that such bonds sell *on an accrual basis*. The seller of a corporate bond is entitled to accrued interest up to the day of the delivery of the bond after sale, currently on the fifth business day, but not including the day of delivery. Corporate bond interest is computed on the basis of 360 days per year, every month being figured as 30 days.

Income bonds, on the other hand, sell *flat*, that is, the buyer pays no interest to the seller for the time that has elapsed since the last payment date. After all, there may be no interest payment. In the bond quotation it would read: Missouri Pacific Railroad 5% 2045f. The "f" indicates that it is an income bond, that it is selling flat with the interest included in the market price. Income bonds, the only bonds that are selling flat besides bonds in default, have an interesting tax feature. Whatever interest has accrued prior to the purchase date is regarded as a return of principal and can be applied to a reduction in the cost base. The appreciation on an income bond bought after interest payment, after it went ex-interest, and sold after six months and one day, can be claimed as long-term capital gain.

From One End of the Spectrum to the Other

By now the reader must have reached one very definite conclusion: The categories and subcategories of bonds are truly legion. Names sometimes convey a fairly accurate idea of the nature of a bond; at other times they are very misleading, not to say meaningless. What is an "income mortgage bond"? A "consolidated mortgage bond"? Yet the "first and refunding mortgage bonds, 4¾% Series T" of the Consolidated Edison Company of New York tell a more definite story. Here is a first-mortgage bond whose proceeds were used to retire a previously outstanding issue; it is a series bond issued under an open-end mortgage.

The use of a term such as "sinking fund bonds" is meaningless. Any bond that has a sinking fund, annual amortization of the debt, is a sinking fund bond. Moreover, a sinking "fund" is no longer set up today. The corporation does not annually put money into a fund in order to "sink" (retire) the bond issue at maturity. It simply gives the corporate trustee the money as required under the bond covenant. The bank, or trust company, will then either call enough bonds or buy them in the market and retire them. Whatever method is cheaper will be used. As long as a bond sells at a discount from par, the trustee will obviously buy it in the open market rather than call it. In view of the current high interest rates, bonds issued over the recent past will very likely not sell at a discount. We can look forward to lower interest rates, so that these bonds tend to sell at a premium. Companies, or their respective trustees, will then call bonds for redemption and/or sinking fund purposes.

There are a few terms which are correctly used. For example, when a corporate debtor merges into another company, the successor company will assume the bonds. They are, thereupon, referred to as *assumed bonds*. The assumption changes nothing in the security's original title and lien, but it substitutes the assuming company's promise to pay in place of the original issuer. Assumed bonds are usually the result of mergers. Of course, the bondholders must agree to such an assumption.

At other times a bond will be guaranteed by one or more other corporations. A railroad terminal may be owned by several railroads; the terminal bonds will then be guaranteed by all the roads that own it. They are then spoken of as *joint* (and several) *bonds* or *guaranteed bonds*. A holding company may guarantee the bonds of a subsidiary in order to permit the latter to borrow more cheaply in the market. If the guarantor is financially strong, the guarantee will improve the bond. Otherwise the bond's quality rests with its own lien security. Some guaranteed bonds reflect an astonishing trust in the stability of human institutions. The West Shore Railroad 4% bonds of 2361 are guaranteed as to both principal and interest by the New York Central, which has now become the bankrupt Penn Central Railroad. The maturity of the Elmira & Williamsport Railroad bonds was 2862.

A Bond Is Whatever the Indenture Says It Is

In a corporate bond issue three parties are involved: the corporate debtor issuing the bond; the lenders, the bondholders; and a corporate trustee, a bank or trust company, charged with the protection of the bondholders' interests. The financial institutions engaged in corporate trust work must have ample capital; otherwise the bondholders would have little protection should the trustee become liable to them. Besides the signature of two officers of the issuing corporation, there appears on the face of the bond a "Trustee's Certificate of Authentication," which is signed by an officer of the trustee. This certification assures the investor that each bond so signed is one of a duly authorized issue of bonds, of a given aggregate principal amount, and issued under the indenture, sometimes also referred to as a debt covenant or deed of trust.

The indenture, quite often a printed document of a hundred pages or more, spells out the rights of the three parties to a bond issue and their obligations to one another. It specifically sets forth the duties of the trustee to protect the bondholders in seeing that the corporate issuer fulfills its obligations under the indenture. This is particularly important in case of a default. The corporation may be unable to meet an interest payment. It may default in the payment of a principal sum. A sinking fund provision may not be honored. The debtor may not live up to some of the conditions set forth in the indenture, such as the maintenance of a certain minimum working capital, or the company may violate a provision against running up additional debt. "Default" is thus a much broader concept than people usually assume.

Bond indentures generally have a provision to modify them. It usually states that "with the consent of the holders of not less than 66⅔ percent in aggregate principal amount of the debentures, modifications and alterations of the indenture may be made which affect the rights of the holders of the debentures and the coupons." The two-thirds majority-rule modification does not, however, apply to a change that would "extend the fixed maturity of the bonds or reduce the rate or extend the time of payment of interest, without the consent of the holder of each debenture so affected." To reduce the 66⅔ percent of bonds required to change the indenture also takes the consent of all the owners of the issue.

A corporation likes to see such a flexible provision in the indenture because it may seek a removal of a dividend restriction or sinking fund clause, or it may wish to sell pledged property that it can no longer use advantageously. When holders of a given issue agree to an extension of maturity of their bonds or to make interest payments temporarily contingent on earnings in order to avoid the burdensome and costly procedure under default and reorganization, the bonds are overprinted to show such changes. They are then known as *stamped bonds.*

The Trust Indenture Act of 1939 gives the Securities and Exchange Commission jurisdiction over bond indentures. The trustee must be an independent trustee with no conflicts of interest; he must have power to act for the bondholders; and he can be held liable for his actions. All indentures must be filed with the SEC to make sure that they comply with the act. In case of default, the trustee must notify the bondholders within ninety days and protect their interests with the skill expected of a prudent man administering his affairs.

Risks of Bondholders

The bondholder assumes several risks. First, there is a *purchasing power risk.* If prices rise in a year by 3 percent, even a luscious 9-percent bond will wind up as a 6-percent *real* rate of return; upon maturity the investor might find that he has lost 30 percent or more of his original purchasing power. Second, there is a *credit risk.* The issuer's credit standing could deteriorate and the market price of the bonds decline, or worse, it could go into receivership. A Moody rating of Aaa, Aa, A, or Baa or a Standard and Poor's rating of AAA, AA, A, or BBB makes bonds eligible for bank and other institutional investment. Ratings of Baa or BBB mean that the bond would be paid under all foreseeable conditions. Ratings of Ba or BB or lower carry, of course, a higher credit risk.

Bonds also have a *market risk.* Sometimes the dealers' shelves are full of bonds, or many new bond offerings are being made. Then bond prices will come down, and yields go up, in order to reduce inventories and sell the new issues.

But even a AAA bond can sell at a tremendous discount from par. When interest rates rise, the price of outstanding bonds must decline. In the summer of 1970 the 2¾-percent American

Telephone and Telegraph bonds due in 1980 sold for 63½ cents on the dollar! This illustrates the *money risk* that even high-quality bonds have.

Figuring Bond Yields

Should the investor buy a newly issued bond bearing 8½-percent interest at par, he can deposit $42.50 on every semi-annual payment date. His yield, his rate of return on the investment, would be 8½ percent. This is the *nominal* or *coupon yield* of the bond. If he can buy a 5-percent bond that was issued when interest rates were lower for $600, his *current yield* would be 8.33 percent. To find the current yield we divide the income ($50) by the cost or value of the investment ($600); thus $50/$600 = 8.33 percent. The *yield to maturity* would even be higher than 8.33 percent, because the bond would be paid off at its face value of $1,000 when due. Let us assume that the 5-percent bond selling at $600 would mature in 20 years. Its yield to maturity would then be 8¾ percent. To the annual income of $50 we add $20 ($400, the capital appreciation over 20 years, divided by 20 for 1 year). The $70 is then divided by the average value of the investment over the 20-year period, or $800. Thus $50 + $20 = $70 and $70/$800 = 8.75 percent.

If a 9-percent bond with a 10-year maturity sells at a premium of, say, $100 at $1,100, we must amortize that bond premium over the life of the bond, over the 10 years ($100/10 = $10 a year). Thus $90 income minus $10 annual bond premium amortization is $80, divided by the average value of the investment over the 10 years ($1,050); this gives us $80/$1,050 = 7.62 percent. Since bonds, once they are issued, tend to trade at either a premium or discount as interest rates change, figuring current yield for a bond has little meaning.

Deep-Discount Bonds

When interest rates are high and it looks as if they may soon go lower, it is advisable to buy so-called *deep-discount bonds*.

They are high-quality, low-coupon bonds whose price changes primarily with changes in the cost of money. They are thus also referred to as *money bonds*. If I purchase a high-coupon bond at par and the interest rate declines, its price will, as a rule, not go beyond the call price. If I buy a deep-discount bond at $800 and the interest rate drops as Federal Reserve authorities ease up on the money supply, my bond could rise by as much as $200! This is why deep-discount bonds tend to sell at a slightly lower yield (to maturity) than newly issued bonds. But the small difference in yield is more than made up by the possibility of far larger capital gains than are possible with bonds bought at or close to par.

Summary

1. Bonds may be bought for long-term investment or for trading purposes.

2. Registered bonds offer protection that bearer bonds do not.

3. The investor can lose his high-yielding bond unless he enjoys call protection.

4. In case of a mortgage bond, how valuable is the property to the company or somebody else?

5. Equipment trust certificates offer perfect protection against an early call.

6. The value of the securities underlying collateral trust bonds should be, at issue, at least 30 percent larger than the face value of the bond.

7. Debenture bonds may be as good as a first mortgage bond if the company promises to put nothing ahead of them, or if it does so, to upgrade the bonds to equally secured and ratable bonds.

8. Interest on income bonds may be skipped without penalty. They are quoted flat and can present some tax advantages.

9. Only the indenture says what kind of bond it is. It is always summarized in the prospectus of a new issue.

10. The biggest risk with high-quality bonds is the money risk. If bought on the eve of a change in monetary policy as deep-discount bonds, they can become a very worthwhile investment.

CHAPTER 13

Are There Advantages in

Government Securities?

How would you like to pay taxes to Uncle Sam with a dollar that costs you only seventy-six cents? You can—if the taxes are federal estate taxes and the payment is made with a deep-discount, long-term Treasury bond. If you don't feel like paying state or local income taxes, don't. Go out and buy United States Treasury securities or those issued by government agencies. The latter fetch a higher yield. The states and their local political subdivisions cannot tax income derived from them.

Even the government savings bond, looked down upon by so many investors, has tax advantages that are not recognized by many people. It depends on how smart you are in dealing with the income from savings bonds whether the tax collector will let your income go untouched for years or whether you get clipped year after year.

Your money should work as hard for you as you have worked for it. To accomplish that is not just a matter of relying on the advice of others. You too must give a little time to your money. Give your money half the attention you give your car, and you might come across something that you had no idea existed, such as, for example, a United States Government security exempt from both the federal as well as the state and local income taxes. There is only one such species.

Besides interesting tax aspects, some Treasury securities are as riskless as man can make a security. The chances that the investor will take a loss on them are about as likely to occur as the comeback of the nickel schooner of beer with the free lunch. Government securities have their place in a portfolio. They should be given more consideration than individual investors, in particular, are apt to give them.

Importance of the Government Securities Market

Money is a perishable commodity. If not invested, it will rot like ripe fruit on the grocer's shelf and must be thrown away. When investors (you are an investor the minute your income exceeds your outgo!) sit on idle cash, the interest they lose, like a rotten peach, is forever gone down the drain. And this is where the market for United States Government securities comes in.

This market is of the greatest importance to our economy, our pocketbooks, indeed to our well-being. Through it, financial institutions, industrial corporations, and individual investors *adjust their liquidity position*. If banks or individuals are more liquid, have more cash than they wish to hold, they may buy short-term government securities and thus exchange cash, a nonearning asset, for a riskless interest-paying investment. If they need more cash than they have, they may sell such securities previously acquired. In the course of a year the buyers and sellers of government securities represent not only the private sector of our economy (profit-oriented businesses and individuals as well as educational and eleemosynary institutions) but also the public sector (federal, state, and local government units). They all have excess funds at one time and invest them to earn something on their money, only to sell them at a later date when cash is needed for other uses. In the interval, income is produced. With today's high interest rates, sitting on unneeded, idle cash is expensive and wasteful. Only the lazy and the stupid do it. We won't for a long time go back to the low interest rates of the 1950s, when Treasury bills on many occasions brought less than 1 percent, so that today the cost of holding unneeded cash, even when only for short, intermittent periods, over a person's adult life time can be truly staggering. But there is more than that to the government securities market.

If we want to reach the second trillion dollars in our annual GNP by the early 1980s, then our national money supply must expand in an orderly fashion. Without an adequate money supply (primarily bank checking accounts and, to a lesser degree, currency), prices will fall precipitously and a recession or even depression could develop. On the other hand, as we have experienced, an overheating economy requires a reduction in the rate at which money is made available to the economy.

When our Federal Reserve authorities buy government securities in the open market, they make "high-powered dollars" available that multiply by way of bank credit expansion. When they sell, the reverse is true. When they tighten up on the money supply, as many hapless investors have found out, this is no time to hold on to common stocks or long-term bonds. For as interest rates rise, stock and bond prices sooner or later *must* come down. The place of refuge is short-term notes. I shall discuss this more fully in Chapter 18, which deals with the money market.

Besides a place through which we adjust liquidity and effect changes in our money supply, the government securities market has one other important function: to assist the Treasury in managing our huge federal debt. Over the next twelve months, over $115 billion of maturing government securities will have to be refinanced, rolled over because the government can't possibly have the money to pay it off. There are also the federal deficits that will have to be financed by raising new money for the Treasury. All these activities in the government securities market influence our complex interest rate structure and the prices and yields available on government securities. They, in turn, affect prices and yields on the government agency securities, municipal securities, high-grade corporate bonds and preferred stocks, and even common stocks held primarily for income.

The Federal Debt

Toward the end of 1971 the total gross direct debt of the federal government amounted to over $412 billion. It was made up of marketable and nonmarketable securities, and special issues held only by United States Government agencies and trust funds in the following proportions:

Marketable Issues

Treasury bills	$ 89.3 billion
Certificates of indebtedness	none here outstanding
Notes	111.5
Bonds	51.8
Total	$252.6 billion

The nonmarketable portion of the federal debt was primarily represented by savings bonds and notes, amounting to almost $54.4 billion. Another $84.3 billion was in the form of special issues held in hundreds of separate government-administered trust accounts, ranging from the various social insurance and retirement accounts, hundreds of Indian tribal funds containing the proceeds of land-claim settlements and oil-lease sales, the Highway Trust Fund, which is essentially a conduit for federal gasoline and tire taxes collected by the Treasury and eventually turned over to the states, to a fund accumulated from private contributions for the establishment of a chapel in a women's prison.

For the investor and the securities markets, only the marketable sector of the federal debt is important.

Treasury Bills. T-bills were first used in December, 1929, and run today for three months, six months, and one year. They do not bear any interest on the face of the security, but are sold through weekly auctions at a discount from par, and they mature at par. On Thursday, unless a holiday interferes, the Treasury asks for tenders on a named total of three-month and six-month bills and at spaced intervals for one-year bills. The bids must be received by a Federal Reserve bank or branch by 1:30 P.M. New York time on the following Monday. Like at any auction, the Treasury, acting through the Federal Reserve banks as fiscal agents, will allot bills to the highest bidders, that is, those willing to take the lowest yield. Noncompetitive tenders may be submitted for smaller amounts, but not below ten thousand dollars; they are accepted at the average price of the successful competitive bids.

Bills can, of course, also be bought in the secondary market for any amount up to a maturity of almost one year. Transactions high in the millions can be effected almost at the flick of a telephone key at the trading desk of a government securities dealer, bank, or nonbank dealer. He may offer to sell bills at a yield of 4.08 percent, meaning that he will discount the bills at an annual rate of 4.08 percent for the number of days they run until maturity, when the buyer will receive their par value. This same dealer might buy bills from you at a yield of 4.14 percent. The spread between the bid of 4.14 percent and the offer of 4.08 percent is the dealer's profit; the shorter the maturity, the larger will be the spread. On the longest maturities, the spread may be only nine basis points, 0.09 percent. On the very short maturities, the spread has to be wider because otherwise the dealer couldn't make a living.

The T-bill market is often misunderstood by individual investors. They know from their stock trading that the bid is always lower than the offer. Now they see a T-bill quoted as 11–30 4.12 bid, asked 3.95. Is this an error? No. These figures represent percentages. They mean that the bill maturing November 30 was being bought by the dealer at a discount of 4.12 percent from par and offered at a 3.95-percent discount. The higher the discount rate, the lower will be the present value. The lower the discount, the higher the present value will be. The bid is therefore still lower than the offer, despite its deceiving look. But do not compare bill yields to bond yields. When I buy the bill, I am getting 3.95 percent on the discounted value, not on the par value. The equivalent bond yield would thus be higher. Moreover, if yield is to be computed as an annual rate of return, then we must allow for the actual number of days the T-bill has to run until it matures.

The small investor should not be tempted by temporarily high bill yields. With the charge that the broker or bank will make, the acquisition cost comes too high. Should he have to sell it before maturity, his yield will be substantially below that paid in a savings account. If he can hold it to maturity, any of the twelve Federal Reserve banks or their twenty-four branches will redeem it without charge. Make sure that you have proof of ownership with you! This should be the delivery slip that shows the numbers of the bills.

A T-bill is about as riskless an investment as man can invent. Suppose an investor buys a 1-year bill of $10,000 at a discount of 4 percent, or at $9,600. Note that he is getting $400 on $9,600 invested! Six months later he needs his money because an emergency has arisen, or he might wish to reenter the stock market. If the interest rate has not changed, he would receive $9,800. The interest rate would have to more than double before he would suffer any loss on the principal amount of the investment. This would be an unthinkable increase in rates. A bond, on the other hand, would drop considerably in price if the interest rate goes up by only 1 percent. This riskless aspect of Treasury bills makes them into such incomparable vehicles for the adjustment of liquidity positions.

Treasury Certificates of Indebtedness. These certificates have a maturity of about one year, but they carry a fixed rate of interest, payable semiannually or at maturity. T-bills can always be sold to the highest bidder, but a new offering of certificates could run into trouble if the rate on the security is below the going market rate. Sometimes bills and certificates are issued as tax anticipation issues, TABs or TACs. They are designed by the Treasury to trap the cash that corporations and individuals accumulate to meet their future tax liabilities.

Treasury Notes. They may carry maturities of one year to seven years. Like comparable private debt securities, they carry a stated interest and pay interest semi-annually.

Treasury Bonds. These bonds mature in excess of seven years. These maturities are strictly defined by the Congress. A note cannot have a maturity in excess of seven years, and a bond is any government debt instrument with a maturity beyond that. The Treasury may sell notes at any coupon rate, but cannot sell a bond with a coupon in excess of 4¼ percent, under a law on the statute books since World War I days. Failure to repeal this law has caused the American taxpayer many additional dollars for interest payments on the federal debt, for long-term securities can often be sold at a lower yield than medium-term notes or bills. In 1971 Congress permitted the Treasury to sell $10 billion worth of bonds at any interest rate.

Treasury bonds, like corporate or municipal bonds, come in bearer or in registered form. What I said about the registration of corporates applies here too. Registered government bonds are much safer to own than bearer bonds. The bonds are usually callable, but in contrast with a corporate bond, which may be callable after five years of issue, they are callable usually five years prior to maturity. An issue maturing in 1983 may be callable from 1978 on.

United States Treasury bonds and notes are quoted in terms of thirty-seconds, not eighths, as is the case with corporates. The 4-percent bonds of 1988–1993 were quoted in the summer of 1970 as 67.16 bid and 68.16 offered. This meant that the 4-percent bonds are callable from 1988 on, mature in 1993, and could be bought at $68^{16}\!/\!_{32}$, or $68\frac{1}{2}$, or $685 per $1,000 par value. The seller would have gotten $675. Of course, we buy the bond at $685 plus accrued interest. Regular delivery for governments is usually the next business day, so that the seller would receive the accrued interest on the trade day; he is entitled to interest up to the date of delivery, but not including it. Interest in the case of government securities is figured on an actual day basis.

Risks

What are the risks of owning government securities? That depends on their maturity. The credit risk is nil. We don't have to worry about the government not paying off a maturing debt. Its unlimited power to tax is pledged. There is, as with all longer-term debt instruments, a purchasing-power risk. But as we have seen, this does not apply to a Treasury bill. The chief risk with notes and particularly bonds is the money risk. As interest rates rise, bond prices must come down. The longer the maturity, the more pronounced is this risk. The T-bills, as was shown, have no money risk. For longer-term notes and bonds there is also a market risk. Heavy supplies of newly offered bonds, corporates and municipals, tend to drag governments down with them.

Nonmarketable Issues

Nonmarketable government securities are primarily in the form of E and H savings bonds and the so-called Freedom Shares, United States Savings Notes, which are no longer sold. They are nontransferable, they cannot be used as collateral for a bank loan, and they can be cashed in only by surrender to the Treasury, directly or indirectly through a bank. About $59.3 billion of them are currently outstanding.

Series E Savings Bonds. Designed for the small investor, they are sold at a discount from par, say $75 for an eventual value at maturity of $100. However, when the interest was raised in 1968 and again in 1970, rather than shorten the maturity period to less than 7 years, the bonds will now mature at a premium. Provided they were held to maturity, the yield was 5½ percent in 1971. The yield is a "perverse" yield. It is realized only if the bonds are held to maturity. The sooner after issue the bonds are cashed in, the lower the yield will be; the later they are cashed, the higher the yield. The full interest rate of 5½ percent will be reflected only in the final interest period.

Series H Bonds. They differ from the E series in that they are sold at face value and pay interest semi-annually by check for a period of ten years. Both E and H bonds are thus registered rather than bearer securities. The H bonds may be redeemed at par after six months from issue date upon one calendar month's notice. As in the case with E bonds, the full rate of interest will not be earned until maturity.

Someone might ask, "Why should I hold such bonds? I can do better elsewhere." Undoubtedly. But before you make your investment decision, you had better look before you leap. The owners of these nonmarketable savings bonds enjoy certain tax and other benefits that cannot be had elsewhere. For example, they may be issued not only in single names, but also in the name of two individuals either of whom is entitled to interest and principal payment, before or at maturity. In case the owner dies, if they have previously been made payable to another person to cover such a contingency, no transfer problem arises. This can be very useful when it is important for heirs to have funds available without the delay and the cost of probate.

Taxation of Government Securities

Federal tax laws apply to government securities—income, capital gains, estate, and gift taxes. Under the doctrine of reciprocal immunity, the states cannot tax income from them. There are, however, certain other peculiarities that should be mentioned.

No matter how long a discounted T-bill is held, the increase in value is never eligible for long-term capital gains treatment, because the capital appreciation here is the form that the income takes. Most government bonds are redeemable at par for the payment of federal estate taxes. Of course, for this reason you would want to buy the longest maturities, which bring the deepest discount from par value.

The 3½-percent bonds due in 1998 could have been bought in the summer of 1970 at about 66 cents on the dollar. In other words, you could pay the estate tax with a dollar that cost you 66 cents. The appreciation of the bond is not taxed, but the bonds are counted for tax purposes as part of the estate—at par. There is only one thing to keep in mind: The bonds must be placed in the estate before the owner dies. The "contemplation of death" provision, as is the case with the gift tax, is not applicable here. The bonds can be acquired twenty-four hours before the owner's death and still could be used at par to pay the federal estate tax. I am always amazed when I see large estates without deep-discount government bonds in them. This is such a good way to reduce the bite of this progressive tax. In early 1972 these bonds were still selling at about a 24 percent discount.

Unique Tax Advantages of E Bonds

The series E bonds possess certain unique tax advantages. They may be cashed in at maturity or earlier and the value accrual may be declared as income at that time, or the taxpayer may report the increase in the bond's redemption value each year. For individuals whose income does not place them in a high tax bracket, declaring the tax on each year's value appreciation is probably the best plan. The tax shouldn't be too heavy, and the maturing value of the bond will be tax-free. For investors in upper tax brackets, particularly those ten or fifteen years away from retirement, tax deferral may be best. The present series E bonds have the privilege of a ten-year extension after original maturity, so that investors may thus carry a large appreciation over into the post-retirement period when income is generally lower and the tax exemptions are larger. By doing that, income will be taxed at a lower rate. At any rate, the taxpayer here can choose how he wants to be taxed—on an annual basis or at maturity, with or without a ten-year extension.

The accumulated value of E bonds can also be converted tax-free into H bonds, which mature in ten years. No income tax will be payable on the accumulated series E interest until such time as the H bonds are surrendered for cash. The investor will thus receive interest on money that really belongs to the tax collector. He is drawing interest on tax-deferred funds for as much as a quarter of a century plus; moreover, the bonds mature originally in 7 years, can be extended for another 10 years, and can then be converted into H bonds for another period of 10 years. At a rate of 5½ percent compounded annually, one dollar gets to be two after about 12¾ years. Instead of paying taxes, you make money off the dollars that are tax dollars!

If you have sizable interest accruals on E bonds, don't accept too quickly the advice of a broker who says, "Look, you can do better by cashing in your bonds, putting the proceeds in a good mutual fund, and withdrawing 6 percent each year." Perhaps the advice is good. First do a little figuring of your own as to what your tax bill will be on the bond's accrued appreciation and the commission on the fund shares. Compute the interest that these tax dollars would give you while you draw the income from H bonds, with possibly a previous extension of the E bonds. These are dollars you would lose by cashing in the bonds.

Two other features of E and H bonds should be mentioned. When the Treasury, in 1959, 1965, 1968, and again in 1970, raised their yield rates, these increases applied to subsequent months and years of all such bonds then outstanding. This is in sharp contrast to any marketable bond. There you get whatever is printed on the face of the bond, no matter how high the interest rates go. If you should have to sell the bond, you would have to sell it at a loss, at a discount. Your H bond can always be redeemed during its life at par, and you know exactly the cash value of your E bond risk.

The Two Faces of Debt

Every debt has two faces: a liability to the issuer and an asset for the owners of the debt instruments. Who today owns the federal debt?

Uncle Sam himself owns over 25 percent of the federal debt of $412 billion. Late in 1971 United States Government agencies and trust funds held $106.5 billion. The Federal Reserve banks had another $67.6 billion, on which the Treasury, however, recaptures interest payments annually of about $3 billion. The banks don't need much of their earnings and thus paid, in 1970, over $3 billion to the Treasury as a sort of franchise tax. The owners of the Federal Reserve banks, the commercial member banks, received a little less than $40 million in dividends that year. This merely reflects the fact that a central bank cannot be privately operated under the profit motive.

As has been said, the Federal Reserve banks provide an expanding economy with needed additional money by buying government securities in the market. Back in 1941 the Federal Reserve banks had about $2 billion of government securities. Over the years, they have and will continue to increase substantially their holdings of government securities, returning annually an increasing amount of the interest payments to the Treasury and thus reducing the burden of carrying our large federal debt. Incidentally, interest on the federal debt is approximately where it was in 1945—about 2 percent of GNP. The servicing of the debt seems therefore well within our financial ability and is not likely to endanger economic stability. If you are one of the individuals who together have over $81 billion of marketable and nonmarketable government securities, you need not worry about the soundness of your bonds.

Other owners of the federal debt in late 1971 were the following:

Commercial banks	$60.0 billion
State and local governments	21.0
Savings and loan associations, securities houses, corporate pension funds, and nonprofit institutions	17.7
Nonfinancial corporations	10.0
Insurance companies	6.5
Mutual savings banks	2.8

Foreign and international accounts possess $42.4 billion. This is primarily the result of our continued deficits in our balance of international payments.

Inflation and the Debt

People tend to associate an increase in the federal debt with inflation. This may or may not be true. It depends on how the government's deficit is financed. There are only four basic ways:

1. Securities are sold to individuals. They reduce their current spending, give their savings to the government in exchange for bonds, and the money is now spent on military hardware or public works. While no increase in the money supply has occurred, a reallocation of resources takes place, from private to public uses. Should individuals withdraw funds from financial institutions to buy the bonds, private spending would not be reduced and the increased government spending could become inflationary.

2. When government securities are sold to financial intermediaries such as life insurance companies or savings institutions, again only a transfer of funds takes place. The collected savings are simply turned over to the government.

3. Under these two methods, no new money is created, so

that regardless of the level of economic operation, no inflationary pressure should arise. But during periods of high employment, if securities are sold to the commercial banks, inflationary developments will not be long in coming. The banks will "buy" them by crediting Treasury tax and loan accounts, Treasury deposits kept with them. When the Treasury calls for and spends these funds, they will return to the banks as private deposits when the recipients of Treasury checks deposit them, subject to multiple credit expansion. The money supply has thus increased.

4. The greatest inflationary impact comes when government securities are sold *directly* to the Federal Reserve banks. They will simply credit the Treasury's checking account with them for the securities. As the Treasury draws down these balances, new reserves for the commercial banks are created that are subject to multiple credit expansion. This type of financing is inherently a veritable engine of inflation. But note: The $61-odd billion of government securities held by our Federal Reserve banks were bought in the secondary open market, not directly from the Treasury. Under no condition must the Treasury be given direct access to the Federal Reserve banks, because they manufacture credit.

If you ever see—but I don't think you ever will—that the Treasury is selling its securities directly to the Federal Reserve, except for a matter of hours, hock your jewels; mortgage everything you can. For the biggest inflation you have ever seen will come. Then everything will be topsy-turvy. The debtors will gain, and gain handsomely, at the expense of the creditors as they repay debts with cheap dollars.

Repayment of Debt

What the impact of federal debt repayment will be depends again on how it is effected. If individuals or private financial institutions receive cash for their maturing obligations, they receive tax money back. This cash can then be used by them for more spending or credit extension. But if the tax money is used to pay off debt held by the Federal Reserve banks, then a net reduction in the money supply is accomplished, for individuals and corporations when paying taxes transfer funds from their pockets via the commercial banks, by writing a check, to the Treasury account at the Federal Reserve banks. Result: The Treasury now has funds to pay its IOUs held by the Fed. We now have a cancellation of debts. Government securities held by the Fed are reduced, and so are deposit liabilities, the Treasury's account. All this is proof that in our modern society "money" is primarily social bookkeeping. Nothing more. It also shows clearly that the best brake against inflation is a federal surplus that is used to repay the government securities held by the Federal Reserve banks.

Will There Be More Inflation?

Whether we shall continue on the inflationary road depends on a proper integration of fiscal and monetary policies, and on debt management. If there is no such integration, base your investment policies on the premise that further inflation is inevitable. Ideally, during periods of full employment, there should be at least a balanced budget or preferably a surplus so that an excessively restrictive monetary policy will not throw us again, as in 1966 and 1969–1970, into the jaws of a credit crunch with excruciatingly high interest rates. Federal debt management, too, must fit into the picture. Maturing obligations must be properly refunded and caution exercised that short-term securities are not recklessly increased.

Right now the average maturity of the marketable federal debt is about four years. Excessive concentration in the short-term sector forces the Treasury to come to the market too often. This disrupts the capital funds market and complicates the job of the Federal Reserve authorities to regulate the nation's money supply and maintain orderly conditions in the capital markets. There is no watertight compartment in these markets. An increased demand of the Treasury for funds may easily create problems for the mortgage or the private and municipal bond market. Too large a floating, short-term debt will force the Treasury at times to pay higher interest rates than would be required by a long-term financing. Moreover, a large volume of short-term debt in the hands of the public is potentially inflationary. It makes the economy too liquid, since T-bills are like money and can be quickly monetized without penalty to the holders, that is, without a loss to principal. This is where the great advantage of the T-bill can become an awful liability.

By using advance refunding, the Treasury has at times avoided market congestion. Holders of securities selected for advanced refunding are given the opportunity to exchange their holdings for a new issue of longer maturity. As a special incentive, the interest rate for such advance refunding, for the to-be-issued securities, can easily be about 25 basis points (0.25 percent) higher than the current market yield on a comparable maturity. This privilege of the holders of the to-be-refunded securities is sometimes referred to as a "right."

Federal Agency Issues

A greater variety and a rising volume of federal agency issues have made them more important to investors. They range from the obligations of the federal farm credit agencies (Federal Land Banks, Federal Intermediate Credit Banks, and Banks for Cooperatives), Federal Home Loan Banks, Federal National Mortgage Association, to the Participation Certificates (PACs) of the Export-Import Bank and FNMA and the bonds of the TVA. Through PACs an investor participates in the lending activities of federal agencies, because they represent a claim against a basketful of loans.

Advantages for the Investor

These securities are not guaranteed by the federal government, but it is difficult to imagine that it would let them go into default. They bring a higher yield than comparable government securities, sometimes by as much as 50 basis points (0.5 percent). With the exception of the FNMA obligation, all agency issues are exempt from state income taxes. Nor are they usually callable prior to maturity, so that the investor need not fear the premature loss of a good income. But the spread between bids and offers tends to be appreciatively larger than on comparable governments, because the agency secondary market is not as well organized in depth as the government securities market. Yet if the investor properly spaces his maturities, this should not bother him, because he will not have to sell prior to maturity. Bad spacing can cause problems. The spread between bid and offer for a Federal Land Bank bond with a 1975 maturity can easily be 100 basis points or $10 per $1,000 bond; the spread for a U.S. Treasury note of the same maturity may be as little as 25 basis points.

A Tax-Exempt Federal Bond

Another type of debt instrument should be mentioned here: the *New Housing Authority Bonds* or Notes. They are not a government agency issue, but a United States Government obligation. They are sold by local public housing authorities and secured by a pledge of their annual net rental income. Should this, in any given case, be insufficient to meet the required interest and amortization payments, an annual contribution contract with the U.S. Public Housing Administration obliges the PHA to contribute annually whatever additional funds are needed to meet the housing authority's payment schedule. Since the faith of the United States is pledged to the payment of these annual contributions, we may say that here is the only United States Government bond that carries an exemption from the federal income tax. In fact, the Attorney General of the United States has ruled that these bonds are direct obligations of the U.S. Government. If the investor resides in the same state as the authority that issues the securities, he will also avoid paying any state and local income taxes.

Summary

1. Investors may use government securities to adjust liquidity positions, and the government securities market helps our Federal Reserve authorities to regulate the nation's money supply.

2. It is unlikely that you will ever take a loss on a T-bill.

3. Aside from small amounts of bonds, the only marketable

long-term government security issued today is U.S. Treasury notes. They carry attractive coupons.

4. Marketable government securities have no credit risk, but the longer maturities carry a money risk, as do all debt instruments.

5. Series E and H bonds are nonmarketable and cannot be used as collateral for a bank loan, but they may save the day for you while waiting for a will to be probated.

6. E bonds pay no income; H bonds do.

7. With $0.76 you might be able to pay $1.00 of estate taxes.

8. E bonds give you a chance to earn income for long periods on the tax collectors' dollars.

9. An increase in the federal debt does not necessarily mean that the purchasing power of your government bonds erodes.

10. The best protection against inflation is properly meshed fiscal, monetary, and debt management policies.

11. Federal agency issues yield more, but bad buying and selling can cost money because of their wide spreads.

12. Yes, there is a United States Government security that keeps you from paying any kind of income taxes—the New Housing Authority Bonds.

CHAPTER 14

When the Tax Bites You, Are You Biting Back?

One of these days I may run into my fairy godmother. If she grants me a wish as my reward for all the years spent in teaching people better ways of handling their hard-earned money, I know what it will be. I want 10 percent of all the taxes that people pay needlessly. What a pile of dough that would be!

The level of economic literacy is not very high in this country, and institutions of higher learning, despite mounting enrollments, don't really help very much. A lot of students never take a course in economics, and when they do, another problem faces them. One of the requirements for a Ph.D. in economics surely must be that the prospective professorial candidate must promise to bore the daylights out of students when he teaches the most important course he will have, namely, principles of economics. And as anybody who ever took such a course will readily admit at the drop of a textbook, economists do quite well in making good their promise. The insipid classroom fare is, in addition, all too often seasoned with attacks on "the establishment" and, as one "instructor" I know does, with lectures on the exploitation of the world by American capitalism. When the poor student graduates, after paying a whopping tuition, he still doesn't know how to use even the most ordinary means that the law provides to ease his or his family's tax burden. One simple way to practice a little tax economy is through the purchase of municipal securities.

Municipal bonds and notes are exempt from the federal income tax, and if bought right, also from state and local income taxes. An illustration: In 1970 the Illinois State University brought out some revenue bonds that yielded 5 percent for the short maturities and up to 7.40 percent for the longer maturities. The bonds were high-quality investment media, rated AA by both rating agencies. Under the federal tax laws a taxpayer with a taxable income of only $8,000 to $12,000 filing a joint return is in the 22-percent bracket. A 7-percent rate of return on a tax-free bond is a taxable equivalent yield of almost 9 percent, exactly 8.98 percent. In the 36-percent bracket with taxable income between $24,000 and $28,000 for joint returns, $12,000 to $14,000 if you are single, a 5-percent tax-free yield would be the tax-equivalent yield of 7.81 percent; a 7-percent tax-free yield, an impressive 10.94 percent. Such yields are usually unavailable without assuming a degree of risk that the rank-and-file investor has no right to assume. And these figures consider only the federal income tax!

In the spring of 1971 you could have bought bonds of the town of Oyster Bay, New York, with a yield of 5.90 percent for the long maturities. Moody's rated the bonds A1, close to AA. A resident of the State of New York could avoid here not only the federal income tax but also the rather burdensome New York State and City income taxes as well.

Have you ever figured out on paper how many weeks or months a year you work for governments, federal, state, and local? It is an impressive figure. Don't you want to work a little more for yourself? One dollar saved, reinvested at 7 percent, compounded annually, would be two dollars in only ten years. You don't have to join a hippie commune to get away from paying income taxes. The investment of your hard-earned savings in the proper municipal securities will do it.

If you want to find out what the term "municipals" really means and what types of municipal securities are available, what their respective strengths and weaknesses are and how they should be bought, this chapter is for you. Just keep reading.

Municipal Securities

In the parlance of the finance industry, municipal securities—or for short, "municipals"—include all debt securities issued by a state and its local political subdivisions, territory, or possession of the United States or by a public agency. The term "local political subdivisions" comprises not only counties, cities, and villages, but also school districts and a host of special districts ranging from water, sewage, irrigation, fire prevention, even to mosquito abatement districts. Increasingly, public authorities or commissions issue so-called municipal revenue bonds; convertible bonds or equities are, of course, not issued, because it is impossible to sell an ownership in public properties. A "public authority" or a "commission" is a municipal corporation formed for the purpose of running facilities such as highways, bridges, tunnels, turnpikes and expressways, rapid transit, airports, waterworks, or other public utilities. Since a public utility has once been defined by a judge as any enterprise upon which the public has become "peculiarly dependent," this includes quite a variety of enterprises: gas and electric systems, hydroelectric power projects, parking facilities, stadiums, auditoriums, parks, ice plants, hospitals, student dormitories, and many others. Such authorities may operate solely within a city or they may extend their operations into one or more counties or throughout a state. Agencies have also been set up by a compact between states and ratified by the Congress, as required under our Constitution. The Port of New York Authority and the Delaware River Port Authority are examples of such interstate compacts.

To give you an idea of the size of the municipal bond market: There are right now probably over 110,000 different issues traded in a year's course. Of course, some issues are not traded every day. Nor are all stocks listed on the New York Stock Exchange traded every day; during the dull trading days of the summer of 1970, as many as 300 securities could be found on a day only in the list of "Closing Bid and Asked Prices of Stocks Not Traded."

Not only is the number and diversity of issues of municipal securities legion, but the size of the municipal debt is equally impressive. There are probably right now over $120 billion of marketable municipal securities outstanding. In 1971 alone, $24 billion of new municipal issues came to the market. Over the recent past, this figure has been smaller ($11.9 billion in 1969) because a lot of issues were withheld. In some cases, coupons could not be issued under existing laws to meet the current high interest rates, and in others, public officials hopefully waited and are waiting for lower interest rates. Result: A sizable backlog of municipal bond offerings exists. This was reflected in the $24 billion of new issues that came to the market in 1971.

In the preceding chapter, I have pointed out that the marketable debt of the United States is $252.6 billion, out of which $67.6 billion is owned by the Federal Reserve banks. Government agencies and trust funds, besides nonmarketable special issues, also own about $22 billion of marketable securities. All these most likely will never come to the market, so that the effective federal marketable debt is probably no more than about $163 billion. It won't take so many years—perhaps ten—for the marketable municipal debt to exceed the federal marketable debt. The services we demand as our per capita standard of living rises are largely provided on the state and local level, so that my figures here will probably turn out to be conservative. At any rate, the importance, the rising importance, of the municipal bond market is quite clear. There will be more municipal bonds and notes outstanding, and more investors will buy them. Will you be among them? If so, will you buy the right ones? So now let's see what types of merchandise are available in this sprawling municipal bond market.

Types of Municipal Securities

We distinguish several types of municipals:

General Obligation Bonds. GOs for short, they are full-faith and credit bonds secured by the pledge of the issuer of his credit and by unlimited taxing power to pay interest and principal. Of the $18.2 billion municipal issues in 1970, almost $12 billion were general obligations. Before such bonds are issued, the voters must approve them, since they will in the end have to foot the bill. Usually these securities are issued as serial bonds, with annual and sometimes semi-annual maturities. There is thus no sinking fund provision, the serial maturities taking care of the amortization of the issue. Originally these bonds were issued as term bonds (now rarely except in case of certain revenue bonds) with a sinking fund. But the experience of investors was bad, as these sinking fund arrangements were often subject to fraud under politically corrupt administrations and some issuers just disregarded them. Moreover, serial maturities provide for better marketing of issues, since investors can choose exactly the maturities they desire and be absolutely sure that their bonds will not be called from them prematurely.

The statement made in our discussion of corporate debt securities that "a bond is whatever the indenture says it is" is not applicable to GOs. There is no indenture. The issuer pledges, in turn, his willingness to use his credit and unlimited power to raise money through taxation to pay off the bonds. In case of default by a county, city, town, or village, the bondholders could bring suit and obtain a court judgment. But what good is it if, as is true in most places, the creditors cannot attach public property "essential to public service," whatever that means? A state cannot be sued without its consent in a state court. Nor in a federal court. Back in 1798 a Constitutional amendment, the eleventh, was adopted that says federal courts have no jurisdiction if, say, a California bondholder wanted to sue an Illinois city. It was originally enacted to keep Tories from suing states to recover their confiscated properties. Willingness to pay, the payment record, is therefore an important consideration when selecting a municipal GO bond.

Limited Tax Bonds. These are GOs, but the issuer's power to tax is limited by constitution or statute to a specified maximum tax rate. Sometimes, however, the tax limit applies only to levies designed for current spending; it permits additional, unlimited taxes for debt service. Once there are limits imposed on the issuer's taxing authority, the resulting type of GO bonds are not as highly rated as the full faith and credit bonds. They will sell at a higher yield because of the increased risk of default. Should general property taxes reach the legal limit over a period of years and no funds, or insufficient funds, be available to pay the bonds as later serial maturities come due, the bondholder would be in a very tough spot. Little recourse would be open to him, since he bought the bonds with such a contingency clearly in the contract into which he entered. No, limited tax bonds are something to be left to very knowledgeable professionals. Even they probably won't like them.

Special Tax Bonds. These are payable solely from the proceeds of a special tax; highway bonds, for example, are payable only from the proceeds of a gasoline tax. The old *assessment bonds* are also in this category. They were sold to finance city improvements such as pavement and sewers. Whenever the assessments imposed upon benefiting property owners failed to produce the necessary funds, the bondholder was again in the soup. For the municipality has in these cases no obligation whatsoever to pay these bonds from other sources. No wonder investors shy away from special tax bonds.

The second largest category of municipal bonds is *revenue bonds.* Revenue bonds are payable solely from revenues derived from highway or bridge tolls; charges for water, sewage, electricity; rents paid by a school authority; admissions to a municipal auditorium or stadium; and so forth. They are issued as term bonds, maturing in a given year, with a mandatory sinking fund or as a combination of serial maturities and term bonds. Where the revenue is quite stable, such as would be the case with electric, sewage, or water revenue bonds, serial maturities are usually issued. Where the revenues supporting such a bond tend to fluctuate or estimated revenue is uncertain as to its exact time of realization, callable term bonds offer greater flexibility. Here the issuer avoids the rigid maturity schedule of serial bonds; on the other hand, if the revenue should come in faster than originally anticipated, more bonds can be called for redemption. In this case the bondholder will receive a call premium in addition to his principal amount.

The basic instrument of security for the investor here is, besides the degree of essentiality of the service rendered by the issuer, the indenture or bond resolution. It sets forth the manner in which the corporate trustee must apply the authority's income to operation, maintenance, insurance, and possibly the payment

to outside consultants or supervisory engineers. Protection is af-
forded in the indenture against diversion of revenue, or against
the city fathers' dipping into the coffers of the authority. The
covenant also requires that charges for the services must be maintained high enough to yield a margin of safety. Proper books
must be kept, and at least once a year there must be an audit of
the properties by a certified public accountant. At times, open-end
indentures permit the issuance of additional bonds for the financing of additional facilities. Usually such permission is confined
to additional funds needed to complete a project. The usual
closed-end indenture prohibits, of course, the issue of new
bonds on par with the outstanding ones. Additional bonds can
only be issued as junior bonds, junior in their claim to revenue to
the older bondholders. Since the investor has no claim to assets,
a tightly, properly drawn indenture is here of the greatest importance.

Originally, revenue bonds were issued largely to circumvent
legal debt ceilings. More recently the difficulties, even for badly
needed projects such as schools, of obtaining the approval of voters for GO bonds have turned governmental units to lease
financing and revenue bonds. A general law is passed enabling
the governmental unit involved to set up a nonprofit authority
for the express purpose of acquiring or constructing facilities
that are then leased by the authority to the local political subdi-
vision or municipality. The authority sells the revenue bonds
and uses the proceeds to construct the facilities. The bonds are
paid out of the contractual lease payments made by the leasing
governmental unit. State supreme courts have held that neither
the payments under the lease nor the revenue bonds issued by
the authority violate any debt or taxing limits that may or will
be in force.

Revenue bonds carry a higher interest rate than GOs, so that
debt ceilings and voter apathy have not only not prevented state
and local borrowing, but have made it more costly. A debt ceiling,
as the fiscal history of the United States shows, is no substitute
for a sound and desirable fiscal policy. The future will undoubtedly see a great increase in revenue bond financing. Such bonds
might well be sold to help fight pollution and solve the problem
of solid waste disposal. Revenue bonds might, in such cases,

be payable out of a charge to your water bill or a fee attached to the property tax bill.

Industrial Revenue Bonds. These bonds have been used by municipalities or local development corporations to raise funds cheaply with which to build industrial plants that are then leased to private corporations. Since the income from all municipals is tax-exempt from the federal income tax, money can be raised more cheaply than through the sale of corporate bonds. The towns and cities, in turn, have the benefit of new payrolls. The company saves money twice: It won't need to sell bonds to build a plant, and it does not own property on which it must pay taxes.

Investors should be clear on one point here: Buying an industrial revenue bond is buying corporate credit under the guise of municipal credit. You are not buying a municipal bond at all. You are actually buying a corporate bond. Any presentation to the contrary is fraudulent. Funds available for payment of interest and principal depend solely on the regular receipts of rental payments by the corporation involved. It has not been at all unusual in the past to see a village of less than a few thousand inhabitants selling tens of millions of dollars of industrial revenue bonds! A lot of them are still outstanding. So watch out!

Under federal securities laws, municipal securities are exempt from registration with the Securities and Exchange Commission. But the Commission feels that private companies benefiting from industrial revenue bond offerings should register with it. Since it is the success or failure of the private corporation that determines the soundness of this security, the investor is entitled to have access to all relevant information concerning it. If the bonds of the leasing corporation are rated highly by the rating agencies, you have nothing to worry about.

In 1967, communities raised over $1 billion with such bonds, more than they did for the whole decade 1956–1965. The Treasury repeatedly stated that it wanted the tax-exempt privilege removed from these bonds, because this type of financing was nothing but a federal subsidy to private corporations. The benefit to industry was achieved only at the expense of the federal tax collector. A lot of people within the ranks of investment bankers didn't like these bonds much, and they expressed their concern over the dangers involved in them. Congress finally acted, and since January 1, 1969, no one issue of tax-exempt industrial bonds can be in excess of $5 million; under certain conditions it might be even less. Such bonds may be used to fight pollution in much larger amounts, however.

Now if a municipality or village wants to help a smaller corporation and in so doing provide well-paying jobs for its citizens, it can still be done. But the practice of a big corporation going to a village which then issues $50 million of industrial revenue bonds to build the plant according to that company's specifications and lease it back, is now no longer possible. But who knows what pressure there may yet be on states to attract United States or even foreign industries. What one Congress takes away, another Congress can give back. I have a hunch that we have not yet heard the last of industrial revenue bonds.

New Housing Authority Bonds. These are treated by most people as municipal obligations. Taking the Attorney General's word, I feel that this is really a United States Government bond. I have therefore included it in my discussion of U.S. Government securities. It really doesn't matter too much, as long as you remember that it is in fact a direct obligation of the U.S. Government, and the interest from it is tax-exempt.

Hybrid Forms. Such types of municipal bonds are also used. A revenue bond may be secondarily protected by the unlimited taxing power of the governmental unit that guarantees payment of the authority's securities. If the revenue is insufficient to pay off the bonds or pay interest, the guarantor will make up the difference from tax revenues. In this case the revenue bond becomes a GO bond. Recently, special assessment bonds have quite often been additionally secured by the city's pledge of full faith and credit and its unlimited taxing power. In that case, the special assessment bonds become GO bonds and assume a totally different investment characteristic.

Investment Characteristics

Municipals are, as a rule, high-grade securities. Probably half of all the GOs brought to the market are rated AAA or AA.

Smaller issues are usually not rated, because they lack sufficient public interest. No doubt they include many top-quality issues. If an issue is not rated, it cannot be construed as an indication of low quality. A large secondary market assures marketability. Diversity of issues and maturities affords the investor a choice of maturity as needed and of geographical selection as desired. A publication known as the *Blue List* shows daily the issues municipal bond dealers have on their shelves.

A municipal bond sells on the basis of price plus accrued interest. As in the case of corporate bonds, interest is computed on the basis of 360 days a year (each month 30 days), and regular delivery is also on the fifth business day, with the seller entitled to the accrued interest up to but not including the delivery day. Serial municipal bonds are usually quoted on a yield rather than a price basis. Reference to a *Basis Book,* a book of mathematical tables, quickly gives the dollar price.

The greatest attraction of these bonds for the investor is their tax exemption. Municipals are not exempt, however, from all federal taxes; only from the federal income tax. They are subject to the federal estate, gift, and capital gains taxes. If I buy a municipal bond in the secondary market at a discount and sell it later on at a profit, this gain is taxable. But if, because of a coupon ceiling, a bond is issued at a discount, the eventual capital appreciation is considered income (interest) to the original purchaser and thus exempt from the federal income tax. Interest is usually also exempt from the state and local income taxes in the state of the issuer. Territorial bonds are exempt from all income taxes, federal as well as state and local.

When tax rates were lower, municipal securities were considered to be the investment medium for the rich. With rising incomes and high tax rates coupled with the attractive yields nowadays available, even people in lower income brackets find them most attractive. It is therefore not surprising that individuals are today the largest municipal bond buyers even though a lot of people still don't know anything about them. If they did, the yields would be lower. Commercial banks are a close second, and casualty and property insurance companies are third. In view of their different tax base, life insurance companies rarely buy municipals. But the banks are erratic buyers. When money is tight, they tend to become heavy sellers of municipals in order to have funds for loans to their customers. This lowers bond prices and ups yields.

Points to Remember

What is particularly important to you is how knowledgeable your broker is. Here is one good test to apply. After you indicate your interest in municipals, if he does not ask you whether you need your income now or later, he doesn't know a great deal. Why? Because if you don't need the income now, but can wait until the bond's maturity, he should suggest a deep-discount municipal. True, your capital gain at maturity is taxable, but despite the tax your yield to maturity on a low-coupon deep-discount bond can be substantially higher, maybe as much as fifty or more basis points, than on a bond selling at or near par. This is a peculiarity of the municipal bond market and is in contrast to the corporate bond market. Deep-discount corporates are usually selling at a somewhat lower yield than newly issued bonds.

Find out how much municipal bond business your broker does. If he does a lot, he keeps in constant touch with his firm's municipal bond department. This means his bond man will inform him of bargains. Every now and then the firm will want to clear its shelves of odds and ends and will price them attractively, the way any merchant does. Another good idea is to check whether the firm with which you do your securities business does a lot of municipal underwriting. Just follow the ads in *The Wall Street Journal*. If its name shows up frequently in the underwriting group, your house can do better for you than your banker —in case you have been buying your municipals through him. At any rate, do a little window-shopping and compare yields quoted to you.

Risks for the Investor

Like corporates and governments, municipal bonds too have a purchasing power risk. But don't let this keep you from buying municipals or, for that matter, any bond. I am not ready to say that price and wage inflation has become a way of life in America.

Moreover, what happened to the people who used to say in 1969 that Washington would be unwilling to take strong action to slow down the economy? Or the ones who insisted that monetary and fiscal actions would not slow the economy, that the demands of consumers and uncontrollable government projects would keep on pushing business up regardless of the policies? By late summer, 1970, they must have changed their tune.

Like all high-grade bonds, municipals have a money risk. When interest rates rise, their prices decline; when they fall, they rise. Lower-quality bonds have a considerable credit risk. A BB (or Ba) rating indicates a big question mark about the issuer's ability to pay interest and principal. No states or major cities are currently in this bracket. Municipals are particularly subject to a market risk. When dealers have large inventories or when there are large new bond offerings, bond prices decline as they clear their shelves of inventory.

Municipals are traded in the over-the-counter market like unlisted stocks. Any amount of less than $5,000, and some dealers say $25,000, is deemed to be an odd lot. Large issues today come out in $5,000 denominations, as bearer or registered bonds, so that three bonds of $1,000 each may be difficult to sell without appreciable price concessions unless the issue is a fairly large one and fairly heavily traded. This should be an important consideration for an individual with relatively small funds to invest. He may be much better off to consider investing in an MIT, a Municipal Investment Trust Fund.

The MITs

With the exception of the sale of tax anticipation notes, which mature in one year or less, state and local governments borrow almost entirely for capital purposes, and the volume of their capital outlays has increased to about six times the level of two decades ago. Over the years to come, the increase will be even more pronounced. About 6,000 new issues will be added annually by our 80,000 state and local governments to the more than 110,000 different issues now outstanding. This makes a rational appraisal of available investment alternatives difficult for many investors and helps to explain the recent popularity of the Municipal Investment Trust Funds.

An MIT consists of a diversified tax-exempt bond portfolio with anywhere from 20 to 40 issues, selected by professionals. The prospectus shows the rating of each individual issue. Result: Safety, diversification, convenience, professional management, tax-free income, and ready marketability are yours.

The funds are divided into "units" of about a thousand dollars each. The investor may receive his income semiannually or monthly. Most likely you will be able to sell your units in the over-the-counter market for an amount in excess of the redemption price, because the sponsors of the funds make markets for them. If this should not be the case, the trustee will redeem the units. He will also mail you in January a statement as to what tax liability there is. The chances are that some bond interest will be taxable by your state or city, since the portfolio contains bonds issued outside of your state.

The MITs come out at intervals. Once they are sold, they can only be bought in the secondary market—if there are sellers. Issues are usually quickly sold out, a sign of how anxious investors are to get them. There is only one drawback, if indeed it is one. Many of the bonds in the portfolio are callable revenue bonds. When one of them is called, the proceeds must be distributed to the unit holders. They cannot be reinvested, or the tax exemption would then be lost. But such a gradual liquidation of an MIT has a compensation: The call premiums increase the yield on your investment.

There is a sales charge of 3½ percent involved. If you need the help of the professional, you have to pay for it. But this charge is, in my opinion, more than made up by the advantages the MITs present to so many investors. How could they possibly make a proper selection from the multitude of bonds available, achieve diversification, have continuous professional portfolio supervision, know instantly what percentage of income is taxable, buy and sell the units at far better prices than if they bought or sold an odd lot, and enjoy a higher and safer yield than they most likely could have gotten by themselves?

The Legal Opinion

The "legal opinion" on a municipal bond is essential, for without it the bond is unsalable. It is an opinion regarding the legality of a particular issue, written by a law firm specializing in the approval of public borrowings. Since about fourteen years ago, it has been printed on each bond, but there are still older issues outstanding that lack such legal opinion, so that it must be furnished with the bond. The bond attorney attests that the issue has been legally issued. In the case of an illegal issue, one taxpayer can petition a court to stop all further interest and principal payments on the bonds. A municipal bond attorney, a highly specialized branch of the legal profession, must retrace every little step in the history of the bond to ascertain that there was compliance with the law.

Should you perchance buy deep-discount bonds, the legal opinion might not be on the bonds, and in this case you will be furnished with one. Don't throw it away. Put it with the bonds. You'll need it should you want to sell the bonds prior to maturity.

Underwriting of Municipals

GOs are sold primarily through competitive bidding to underwriting groups formed for that purpose. *The Daily Bond Buyer*, the municipal industry's trade paper, carries the advertisements for coming municipal bond sales. Many revenue bonds are marketed through negotiated sales, direct arrangements between issuers and underwriting firms. While commercial banks are restricted to the underwriting of GOs, they would like to be permitted to participate also in the underwriting of revenue bonds. The public issuers would welcome this; it would bring in more bids for their bonds. But to what degree such freedom for the banks would involve a conflict of interest for them is another question again. Suppose an issue moves slowly; could it be placed in a trust account?

The Rating of Municipals

The issuance of GOs should be confined to borrowing for capital expenditures, and the maturity of the bonds should be adjusted to the economic life of the property acquired. Refunding a debt or funding an operational deficit causes rating agencies to lower the issuer's rating. When, a few years back, New York City behaved in such an unapproved manner, the two biggest and most widely known rating agencies, Moody's Investors Services, Inc., and Standard and Poor's Corporation, lowered the city's rating from A to Baa (S and P's rating is an equivalent BBB), which has probably so far cost the city a good $20 million in additional annual interest charges. Moody's downgraded the Newark, New Jersey, rating from A to Baa long before that city's summer riots. The absence of a long-range capital program, an inadequate capital plant, a rising welfare load, a declining middle class, and a population unsuited for skilled labor were all items that entered into the rating decision. When a rating is lowered, the outstanding bonds will, of course, drop in price.

Some public administrators have been highly critical of the two rating services and proposed that a public agency be given such a rating function. A public rating agency for public issues would probably not enjoy the confidence of the investment community that an improved private rating system inspires.

Can Washington Take Away This Tax Exemption?

As far as currently outstanding bonds are concerned, this could not be done. It would be an *ex post facto* legislation. Under Section 9 of the Federal Constitution, "No . . . ex post facto law shall be passed." But what about the future?

In addition to express statutory exemption, the interest on municipal securities is exempt from taxation under the court doctrine of *reciprocal immunity*. It is deeply embedded in our legal structure. The Supreme Court, in the case of *Collector v. Day,* said:

> It is admitted that there is no express provision in the Constitution that prohibits the general government from taxing the means and instrumentalities of the states, nor is there any prohibiting the states from taxing the means and instrumentalities of that government. In both cases the exemption rests upon necessary implication, and is upheld by the great law of self preservation; as

any government, whose means employed in conducting its operations, if subject to the control of another and distinct government, can exist only at the mercy of that government. Of what avail are these means if another power may tax them at discretion?

Since 1871, when the above decision was handed down, the Supreme Court has restated the position clearly on four more occasions. The preponderant opinion is that the authority for the federal government to tax *future* issues of municipal bonds, including revenue bonds issued by authorities, requires an amendment to the Constitution. There is mountainous doubt that such an amendment could muster a two-thirds vote in both houses of the Congress, not to mention the obstacle of ratification by three-fourths of the states. The possibility of a national convention being called to propose such an amendment is also remote.

Summary

1. If you want a second income, don't let it throw you into a higher tax bracket. Get it tax-exempt.

2. There are over 110,000 issues to choose from, and the secondary market for municipals is active and huge, assuring liquidity.

3. Before long the municipal bond market will be more important than the government securities market.

4. General obligation bonds are backed by the issuer's unlimited power to tax.

5. Better stay away from limited tax bonds and special tax bonds.

6. You can get a higher yield on revenue bonds. The indenture is important here.

7. A serial GO gives you perfect call protection.

8. Check how knowledgeable your broker is about municipals.

9. If you don't need income now, buy deep-discount bonds. The chances are you can improve your yield, despite the tax on capital gains.

10. For busy people and for small investors, the MITs are better. You buy professional selection, diversification, and supervision and enjoy the highest degree of liquidity.

11. Watch the ratings on bonds. Perhaps you don't want to go below an A-rated bond.

12. Apparently, tax exemption on municipals is going to be with us for a long time to come.

Part IV

What Strategies and Tactics?

CHAPTER 15

What Tools Can I Use to Make Big Money?

"Investigate before you invest," the New York Stock Exchange admonishes. There are always plenty of facts available, but they must be properly utilized or the investor's judgment will be faulty and thus costly. You won't make out well investing unless you know a few fundamental principles on the evaluation of companies. How strong is a company financially? Will it run out of cash before it can translate its glorious plans into dividends? Maybe it won't be able to pay its bills when credit gets tight. But where is a good starting point to lay a foundation before putting on the roof? To that, there is a very simple answer.

Write to the company that has caught your interest and ask for a copy of the last annual report. If you can't find the address, your broker can look it up for you in Standard and Poor's or Moody's publications. You will probably receive the report plus the latest semi-annual or quarterly statements. For the price of a postcard, any publicly owned company is delighted to send anyone such reports. And for a simple reason: The great economic expansion ahead demands more capital and more shareholders.

To the knowledgeable, annual reports can make profitable reading. Don't believe that the so-called smart money crowd discounts everything in Wall Street. Not by a long shot. Managements are quite often very frank with their shareholders in their annual reports. I remember one that said, "We have now written off all of our developmental charges." It was a big chunk of money. In other words, what management said was this: "Look at us. We are in fine shape. Sales are going up and with everything now charged off, next year's earnings should be a lot higher." And they were, right on schedule. But for several months the stock didn't move until people began to discover what a bargain it was. During 1969–1970, common stock prices were so low in many cases that it was difficult to see how they could go much lower. Quite a number of managements took advantage of the situation and charged off whatever they could, including past errors that had been swept under the rug. Other managements bought up their own stock at bargain prices. Both will look good in the years to come. As long as you buy values, you will make *money*—sooner or later.

The annual report provides you with two basic tools: the company's balance sheet and the income statement, formerly called profit and loss statement. Take a good look at both of them.

The Balance Sheet

A balance sheet is a photograph of the business, in our case as of December 31, 19—. Like any other photograph, it is something static. The next business day, things can look quite different. Checks are received and sent out in the mail; raw materials are delivered to the factory; sales are made over the telephone; new equipment is bought; and so forth.

The balance sheet won't tell you whether the company can make a lot of money. But it can tell you whether it is healthy or not, and if it is sickly, how deep the disease goes.

Take a look at the BZB Manufacturing Company's statement. See how the assets are listed. First come those that can be converted into cash within one year or less—the current assets. After that, intermediate assets, investments in subsidiaries. They could be sold to keep the company afloat. But its earnings would then fall off quite a bit, since these subsidiaries play an important part in the company's organization. Finally come the fixed assets, particularly plant and equipment. They are the most illiquid assets.

The liability side is similarly arranged. First come the liabilities due within one year or less, and then the long-term debt followed by the money the owners have in the business. An electric company's balance sheet will show assets and liabilities in reverse order. Why? Because plant and equipment are so much larger than the liquid assets and there is no appreciable inventory. The accounts receivable are also of quite a different nature. An electric company has few problems collecting its bills. On the utility's liabilities side, the equity is listed first, followed by the bonds. Current liabilities come last.

The Company's Liquidity

The balance sheet (pages 246–247) will help you to find out whether the company can pay its bills promptly; whether it can expand its operations as new opportunities present themselves without resorting to new financing in adverse equity or bond markets, when stocks are selling at low P/E ratios and bonds at high interest rates; and whether it can face emergencies or losses without becoming financially embarrassed.

During the credit crunch of 1969–1970, many articles appeared on the dangerous decrease of corporate liquidity. Most of it was a lot of nonsense. The liquidity ratio is too often expressed as cash and government securities to current liabilities. But when such other cash equivalents as commercial paper and bank certificates of deposit are included, corporate liquidity ratios don't look so bad. Furthermore, this ratio has been going down for the last twenty-five years as management became more efficient in handling its cash and tens of thousands of computers were added. The fact that there will always be inefficient managements that won't be able to pay their bills is hardly news.

In financial statement analysis, we translate dollars into ratios that pinpoint important relationships in the balance sheet and income statement. But keep in mind that ratios raise more questions than they answer. A ratio that is out of line could indicate something very good or very bad. You'll have to examine it further, interpret it in the light of its relation to other ratios. One figure never means very much; neither does one ratio. What is important is the trend.

Working Capital and Current Ratio

The working capital of the BZB Company is found by deducting from the current assets ($96 million) the current liabilities ($37.5 million), leaving $58.5 million. The current or working capital ratio is obtained by dividing total current assets by total current liabilities; in our case it is better than 2.5:1. For industrial companies a 2:1 current ratio is standard. A current ratio for utilities has little or no meaning. Even if the BZB Company were to take a 50-percent loss in the value of its receivables and inventories, it would have no problems paying its bills.

THE BZB MANUFACTURING COMPANY
BALANCE SHEET

December 31, 19—

ASSETS

Current assets

Cash	$ 4,000,000	
U.S. short-term government securities	14,000,000	
Accounts and notes receivable	23,000,000	
Inventories	55,000,000	$ 96,000,000
Investments in subsidiaries:	$ 12,000,000	$ 12,000,000
Property		
Buildings, machinery, and equipment at cost	$210,000,000	
Less accumulated depreciation	89,000,000	
	$121,000,000	
Land	2,000,000	$123,000,000
Miscellaneous items		
Prepaid expenses	$ 50,000	
Deferred charges	450,000	$ 500,000
TOTAL ASSETS		$231,500,000

LIABILITIES

Current liabilities

Notes payable—banks	$ 2,000,000	
Accounts payable	12,000,000	
Accrued liabilities	1,500,000	
Current maturity of long-term debt	2,000,000	
Income taxes and other taxes	18,000,000	
Dividends payable	2,000,000	$ 37,500,000
Reserve for plant expansion	$ 40,000,000	$ 40,000,000
Long-term debt:		
6% debentures due 1980	$ 30,000,000	$ 30,000,000
Stockholder's equity		
6% cumulative preferred stock ($100 par)	$ 12,000,000	
Common stock ($10 par)	48,000,000	
Earned surplus	64,000,000	$124,000,000
TOTAL LIABILITIES		$231,500,000

Any time you see a low current ratio, say 1.2:1, stay away from the stock no matter what others tell you. If you are unfortunate enough to own it, sell it. A small loss or failure to collect receivables could force the company into technical insolvency. The Penn Central's assets exceeded its liabilities by a good margin, but it couldn't pay its bills and became a bankrupt company. From a high of 86½, in 1968, the stock tobogganed to 5½ in 1970. The Douglas Corporation had working-capital trouble and became the McDonnell Douglas Company, and look what has happened to Lockheed with its working-capital problems in 1970.

Is a 5:1 ratio, therefore, very good? Not necessarily. An examiner of the Federal Reserve Bank of Boston once showed me a company with a current ratio of 8:1 that went broke because most of the working capital was in unsalable finished inventory goods. If accounts receivable include past due and uncollectible accounts, a high current ratio doesn't mean much. The BZB has a lot of money in inventories. What is it? Heavy raw materials inventories bought at inflated prices, or bought very advantageously? A lot of work in progress? If so, BZB should bring in a top-notch production engineer. Is BZB a seasonal business that has to manufacture for inventory until goods can be moved? Or are there in the inventory finished goods that can't be sold? A good company will give a breakdown in footnotes with the balance sheet.

An unusually high current ratio is always of interest to the investor, particularly when a great deal of the current assets is in cash or cash equivalent. Why does the company have all this money? Is it going to buy up other companies and increase its earnings without diluting the equity or adding to its long-term debt? Such a stock would surely rise before long. The excess cash is bound to be put to more productive use in the business and thus increase earnings.

Because of the inventory problem possibilities, we apply a so-called acid test, or quick ratio. It is the ratio of current assets minus inventories to current liabilities. This ratio should be at least 1:1. In our case it is a shade better. Be cautious when cash items and receivables are less than the current liabilities.

An inventory in excess of one year's requirements should be shown as a noncurrent item for the excess, just as an adjustment should be made when receivables are based on installment sales in excess of one year. In either case not all the current assets will return to cash during one year. What is even more important is the method used in evaluating the inventory items. If during periods of rising prices, a FIFO (first-in-first-out) inventory costing method is used, reported per-share earnings will be higher than when the LIFO (last-in-first-out) method is used. Under FIFO we work off low-cost inventory; under LIFO, high-cost inventory. A company using FIFO during periods of rising prices could have difficulties meeting its competition when prices start declining again and it is forced to work off its high-cost inventory. Look for the note that will explain what method has been used in compiling the value of the inventories. If GE had used FIFO instead of LIFO in valuing inventories in 1970, its earnings could have been over $230 million higher!

Whether a high ratio of inventory to working capital is good is not only a matter of price trends, but also a question of the collectibility of the receivables. A lot of money invested in inventory when accounts receivable can be easily and quickly collected and prices are rising, is not bad. The reverse is the bad feature. The inventory ratio will also differ with industries; it is much higher in tobacco and farm machinery than in automobiles and food industries.

Other Balance Sheet Ratios

Net worth–fixed assets ratio, found by dividing net worth by the fixed assets, indicates the proportion between the owners' equity and funds not invested in current assets. A very low ratio calls for a thorough look, because if too much has gone into fixed assets, the company might find it hard to meet the demands of creditors.

If this ratio is steadily declining, don't get in or, if in, get out of the situation. Such a company can show lovely, rising earnings, but everything is plowed back and current assets are diverted into fixed assets. Plant capacity is increased to meet continuously rising sales. Then comes the day when the company can't pay its bills, and it becomes a merger candidate on very unfavorable terms for the owners.

The net worth–debt ratio (current as well as long-term debt) is found by dividing the net worth by the total debt. In the BZB case, we must add to the $124 million stockholders' equity (permanent capital) the $40 million reserve for plant expansion, giving us $164 million:$77.5 million (current debt plus funded debt), or a 2:1 ratio. The pressure of debt is not too strong. The company could, in case of need, raise additional funds through debt and thus increase its financial leverage. BZB seemingly is annually retiring $2 million of its long-term debt and paying off its bank debt.

We could make two adjustments: One, the $50,000 prepaid expenses could be listed under current assets. There is a cash value here that would be realized upon surrender of a contract, for example, a long-term property insurance contract. The company could act as a self-insurer. Two, deferred charges, like any intangible, should be deducted from the equity. A deferred charge is not an asset at all. It represents money already paid out for which no specific services will be received by the company in the future, but such items can be considered proper charges to future operations. An airline may show deferred charges of $8 million as the cost of introducing its new jets. Let's say the cost was $10 million and only $2 million were charged as expense to revenue the first year; the balance is charged off over 4 years. Another airline might charge off the entire amount the first year. Needless to say, the companies' stock will not sell at the same P/E ratio. Since the deferred charges make for higher reported earnings, the one selling at the lower P/E ratio is not necessarily a bargain.

Deferred charges can become troublesome, indeed disastrous. A computer company had large amounts of capitalized development costs that remained to be charged off. At the same time, it reported earnings containing appreciable amounts of anticipated future rental income from a subsidiary. Before long the stock dropped 50 percent.

Bad debt ratios usually mean the company is entangled in all kinds of creditors' restrictions on its freedom to operate or pay dividends. Bad earnings or a loss can really cause trouble here.

Watch out for secondaries of companies with bad financial ratios, when insiders get out while the stock is still high. Sometimes a "fringe" underwriter will have parlayed the stock up. Read your prospectus carefully before buying.

Voluntary Reserves

Voluntary reserves, such as a reserve for plant expansion or modernization or for the retirement of the preferred stock or simply a contingency reserve, should be added back to the equity, as was done in the BZB account. Such reserves represent neither an obligation to pay nor a definite deduction from a particular asset. The company only has $18 million in cash, so how could it shell out $40 million for a new plant? Nothing can be paid out of a liabilities item.

The unsophisticated often look upon a big surplus as a source of increased dividend payments. They say, "The company can pay more. Look at the big surplus." A cash dividend can only be paid out of cash. If the company hasn't got it, it can't be paid. Of course, a stock dividend can be given. All that is needed is to increase stock outstanding and decrease the earned surplus account. In order to reduce the surplus, so people won't get ideas of bigger dividends or higher wages, management sometimes has set up such voluntary surplus reserves. We throw them right back into the equity account out of which they came.

Static and Dynamic Ratios

All the ratios so far given here, all the tools for a look into a company's affairs, are so-called static ratios, balance-sheet ratios; they indicate a condition. Ratios taken from the income statement are called dynamic ratios; they indicate the efficiency, or lack thereof, with which a company conducts its affairs. For example, sales–fixed assets ratios indicate the productivity of the fixed assets, plant and equipment, or the justification for having invested in them. A low ratio might be interesting. Maybe a better management could make these assets more productive. On the other hand, the low ratio may be the result of an old plant.

The Principles of Consolidation

Watch out for consolidated balance sheets and income statements. Go to the notes to the financial reports and find out what principles of consolidation were used. Are all subsidiaries included? What about foreign subsidiaries? Is the investment in such subsidiaries, as shown by the parent company's books, reported on an original-cost basis or on an underlying-book-value basis? If on a cost basis, there could be big values that are not reported. If on an equity basis, there could be problems. Suppose a company has Latin American subsidiaries that earn good money, but everything is reinvested in these countries. In view of anticipated future devaluations, how realistic is an evaluation in American dollars, as one company reports, "at rates of exchange in effect in each of the foreign countries"? Black, gray, or free market rates might be much lower than the official exchange rates.

The Income Statement

While the balance sheet is a snapshot of the business at a particular point in time, the income statement covers an entire period of operation, a year in our case. It shows how efficiently or inefficiently the firm has conducted its affairs.

For the BZB Manufacturing Company, the first item on the income statement is net sales—$230 million. We are never interested in gross sales, for there could have been substantial returns of merchandise. The first item to be deducted is the cost of goods sold—$140 million. This can be a very slippery concept, since it involves the evaluation of inventory. Did the company use the LIFO, FIFO, or an average inventory costing method? As we said before, the earnings will be quite different if, during a period of rising prices, LIFO rather than FIFO is used. The subtraction of selling, general, and administrative expenses presents no particular problems.

Depreciation and Depletion

Depreciation and, with a resources company, depletion are extremely important concepts. No one can follow the operation of the modern corporation without thoroughly understanding them. They are costs to the company as real as any other cost, but the money involved is not expended. They are expenses, but no expenditures. This is internally generated cash that stays in the company and can be used to acquire new earning assets.

Suppose BZB had a machine for which it originally paid $1,000. At the end of 10 years, its value is zero. In order to recover the investment, the company charges itself $100 a year. Visualize the sales revenue coming in. We dip into it and pay our suppliers, employees, and officers, heat, light, and power, and so on, and then we take out $100 for the depreciation of the machine. It can be immediately reinvested. An oil company receives annually tens of millions of dollars from the writing down of its oil and gas wells as they are being depleted.

THE BZB MANUFACTURING COMPANY
Year Ended December 31, 19—

STATEMENT OF INCOME

Net sales revenue		$230,000,000
Less:		
Costs and expenses		
Cost of goods sold	$140,000,000	
Selling, general, and administrative expenses	20,000,000	
Depreciation	30,000,000	$190,000,000
Income from operations		$ 40,000,000
Interest charges		1,800,000
Income before income taxes		$ 38,200,000
Provisions for federal and state taxes on income		$ 17,500,000
Net income for the year		$ 20,700,000
Dividend on preferred stock		$ 700,000
Net income		$ 20,000,000

STATEMENT OF EARNED SURPLUS

Balance at the start of the year	$ 53,600,000
Net income for the year	20,000,000
	$ 73,600,000
Less dividend paid on the common stock, $2.00 per share	9,600,000
Balance at end of year	$ 64,000,000

Read now the chief executive's message in the annual report to the shareholders. What are the plans for expanding the business? Suppose BZB intended to spend $35 million in the following year for plant expansion. Take a good look at the income statement. It would not require outside financing, because the internally generated cash is over $40 million—$30 million from depreciation and $10.4 million retained earnings. This, incidentally, is quite typical. For many companies, the cash throw-off from depreciation and depletion is far greater than the amount derived from the net earnings. Always look for the announcement of management's goals for the future. Where will the money come from? Must bonds or common stock be sold to raise the needed cash? See if the expansion can be financed from internal sources—retained earnings and depreciation and depletion. Sometimes funds will accrue from the sale of property no longer needed for the efficient operation of the business, but this will be a one-shot affair. If bonds or preferred stock will have to be sold to finance the expansion, the company's financial leverage will increase and with it profit possibilities and risk. In that case, find out how much money will be needed to pay interest and dividends and sinking fund payments on the bonds that, like preferred dividends, come after taxes. If common shares will have to be sold, the equity will be diluted. If convertible securities are sold, the potential dilution of the equity, the potential increase in the supply of the stock, will hang over the stock and might keep it from rising for quite a spell.

A company's cash flow is also a good guide to future dividend policy; it is really a better guide than the reported net income. For cash dividends can be paid only out of cash, never out of a surplus account on the liabilities side of the ledger. Therefore a large cash flow assures management that the cash will be there to pay higher dividends as earnings increase. But this assumes that the company has a good current ratio, not less than 2:1, an adequate working capital, and that projected plant and equipment acquisitions are properly budgeted and don't use up all the cash flow. From what I have been giving you in the way of tools, you should have no problem checking it out now.

When it comes to depreciation, things are a little complicated because there are several methods of depreciating equipment. Which does your company use? The straight-line method, under which an equal amount will be charged off each year over the economic life of the equipment? Or an accelerated method of depreciation, under which more is charged off during the early years and progressively less as time goes on? If an accelerated method is used, three important results will follow: (1) The depreciation costs on the income statement will show a larger figure during the earlier years of the equipment, and the reported net income will of course be correspondingly less. (2) The cash throw-off, the available cash for expansion, will be consequently larger. (3) Taxes will be less because deductible expenses of doing business, depreciation, will be larger.

Should the day come when the company using the accelerated method slows down its expansion, the cash throw-off will be much smaller as the deduction for depreciation decreases rather rapidly, and income taxes will rise since the tax-deductible expenses will be less. This is why you will see, at times, an item on the balance sheet called deferred income taxes as an intermediate liabilities item, after current liabilities and before the long-term debt. For a rapidly expanding company, the deferred income tax item might well be considered part of the equity. It will never be repaid, for as the company expands its operations it will continue to have heavy, increasing depreciation charges, and possibly depletion charges, as tax-deductible items.

My crystal ball says that the 1970s, and for that matter the rest of this century, will see a rapid economic expansion. So invest in companies that expand as fast as GNP, preferably faster, and watch their cash flow. You won't have to worry about its slowing down.

Expanding Sales

How shall we judge expanding sales? That will depend on what the prices, the industry of which the company is a part, and national economic trends are doing.

If prices went up by 6 percent in a given year and the firm's sales by only 5 percent, the company has lost ground. Unit sales will have actually decreased. This is why many companies today also publish unit sales as supplementary information. If industry sales rise by 12 percent and your company's by only 7 percent, there is something wrong here. What happened? Did the company have a strike? Was it indirectly affected by a supplier being struck? Did a hurricane knock out a key plant in the organization? Check it out. If you don't find a satisfactory answer, you had better sell the stock and look around for a better opportunity. If the GNP grows by 4 to 6 percent real increase and 2 percent price level increase—and your company's unit sales have jumped 15 percent—you might call your company a growth company, assuming that further increases above the national economic growth rate are also projected for the future.

But sales increases, in dollar or real terms, are one thing; profitability of operation could be quite another matter. There are two tools for measuring profitability: the pretax profit margin and the operating ratio.

The Pretax Profit Margin

The pretax profit margin is the ratio of profit, before interest and income taxes are paid, to net sales. It is found by dividing the operating profit by sales; it is a percentage figure. Take another look at the BZB's income statement. Our operating profit (the company calls it income from operations) was $40 million: $230 million (our net sales), or 17.4 percent. That is quite good.

In some cases, be careful. This is income from operations. Don't ever include nonrecurring income or nonoperating income in the sales or revenue figures. Nonrecurring income does not come along again next year to boost your margin; an asset can only be sold once. Nonoperating income could be from rental income, from fees received from grants of patent licenses, or from oil and gas royalties. This has nothing to do with a manufacturing company, which is the basis on which we judge the BZB company. If you want to invest in a real estate trust or an oil company, go ahead and do so. But as long as your money is tied up in a manufacturing company, judge it as such.

Let me introduce a note of refinement: There are times when we should treat part of the sales as nonrecurring. During the top of a boom, a marginal company may be able to make substantial sales that it can't make under more ordinary conditions. High operating costs or distant location from markets prevents it. These companies are often highly leveraged, and when they can make these additional sales, net profit per share zooms. Don't let anybody sell you a bargain because these stocks tend to sell at a relatively low P/E ratio for these high earnings. The reason that the P/E ratio is low is that the market discounts such "nonrecurring" earnings. A bum may dress up to look like a gentleman, but sooner or later the bum will show through.

Compare your company's pretax (gross) profit margin with that of other companies in the industry, and above all, see what happened to that margin over the last ten years. Standard and Poor's stock reports show this. Is it improving? Getting worse? The trend will be far more important than the magnitude in a given year.

Sometimes it is difficult to compare companies because one will use one method of depreciation, and the other company another. In that case we can compute the gross profit margin without including the depreciation charges as part of the costs.

At what percentage of rated capacity is the company operating? If it can expand without adding greatly to its fixed costs such as depreciation, interest, and certain other costs, the fixed costs can be spread over a larger sales volume, thus reducing costs and increasing profits.

The Operating Ratio

The operating ratio is found by dividing sales (operating revenue) into operating expenses. Our total operating expenses were $190 million divided by the net sales of $230 million, or 82.6 percent. This is, of course, describing operating efficiency another way. Expenses took 82.6 cents out of every sales dollar, and we therefore wound up with 17.4 cents as gross profit.

Now we shall discuss a few more tools that you can easily use.

The Sales–Receivables Ratio

It shows the volume of sales for which payment has as yet not been received. We get it by dividing the net sales by the total amount of the accounts and notes receivable: $230 million: $23 million = 10. Such an unusually high ratio indicates good collection and a position favorable to creditors. A low ratio poses all kinds of serious questions: Is something wrong with the firm's credit administration? Is there cooperation between the sales manager and the credit manager? Are the stipulated terms of sale unrealistic, and should they be changed? Maybe some of the accounts are uncollectible and should be charged off. If receivables have been sold by the company, with or without recourse to the firm in case of nonpayment, the ratio has lost its usefulness.

The Sales–Inventory Ratio

The higher this ratio is, derived by dividing net sales by inventories, the higher is the merchandise turnover. A good turnover rate indicates highly salable merchandise, good pricing policies, and a much smaller risk in the event of adverse retail or wholesale price fluctuations, sudden changes in consumer taste, or technological changes.

A low ratio or a downward trend in it are warning signals. Is management speculating in inventory? Is part of the merchandise unsalable or unsalable at the asked prices? Maybe pricing or credit policies are out of line, and prices should be cut and more credit extended.

In the BZB company's case the ratio is $230 million:$55 million, or 4.2. As I have said before, this large inventory raises some questions. The ratio is too low for the average manufacturing company.

Net Income to Net Worth

This is the last and one of the most important tools I can give you. It answers the question: "How much is BZB earning on the investment of the owners?" We find the answer by dividing net income by the total of preferred and common stock and surplus accounts.

Preferred stock	$12,000,000	
Common stock	48,000,000	
Earned surplus	64,000,000	
Reserve for plant expansion	40,000,000	$164,000,000

The net income is $20 million:$164 million = 0.122 or 12.2 percent. This is a good rate of return, better than average. A large and particularly increasing ratio is good for both owners and creditors. Good earnings mean a good coverage factor for the bondholders and a good bond rating, so that borrowing can be done on a low-cost basis. If the trend is up, the rating agencies might up the rating so that borrowing can be done still cheaper and the bonds' price might rise. Dividends might be raised and more money plowed back to make more sales and profits as the nation's economy expands. Many managements deem expansion unwarranted and unwise unless an annual return of 10 percent on the new assets can be expected.

In Conclusion

Companies don't go broke overnight. There is always a trend. You now have some very important tools to spot good and bad trends. Take a sharp look at a break in a trend.

Read the annual reports of companies that you think you are interested in and apply the tools given here. It is more fascinating, and pays much better, than doing crossword puzzles.

Summary

1. Before investing, take a look at the company's annual report and use the tools given here. It will pay off.

2. The balance sheet will tell you whether the business is healthy; the income statement, whether it will stay healthy and become wealthy.

3. Industrial companies with low current ratios and low working capital will cause you grief, defined by Webster as "intense emotional suffering."

4. A high current ratio is bad if there is something wrong with a large inventory.

5. If the quick ratio is less than 1, grief very likely will again come your way.

6. Voluntary liabilities reserves must be treated as part of the

equities. It's important to figure the return on the owners' investment in the business.

7. If it's a consolidated statement, check on the principles of consolidation.

8. Depreciation and depletion charges are vital in the company's cash flow. They might tell you whether the dividend will be raised.

9. The gross profit margin must be computed from operating income.

10. Sales–receivables and sales–inventory ratios can give you warning signals if something is wrong.

11. What the owners want to know is: "How well are we doing?" The net income–net worth ratio (make sure you include everything!) will answer the question—one of the most important tools in your investor's kit.

12. Companies don't go broke overnight. There is always a trend. Try to spot it with the tools given here. And if the trend points up, be the early bird that gets the worm.

CHAPTER 16

Is Short Selling and Margin Buying

Only for the Professionals?

The answer is a ringing NO. I suppose the reason that more people don't go short at times in the market is ignorance of procedure. Ignorance scares them off, and since Americans are fundamentally optimistic, they marry their stocks for better or for worse. Often it gets a lot worse than they had thought; then come fear and eventually panic. Stocks are thrown on the market for whatever they may bring. Usually that kind of selling climax is a sign that the market is now turning up.

When to Go Short

There are signs when the market has only one way to go and that is down. For example, when monetary indicators point to a credit crunch, to tighter money conditions, when interest rates go higher and higher, this is no time to stay in stocks unless a special situation exists in a particular company. Sell your stocks and your bonds too, and at the same time go short. You can short any bond—government, municipal, or corporate. Shorting bonds can be very profitable when you think the time is here for interest rates to go much higher than they are currently. For as they advance, bond prices must come down under the laws of financial physics.

With the growing money tightness during 1969 and 1970, the high P/E ratio of stocks, and the unpopularity of the conglomerates, these stocks just had to come down. The investor who sold Walter Kidde short in 1969 and covered (bought himself in) in 1970 did quite well. The stock's high was 66½ in 1969, down already over 20 points from the 1968 high; the low in 1969 was 34½, and this was cut in half again in 1970. The highs over these years, 1968–1970, for Litton Industries were 120, 74½, and 38. The low in 1969 was 35, and that was more than halved in 1970. This shows there is ample opportunity to make money in a bear market, even if you don't catch your stocks anywhere near their highs and lows, which of course is something that is rarely ever done. The records of Gulf and Western Industries, Fuqua Industries, and such troubled companies as Ling-Temco-Vought or Lockheed amply illustrate the opportunities that exist in going short to make money.

If you owned one hundred shares of any of these stocks and you decided that there was good reason to get out because you thought the stock, on the evidence available to you, could only go down, then why not sell the long shares in your possession and sell short another hundred shares? I shall tell you in these pages how you can sell something you haven't got. Incidentally, there are other uses for using the short sale device than speculative. You might want to use it for protection or to put yourself into a more advantageous tax position.

Buying on Margin

If you feel confident that a stock will go up and you have tangible evidence for your judgment—not just a hunch or, worse, a tip—then why not buy more than your funds will permit you if you buy the stock outright? In other words, buy on margin. Using the 1971 initial margin requirement of 55 percent for stocks, your $10,000 would buy close to $18,200 worth of stock. Instead of buying 200 shares of ABC at $50, you can now buy about 360 shares. If the stock moves 15 points, you have made $5,400 instead of $3,000—a 50-percent return on your investment of $10,000 instead of 30 percent. This is leverage working for you if your judgment was right. You could further increase it by also buying a call option or two on the stock.

What happens when the stock goes down? The chance that your broker will ask you to put up more money is slim. Moreover, you should sell the stock if it goes down by 10 percent. It shows your judgment was wrong. Always cut your losses the way the professional does; he also lets his profits run. Try to learn what went wrong and benefit from the error. Then try again—on margin, on the long or short side of the market.

Avail yourself of all the tools that the securities markets put at your disposal. There is more than one way of selling short; more than one way of buying something on margin. Let me first discuss short selling, and then devote the other half of this chapter to margin trading.

There are four types of short sales: the speculative short sale, the short sale against the box, the technical short sale, and the hedging short sale.

The Speculative Short Sale

Suppose you thought Lockheed Aircraft was overpriced at $40 and you decided to sell 100 shares short at that price. Seven months later, you bought yourself in at $20, making a profit of $2,000. How can you sell something you do not have in your possession? It is quite simple. Here are the rules:

1. You have to put up 55 percent of the stock's value, or $2,200.

2. A speculative short sale can never be executed on the floor of an exchange on a down tick or a zero minus tick, only on a plus tick or zero plus tick.

The following trades occur in Lockheed stock: 40, 39¾, 39¾, 40, 40. The sale at 39¾ is a down tick or a minus tick; the second 39¾ is a zero minus tick. The following 40 is an up tick or plus tick; the second 40, a zero plus tick. No speculative short sale can be made on a down tick or a zero minus tick; short sales can only be executed on an up tick or a zero plus tick. This SEC rule is to prevent the bears from clawing down the market. The required ⅛ markup, if the last sale was down from a previous price, can be quite an obstacle. On the floor of the Exchange, the lowest offer (and highest bid) always has the floor. Suppose the last sale was $50 and now someone offers long stock at 49¾. You cannot sell short at 49¾. You can sell short only by offering stock at 49⅞, after a sale at 49¾. But who would buy it from you if other stock is offered at 49¾? Besides, your broker couldn't be in that auction, because the lowest offer has the floor and is entitled to execution. If no up tick comes along, no short sale can be made. But there is no limit as to how many short sales can be made on an up tick or a zero plus tick. To enter a short sale knowingly and willfully as a long sale is a criminal offense.

3. Your broker must borrow stock for you. You sold 100 shares of Lockheed short; somebody bought them. He couldn't care less whether you sold long or short. On the fifth business day he wants his stock because he has to deliver it to the buyer, his client. To make regular delivery, your broker has to borrow stock. The stock may be "in the house" or he may have to go out and borrow it from another broker.

4. You can never make a long-term capital gain on a short sale, no matter how long you have been short the stock.

5. You cannot sell stock if the stock is not available to be borrowed from somebody. This is why it is not always possible to sell over-the-counter stocks short. Usually you should be able to sell a listed security short, but even here you could have borrowing problems. Check it out with your broker.

6. When you cover and stock is returned, any cash or stock dividends payable during the "short" period must be returned with the stock. If the stock splits 2 for 1, then of course 200 shares would be returned.

Borrowing Stock

When Broker A borrows stock from Broker B, usually no compensation passes either way, because it is lent "flat." The proceeds of the sale of 100 LK at 40, the $4,000, go to the lender as a cash collateral. Should the stock now go to $50, and you still were short the stock against my advice, the lending Broker

B would send a "mark-to-the-market" notice to Broker A, saying in effect, "Give me another $1,000 cash." In that case, you would now have a debit balance of $1,000 with your broker on which he will charge interest.

In short selling, the loan of the stock is to be secured at all times by about 100 percent of the current market value of the stock. Should the stock go to $30, the borrowing Broker A would send such a mark-to-the-market notice to Broker B, saying, "Give me back $1,000." The incentive to lend stock under these conditions is that the lending broker receives interest-free money that he can use in his business, possibly to lend to a margin customer who will pay him the going rate of interest.

If you were long the stock in your cash account, could you lend stock through your broker? Certainly. But if you wanted to use the $4,000 to trade in securities, the loan would come under the federal margin regulation. It says that as long as the initial margin requirement is 55 percent, you can use only 45 percent of the deposited cash collateral, or $1,800. When individuals lend stock, they can use the cash deposited only to the amount of the current loan value of stock, which is 45 percent.

Sometimes stock is very difficult to borrow. It may then be lent only "at a premium," so many dollars per 100 shares.

The Short Sale against the Box

Let us assume that you had bought 500 shares of ABC in September, 1971, at $30 and by December the price had risen to $40. You want to keep your $5,000 profit, but you don't want to declare it on your 1971 income-tax report; you want to carry it over into 1972, when taxes are lower or you might be in a better tax position. Accordingly in December you would sell 100 shares of ABC short at $40. In January you can then instruct your broker to deliver the long stock to the lender of the stock. Your long and short positions are now both closed out. On your 1972 income-tax report you would list this $5,000 short-term capital gain. You cannot carry over a long-term gain from one year to the next.

A short sale against the box, "the box" being the broker's

vault, also cannot be made on a down tick or zero minus tick. It must be marked up ⅛ of a point, the minimum variation on the Exchange. This type of short sale, in this respect, is treated like a speculative short sale.

The Technical Short Sale

An illustration of a technical short sale would be an arbitrage transaction. The bond is convertible into 25 shares of stock that is currently selling at $46; the bond is selling at $1,100. Here an arbitrage profit can be made. The trader buys the bond and simultaneously sells the stock at $46 in order to nail down his profit of $50 per bond. The 25 shares into which the bond purchases at $1,100 can be converted have been sold for $1,150— 25 × $46. Since converting the bond into stock takes considerable time, the seller cannot possibly deliver the stock on the fifth business day as required under regular delivery rules. He can only make such an arbitrage transaction as a short sale; stock must be borrowed for the delivery. When the stock from the company's transfer agent is received, it can be used to close out the short position.

Two things are important for the technical short sale: (1) A technical short sale can be made at any time; the up-tick rule does not apply. (2) The sale is entered as a "short-exempt" sale. Since all sell orders must be marked "short" or "long," this type of short sale must be marked "short-exempt," exempt from the short sale rule.

Other types of technical short sales would occur in connection with an arbitrage transaction between the rights and the stock or between warrants and the associated stock, or if one is trading on two exchanges (that is, the stock is bought in New York, where it is cheaper, and sold on the Pacific Coast Stock Exchange, where its price is higher). As a general rule, the differences are usually so small that only professionals, who pay lower commissions, can make them. However, every now and then professionals, for one reason or another, show no interest, and a member of the public can make them. All these enumerated arbitrage transactions involve no risk whatever. But there is another type of arbitrage, merger arbitrage, that carries a big risk. The risk is that something will happen between the cup and the lip and the merger won't go through.

In 1970 a merger was proposed between White Consolidated Industries and the White Motor Corporation; it was announced after the market closed on Monday, August 14. The terms provided for the exchange of 1.4 shares of White Consolidated for one share of White Motor. The closing price of White Consolidated on Monday was 13⅛; that of White Motor, 15⅜ (1.4 shares at 13⅛ is 18⅜). So here was an attractive differential, seemingly a quick buck—$300 per each 100-share transaction—and money was hard to find on The Street that summer. We could sell White Consolidated short, buy White Motor stock, and deliver it against our short position. So one would expect at the opening the next day a lot of buying of White Motor and selling of White Consolidated Industries.

What happened actually? Absolutely nothing. On Tuesday, White Consolidated closed unchanged at 13⅛; White Motor declined to 15¼. The arbitrage opportunity was still there. On the third trading day White Consolidated dropped to 12, and White Motor to 14⅜. At these prices, if the merger went through as announced, White Motor stock could be bought at 14⅜ and exchanged for $16.80 worth of White Consolidated stock. Wall Streeters just weren't interested. Maybe they thought this type of arbitrage was too risky. Maybe the lean days of 1970 had made them too cautious. As it turned out, the merger did not go through.

No one knows when arbitrage transactions come down the pike. Professionals won't make them all. Keep your eyes open and know the procedure. There will be in this decade, too, a lot of mergers and quite a few demergers.

The Hedging Short Sale

A short sale can also be used for protection. A security owner has a sizable portfolio that shows substantial appreciation. He does not wish to sell anything, but he has his doubts about the business outlook or the market in general. What such an investor can do is to sell short a group of market leaders or possibly stocks in the Dow-Jones industrial averages. Should the market decline, he would make money on his short contracts, but what he gains on them he would lose on his portfolio. Should the market rise, he would lose money on the short sales, but his portfolio would gain in value. What he loses on one he gains on the other. In other words, he has protected his investment. That is the purpose of any hedge: protection. Note, however, that this is not a perfect hedge. He has not sold the same securities as are in the portfolio. If he had, it would have been a sale against the box. It is therefore quite possible that the short securities will rise more than the issues in the portfolio or fall less than his stocks.

All short sales, with the exception of the technical short sale, are subject to the rule that they cannot be made on a minus tick or zero minus tick. In the speculative and hedging short sale I sell something I do not own and don't intend to own until I am good and ready. In the sale against the box I sell something I own, but I do not want to deliver it. In the technical short sale I sell something I have and I am willing to deliver it, but it is temporarily not in deliverable form.

Trading Rules

If I have interested you in short selling, keep the following rules in mind:

Stocks should not be sold short unless they seem overvalued and a downside correction seems to be around the corner.

Stocks that have a limited floating supply are bad candidates for a short sale. It may be difficult to cover the short position at what seems to be the ideal time.

Better candidates for short selling are stocks with histories of wide fluctuations and a record of moving faster and farther on the downside than on the upside.

When somebody is long stock, he knows what his maximum loss can be: his investment. But when he is short, the sky is the limit. For this reason, low-priced stocks should not be sold short. If you sell a $4 stock short, your ratio between risk assumption and potential gain is too far out of line.

The short seller can try to protect himself against a sudden upward thrust of the market by placing a stop order with his broker, an order to buy him in at a specified price.

Margin Trading

As long as short selling is permitted, margin trading must be permitted, and vice versa. It is necessary for balance. Buying on margin increases the demand for stock; short selling, the supply. The short seller can put a brake on a rising market and keep it from degenerating into a runaway market and later collapse. The margin buyer props up a market and thus enables corporations to sell their shares to raise new equity money for expansion.

There are two main types of margins: the initial margin and the maintenance margin.

The *initial margin* is the amount the buyer must give the broker when he purchases securities. It is his equity and it is set by the Board of Governors of the Federal Reserve System. In the summer of 1971 it was 55 percent for registered nonexempt securities, that is, for issues traded on any national stock exchange. If you were to buy 300 shares of ABC at $50, the *contract price*, exclusive of commission, would be $15,000; the initial margin, your *equity*, would be 55 percent of $15,000, or $8,250. The broker could lend you 45 percent of $15,000, or $6,750. This is the *debit balance* in your general (margin) account. As the value of the stocks in the account fluctuates, so will the equity in it; the debit balance remains fixed unless you pay part of it off or add to it.

The *maintenance margin* is set by the New York Stock Exchange. Whereas the initial margin is to protect the broker, the creditor, as well as the margin trader against getting in too deep, the maintenance margin is to ensure that there remains a minimum equity in the account at all times. The minimum equity for opening a margin account is $2,000.

The maintenance margin is 25 percent of the current market value for all securities owned by the customer on margin, no matter what the price of the individual securities is. With securities he is short; the story is different. Here the maintenance requirement is 30 percent of the current market value for stocks selling at $17 or above. On the lower-priced stocks it is $5 a share. For a short position of 200 shares of a $5 stock, the maintenance requirement would be $1,000. Should the stock sell below $5, the maintenance margin is 100 percent or $2.50 a share, whichever is greater. Low-priced stocks carry a higher maintenance requirement than initial requirement. This is a reflection of the high risk that a short position in a low-priced stock carries. Brokers set their own maintenance requirements somewhat higher; possibly 35 percent on a long position. The less diversified a margin account is, the higher will be the broker's maintenance requirement.

When undue speculation occurs in a stock, the Exchange might set a 100-percent margin for it. In this case the security, temporarily, cannot be bought on margin.

Exempt Securities

For so-called exempt securities, United States Government and municipal securities as well as straight corporate bonds, the Federal Reserve authorities set no initial margin. The initial margin requirement for these securities is set by the New York Stock Exchange. It requires an initial margin for United States Government securities of 5 percent of par value. The Treasury's 3½-percent bonds due in 1998 were selling in mid-summer of 1970 for $650 per $1,000 bond. They could have been bought on a margin of 5 percent of par or $50 per bond according to these rules. Your broker, however, will probably require 10 percent of par. This prevents a margin call when he debits you with an interest charge.

If you can catch the bond market at the right turn in the interest rate cycle, trading government bonds on margin can be quite profitable. Suppose you had bought $100,000 par value of the 3½-percent bonds of 1998 in the summer of 1970 for $65,000 and put up $10,000 as margin, 10 percent of par. The remaining $55,000 would have been financed by your broker. In early 1971 you could have sold the bonds for better than $72,000—a nice profit of $7,000-plus on an investment of $10,000. Part of the interest charges would have been taken care of by the interest payment and accrual on the bonds.

On municipals the initial Exchange requirement is 15 percent of par value or 25 percent of market value, whichever is less. The Chicago Calumet Skyway 3⅜-percent bonds due in 1995 were selling in August, 1970, for about 40—$400 per $1,000 bond. The initial margin for such a bond was 25 percent of $400, or $100 per bond, rather than 15 percent of par, which would have been $150. Here, too, a broker might require a deposit of funds equal to $200 per $1,000 face value of the bonds.

There is nothing wrong with buying AA bonds on margin or selling them short if you can catch a turn in monetary policy— from tight to an easier money supply or vice versa. Interest rates must come down as the money supply increases, and bond prices must rise. If the money gets to be less available, interest rates must rise and bond prices must decline. But if you trade municipal securities on margin, you cannot deduct the interest charges. The Treasury says you cannot deduct interest charges incurred in the carrying of tax-exempt securities. You cannot claim both tax-exempt income and deductible interest charges.

For nonconvertible corporate bonds, the New York Stock Exchange wants an initial margin of 25 percent of the current market value of the long position or 30 percent of the current market value of the short position in the account. The initial margin for convertible bonds, as was previously pointed out, is 50 percent and is set by the Federal Reserve Board. For listed nonconvertible bonds, a broker probably wants 35 percent of the market value.

Any margin requirement, initial or maintenance, regardless of who sets it, for any type of security can always be met by depositing cash or collateral with a loan value equal to the required amount. If I want to buy 100 shares of ABC at $50, I can deposit in cash $2,750, 55 percent of $5,000, or about $11,000 of registered nonexempt securities, which have a loan value of $5,000. But bonds cannot be put with stocks into the same margin account. Straight bonds, corporates, municipals, and governments are in a special bond account, and convertible bonds are in a special convertible debt security account.

Over-the-Counter Securities

Over-the-counter securities, also referred to as unregistered nonexempt securities, cannot be bought on margin unless they are among 390 unlisted, over-the-counter stocks that fall under the Federal Reserve's credit rules. The Fed's list ranges from Aits, Inc., a tourist travel service, to Woodward and Lothrop, Inc., posh department stores; it also includes quite a number of insurance companies and banks. But the mere fact that the Federal Reserve authorities say these 390 stocks can be bought on 55-percent margin does not mean that your broker will let you do so. He may have his own substantially cut-down list. As time goes on, the Federal Reserve authorities will, no doubt, lengthen this list; originally, there were only about 265 stocks on it. The lists of the brokers will also get larger; competition will bring that about.

Under federal credit rules, any over-the-counter security can always be sold short under the same margin requirement as registered nonexempt securities. After all, you, the short seller, put up 55 percent of the contract price, and no credit extension is involved here. Whether your broker will go along with you is again quite another question. The stock you wish to sell short may be hard to borrow.

Regulation U

Brokers come under Federal Regulation T. There is a companion Regulation U for the commercial banks and a Regulation G covers factors. A bank cannot give more credit on securities as collateral than a broker *if* the purpose of the loan is to carry securities. But it is free to lend on securities whatever its judgment dictates for a so-called nonpurpose loan—that is, a loan whose proceeds are applied to other uses than carrying securities.

Please don't be tempted to tell the bank a story. Don't say: "I need the money in my business" when you want it for speculating in a few "hot" stocks. You could find yourself in considerable trouble. The Federal Reserve authorities take a dim view of such prevarications. Besides, in the days of computers, it is a stupid thing to hurt one's credit standing.

Interest Costs

Opening a margin account gives you leverage, as any debt does. As long as you can make more money on the borrowed funds than the interest charges are, you will always be better off than had you stuck to a cash purchase. What will be the interest cost on the debit balance in a margin account?

That depends primarily on two things: the size of the debit balance and the cost the broker incurs in borrowing from his bank to accommodate the margin customer. The larger the debit balance, the lower will be the rate the broker will charge. But don't badger him. The Exchange says that the minimum rate at which he can let you have the money is 0.5 percent above the call loan rate on stock exchange collateral. If that rate is 6 percent, he cannot charge less than 6.5 percent, even to his best customers. But if the debit balance is only $5,000, don't be mad at him if he charges you 7 percent or more. After all, he has a lot of expenses carrying your account, collecting dividends, rights, and so on. If the broker charges 7.5 percent when the prime rate is 4.5 percent, change brokers!

The "truth in lending" rule requires that the broker disclose to you the interest rate charged on the debit balance and any other charges before the account is opened, prior to the execution of the first credit transaction. If you are not furnished with this information (probably it is all printed on a card), you have the right to cancel any transaction.

Excess Equity

In the spring of 1970 you bought 400 shares of Mobil Oil on margin at $40. In August the stock was $50. What would be the status of your account? The initial margin then was 65 percent.

	Market Value	Initial Margin	Debit Balance
At purchase 400 MOB at $40	$16,000	$10,400	$5,600
In August 400 MOB at $50	20,000	13,000	5,600

There is now an excess equity of $1,400 in the account that you could withdraw in cash and use for a fishing trip to Nova Scotia. You could also use the $1,400 excess equity as another down payment on $2,150 worth of securities. Why?

When MOB reached $50, the value of the securities was $20,000. To have the account properly margined, we need $13,000 —65 percent of $20,000. The debit balance is $5,600; that stays fixed. Then $13,000 + $5,600 = $18,600, leaving a balance of $1,400. The formula to figure out the buying power of cash or excess equity is: Add a zero to the amount of the funds and divide it by 6.5. Thus $14,000/6.5 = $2,150.

If you were to sell the securities now, you could withdraw $14,400—$20,000 minus $5,600 the broker advanced to you. Had you bought 250 shares outright, your profit would have been $2,500 on $10,000 invested, or 25 percent. Buying 40 shares on margin boosted your rate of return to almost 40 percent on an invested capital of $10,400. This is what leverage does when it works for you.

A Restricted Account

You bought 400 shares of a swinger like Natomas at $40 and in August, 1970, the stock was down to $30. What would be the status of the account?

	Market Value	Initial Margin	Debit Balance
At purchase 400 NOM at $40	$16,000	$10,400	$5,600
In August 400 NOM at $30	12,000	7,800	5,600

The account is now below the 65-percent margin requirement; it is restricted. The equity is only $6,400—$12,000 market value minus $5,600 owed to the broker. The equity should be $7,800. So the amount of the restriction is $7,800 minus $6,400, or $1,400.

Since the equity is still over 50 percent, way above the maintenance requirement, the broker will not ask for additional cash or acceptable security collateral. The Federal Reserve authorities have no objection to a restricted account being carried on a broker's books as long as changes in the equity reflect market changes. But you cannot carry on trading activities in the account that would increase the amount of the restriction. You can buy and sell, long or short, just as long as the amount of the restriction does not increase.

If the amount of the restriction increases, say, from $1,400 to $5,000, the difference, $3,600, must be fully margined. If a day trade is made and the same security bought and sold brought a loss to the account, 100 percent of the loss must be deposited in cash or its equitable in acceptable securities.

Should the market decline and the equity fall below the broker's maintenance requirement, a maintenance margin call would be sent out. Every afternoon, when the closing prices are in, the credit department of the broker will "mark" the margin accounts "to the market" to see what excess equity, buying power, and amount of the restriction may be. In case of a highly volatile security in a "down" market, any price during trading hours may be used.

If the amount of the restriction in an account is $4,000 and the customer sells 100 shares of NOM at $30, he could withdraw no more than 30 percent, or $900. This is the so-called Federal Reserve retention requirement, which is 70 percent. Cash or stock dividends may be withdrawn not later than 35 days after they have been credited to the account. But a stock dividend or a spin-off must not exceed 10 percent of the market value of the security involved.

The Special Subscription Account

Newly issued securities, and that includes mutual fund shares, cannot be bought on margin, nor can securities be bought on the installment plan. But to every rule there seems to be an exception. An investor may subscribe on margin to listed securities by exercising his rights. Such a security can be bought on a 25-percent margin.

The BZB Company offers to stockholders of record new common shares at a subscription price of $42. The market price is $48. Rights have no value in a margin account. You must either have the requisite number of rights to subscribe to, say, 100 shares or give your broker the money to buy the rights. If there is an excess equity in your margin account, he could siphon enough off to pay for the rights. Once you have the rights and have deposited the required margin, the subscription can be made.

The 25-percent margin is figured as follows: 25 percent of the market price of $4,800 is $1,200 minus the difference between the market value and the subscription price ($4,800 – $4,200), $600. That is the amount you must put up to subscribe to 100 shares, $4,800 worth of market value. The debit balance will be $3,600–$4,200, the subscription price, minus the $600 down payment. If your broker is in the underwriting group, you can't buy the stock through him on that basis. You have to go to another broker.

During the next twelve months, after subscription, the difference between the initial margin of 55 percent of the value of the securities at the time the 25-percent margin was computed and the equity must be paid in four equal quarterly installments. Fifty-five percent of $4,800 is $2,640, minus the original equity of $1,200 ($4,800 – $3,600 debit balance) = $1,440. One-fourth of that, or $360, would have to be paid each quarter. When the securities are fully margined, after one year, they can be sold or must be transferred with the debit balance of $2,160 to the general account ($3,600 minus the four quarterly payments). No trading and no withdrawals are permitted in a special subscription account.

What happens if the subscribed stock should go, after four months, to $60? Can it now be sold?

Fifty-five percent of $6,000 is $3,300, the required margin that must exist before the securities can be sold. But the equity, at this time, is only $2,760–$6,000 (market value) minus $3,600 (the original debit balance) plus one quarterly payment of $360. The client would still have to give the broker a check for $540 before the securities could be transferred to the general account and sold. Such a request is sometimes hard for people to understand when the stock shows a substantial appreciation.

When-Issued Securities

Any security that has been authorized but not as yet issued can be bought on the same margin or sold short as any other registered nonexempt security or eligible over-the-counter security.

A decrease in the value of a when-issued position will contribute to the amount of the restriction. Any appreciation will reduce the amount of restriction only up to the point at which the increased value of the security becomes equal to the required margin. Beyond that, any further appreciation cannot be treated . as excess equity and withdrawn or used as buying power for additional trading.

Short Sales against Convertible Securities or Warrants

When a trader sells short a common stock versus a long position of convertible bonds, warrants, or rights, there is a Regulation T requirement on the long position only—the short position is, of course, marked to the market.

Suppose the client is long low-valued warrants and short a comparatively high-priced stock. In that case, the broker will probably require a maintenance requirement of 35 percent on the short stock. Such a maintenance requirement then could easily be higher than the 55 percent on the long position. When contemplating that type of transaction, make sure you have the funds.

If you purchase any convertible bonds, on 50-percent margin, with the intention of converting them, keep in mind that they cannot be converted in the special convertible debt security account. Prior to conversion they must be fully margined (55 percent) and transferred to the general account.

Day Trades

Sometimes people overlook good opportunities to make money. They don't realize they have buying power in their margin account even though it is restricted. Under these conditions, a day trade can be made on a 25-percent margin. To illustrate:

400 shares NOM at $25 Value	$10,000
Debit balance	5,000
Equity	$ 5,000
Required margin—65% [then]	6,500
Amount of restriction	$ 1,500

Despite the restriction, there is here a $10,000 buying power for a day trade. On August 21, 1970, the trader could have bought 165 shares of Polaroid (PRD) at $60 on the opening and sold it at the close at 64¼. National economic and international news as well as money market news was very good the day before, so that the market had to go up. The Dow-Jones industrial averages shot up almost 16 points. PRD had been beaten down in 1970 from a high of 130¾ to a low of 51. It was bound to come back at least somewhat. The status of the account is now:

400 shares NOM plus 165 shares PRD—about	$20,000
Debit balance now	15,000
(Broker advanced the $10,000 for the trade)	
Equity—meets NYSE's minimum maintenance margin	5,000
Profit minus commissions, odd-lot differential, and taxes	742

But remember three things: (1) Never use a limit order with a day trade. If the round trip is not completed, you have to cough up the full margin on the one position. (2) The fourth-day trade you make in any twelve-month period has to be fully margined. You are allowed only three such trades during any such period on 25-percent margin. (3) Don't try to "free ride." You cannot sell a security before you have paid for it. With all the money that can be made in the market in the 1970s, don't play funny games with your broker. It doesn't pay.

The SMA—The Great Unknown

Every margin account has an SMA—a special miscellaneous account. It is simply a penciled memorandum, a piece of paper kept in the margin (credit) department. It can never work against you. Suppose you bought 400 shares of XYZ at $25 and put up the proper margin of $6,500. The stock now goes to $30, giving you an excess equity of $700 or a buying power of close to $1,100. (Appreciation is $2,000 minus $1,300 for 65-percent margin = $700. Now $7,000/6.5 = $1,070.) If you don't want to use it, never mind. It is put on ice for you in your SMA. If the stock keeps on going up, every night your buying power grows. Your account executive should be able to tell you, before the market opens, what your buying power is that morning. Should the stock go down, it would not affect your buying power in the SMA. That sits there, waiting for you to use it. As long as your margin account meets the broker's maintenance requirement, probably 35 percent, you are free to withdraw or trade on your SMA balance. You can refigure this in the light of the current 55 percent initial margin requirement.

Summary

1. There is no reason why you should not buy on margin or sell short. Keep the rules cited here, and the odds are very much in your favor.

2. Short selling can be used for speculation and protection.

3. In contrast to other types of arbitrage, merger arbitrage can be risky.

4. Before you sell a stock short, study its history.

5. Your broker will not ask you to put up more money if the equity in your margin account falls between the initial margin and his maintenance requirement.

6. You can trade in a restricted account, but if the amount of the restriction increases, the increase must be fully margined.

7. Municipals, like other bonds, can be traded on margin, but interest paid to the broker for carrying tax-exempt securities is not tax-deductible.

8. Over-the-counter securities can be sold short on margin if your broker lets you. But only a handful can be bought on margin.

9. Excess equity can be withdrawn or compounded into more buying power.

10. Yes, stocks can be bought on the installment plan—25 percent down and the balance in four equal quarterly payments *if* it's a rights offering.

11. There can be lots of buying power in a restricted account for a day trade.

12. The SMA will never work against you. Check what your buying power is. It is probably larger than you think.

CHAPTER 17

What Determines the Prices of My Securities?

The prices of securities are determined by fundamental economic and political conditions on the one hand, and on the other, by the technical conditions prevailing in the market itself. But the stock market is not only a barometer of the politico-economic situation; it is also a barometer of the prevailing mood of the security-buying public.

Measured by the Dow-Jones industrial averages, the market declined 27 percent during 1961–1962; 25 percent during the credit crunch of 1966; and 36 percent during the money-tight 1969–1970 period. In each of these cases, unbridled optimism had pushed up the market to unjustifiable high levels before an economically neurotic public generated a pervasive gloom that pushed down the market to equally unjustifiable low levels.

The high for Control Data was 159 in 1969; the low, 28¾ in 1970. By Easter, 1971, CDA had recovered; it was then selling for 68½. But $159 for $3.20 worth of current earnings was too high a price to pay for the stock. It was rampant optimism in anticipation of future higher earnings. Earnings temporarily declined by about 20 percent, and the same management and plant facilities all of a sudden were selling at less than 12 times earnings. By the end of September, 1970, CDA was at 42¼, a 50-percent corrective price increase. Memorex reached a dizzy 173 in 1969 on $2 worth of earnings. In 1970 it declined to 44½, and by the end of September, 1970, it had again doubled in price at 89¾. Because of questionable reporting practices, the stock plummeted to 26¾ in 1971. What is the moral of these two stories?

When enough stock buyers become overly optimistic about fundamental economic and political conditions or about the future of specific companies, they will buy stocks and drive their prices to unwarranted heights. When they become overly pessimistic, they will sell stocks without rhyme or reason.

The investor therefore should know that paying 30 or 40 or more times current earnings for a stock is paying a high price even for a growth stock. But how high is high? Electronic Data Systems Corporation sold in March of 1971 at a P/E ratio of 132.8. That's a high price to pay even for Mr. Perot's company. In 1961 International Business Machines sold at 80 times its indicated annual earnings. When your stock reaches a P/E ratio of 40 or 50, take a hard look. Not wanting to pay capital gains taxes is a poor reason for holding on to a stock if there is no other. Maybe it ought to be sold. Once the Dow-Jones industrial averages start reaching P/E ratios in the low twenties, the market is high by historical standards. While I don't like to say history repeats itself, I do say that like causes tend to have like effects. Don't stay in the market under those conditions, particularly when you see money is getting tighter and interest rates keep moving higher and higher.

Unfortunately, there is no one theory which tells us at what P/E ratio to buy or sell. You can pay more for a growth company that shows great stability and a steady uptrend in earnings and dividends such as a food stock than for a cyclical stock such as autos and steels. Buy the good-acting stocks, those that show better than average resistance to a market decline and an exceptional or good performance when the market again comes to its senses, as it always has and will.

So what then is a stock worth? Whatever the buyer wants to give. But the expression of a stock's worth in terms of an earnings multiple does not float around in a vacuum. Most of the time it is anchored fairly well to economic and political fundamentals. Except in periods of euphoria or manic-depression, the market does respond to economic statistics and messages from the White House, but often with a lag, and at other times in anticipation of actual events.

Economic and Political Fundamentals

A change in the economic and political climate for the economy as a whole or for given industries or companies tends to affect corporate earnings, and they in turn tend to affect dividends. It really doesn't make much difference whether the company in question pays cash dividends or plows the earnings back. Retained earnings lead to expansion, to higher sales, higher future earnings, dividends, and stock prices. Stock prices and corporate earnings, however, do not correlate too well. Sometimes a stock will go up faster than earnings; at other times its price movement will lag behind earnings. There are even times when earnings trends and stock prices move in opposite directions. But over the long pull, stock prices do move with business and economic trends.

By the early summer of 1970, common stock prices had fallen almost 23 percent from their 1969 average. Consumer prices had risen by about 6 percent. So where was the anti-inflation hedge that common stocks, properly chosen, will provide? It was still there. If we take the whole decade 1960–1969, common stocks had risen by about 70 percent, while consumer prices rose by about 25 percent. During this decade, GNP and other economic indicators moved up and so did the market, and as we march toward our second trillion dollars in GNP, the market will continue to reflect that too.

Some stocks reflect the growth in economic aggregates and in business statistics. Others will even do better. Take a good look at your bank. How has it done over the last ten years? This is a service economy, and banking services will continue to expand as the economy gets bigger and per capita income rises. Maybe you ought to buy some bank shares. The First National City Corporation, the holding company of the First National City Bank, raised its dividend in every year of the 1960s. The Black and Decker Manufacturing Company, the leader in the portable power tool field, has been growing more rapidly than GNP.

Between 1955 and 1969 earnings rose at an annual rate of better than 11 percent. Dividends were upped almost every year. And the power tool market is far from being saturated as more and more do-it-yourselfers come along. More retired people, more leisure time, a higher marriage rate, and the ever-puttering suburbanite—all these push up the demand for portable power tools.

Economic Fundamentals

What is happening to GNP, the total output of goods and services? Figures on it are released quarterly. These data are seasonally adjusted totals at annual rates and are given out first as preliminary figures. It is quite possible to read a report of a couple of billion dollars' decrease, and when the revised figures come out, they might show a $2 billion *increase*. In view of the magnitude involved, a billion dollars is a very small percentage, so that such discrepancies are bound to occur and must be expected. When this happens, the market might sell off at the opening as some investors react to this front-page news. During the day saner elements prevail, and buyers come in who take advantage of this weakness.

If GNP expands, so must personal income, and particularly *disposable personal income,* income after taxes, meaning spendable money. A higher personal income tends to boost *retail sales.* What is then happening to *durable consumer goods* sales? Are people buying TV sets, stoves, refrigerators, freezers, and cars, or are they spending more on clothing and other nondurables?

Are people *saving* more and putting more money into mutual savings banks and other thrift institutions? If so, earnings of savings and loan institutions will not only increase, but mortgage money will become more freely available at a lower rate and *housing starts* will turn up. Watch for news on *construction* activities. The construction industry is very big in terms of employment and its demand for equipment and materials.

What is *business spending for plant and equipment?* Money spent in this sector is very potent. An increase shows that management is optimistic about the near future and is willing to add to plant capacity to be able to meet anticipated bigger sales in future. Check the Federal Reserve Board's *Production Index.* It is the only important physical index we have that is not influenced by price level changes. A rising production index after several months of decline would be very bullish for stocks. Rising *inventories* could be bullish or bearish. If business is building up inventories on the retail, wholesale, or manufacturing level in anticipation of greater sales, it is good. But if inventories rise because sales are lagging behind business expectations, that is bad.

What is the *federal government* doing? Is it increasing spending? For defense or for nondefense projects? An increase or decrease will affect industries and companies. Is there a balanced budget, a deficit, or a surplus? If the budget is in balance, the government will simply put back into the economy what it took out of it. If a deficit exists, the effect will turn on how the deficit is financed. And if a surplus should exist, the effect will depend on whose maturing IOUs are paid off.

State and local governments are spending more money for goods and services purchased than the federal government. It has been that way for some years. A 1966 study by the Joint Economic Committee of the Congress, adjusted for price level increases, projects that capital requirements of state and local governments for upgrading and expanding public facilities will rise to more than $50 billion by 1975. Assuming a normal pattern of financing, the states and local political subdivisions will need to sell in 1975 nearly twice the volume of long-term bonds that they marketed as recently as 1968—about $33 billion.

New orders are another important fundamental indicator. As they rise and orders on the books grow bigger, people become more optimistic. These orders spell for tomorrow higher employment, higher incomes, and thus a greater demand.

Wholesale commodity prices foreshadow other price changes and thus influence stock prices. Rising prices mean inventories can be sold directly or indirectly at higher prices. Falling commodity prices indicate future losses. Rising wholesale prices spell future higher consumer prices. As indicators of stock prices, however, commodity prices are not very reliable. Yet changing commodity prices do point up problems or benefits for certain in-

dustries or companies. For example, rising corn prices because
of a blight could affect the earnings of food processors substantially.

This baker's dozen of economic road signs given here deserve
to be watched. But always look for confirming signs. A rise in
wholesale prices might be short-lived if the Federal Reserve authorities are out to wring the steam out of the economy. And
there are times when the stock market is not only not a barometer,
it isn't even a thermometer. In 1946 the market broke sharply,
and the 1946 highs were not reestablished until 1950. Yet the
economy was then poised for the greatest expansion in its history.

What happens when all the economic indicators are on GO
and a *strike* threat or actual strike comes along? Don't get excited
and sell your stocks. Axioms in Wall Street are a dime a dozen,
and with a few notable exceptions, they mean little if anything.
One of these exceptions to the rule is "Never sell on strike news."
Losses in production, sales, and profits are usually made up
quickly and often more than just made up once the strike is
settled. A higher rate of operation after the strike spreads fixed
costs over a larger volume of output and hence lowers them and
improves the profit margin—despite a hefty wage hike. Management might also go into a collective bargaining meeting with its
earnings looking as bad as it thinks it can get away with. The
newspapers invariably blow up the loss in production and wages
caused by the work stoppage, blissfully unaware that cyclical
and seasonal declines have the same effect. Often a strike merely
reduces cyclical and seasonal swings, the result of the much-
higher-than-normal capacity utilization after the strike. Maybe
that is the reason why labor and management often take such a
long time in hammering out a new contract.

Political Fundamentals

In contrast with economic fundamentals, which are almost
always discountable, political fundamentals cannot often be discounted, except perhaps for a Presidential message to the Congress, news of which has been leaked for months to the press. A
Supreme Court decision could have a tremendous impact on an

industry, but we won't know what it is until it is announced. An invasion of Cambodia or an American police action in the Middle East usually comes without advance notice. The impact of a Congressional act is often very difficult to assess because a regulatory commission might take its time in administering it or will take months to develop guidelines for its implementation. Congressional mills usually grind slowly, and the result is often quite different from the harum-scarum original predictions on the part of the "experts."

When it comes to political fundamentals, Grandmother's saying, "The soup is never eaten as hot as it comes off the stove," applies. Before selling, watch things a little. On the other hand, don't fight the market. If selling comes in after a particular political event and lasts for a few days, maybe the smart thing is to get out. Wait it out on the sidelines. Don't average down. That usually turns out to be a sucker's game.

Technical Factors

Technical conditions arise in the market itself, as contrasted with economic and political fundamental conditions, which develop outside the stock market. A trader concerned with technical conditions tends to be interested in capital gains in a day trade, or he hopes to make his profits during a week or month or even longer.

The Short Interest Ratio

We say that the market is technically strong when there is a heavy short interest. About the middle of the month the stock exchanges release the "short interest" figures, that is, the number of shares that have been sold short since the previous monthly report as well as the total number of shares currently held on the short side. The shares sold short must sooner or later be repurchased. Thus it is considered a favorable market factor if the short interest is high, because if the market should rise (and the shorts are often wrong!), the shorts would rush in to buy to cover their short positions. The large short position was a big factor in the August, 1970, rally of the market. But watch it. If there is a big volume of short selling to arbitrage or against the box, the theory does not apply. For these short sellers have the stock; they don't need to rush out and cover their positions.

Look at the short interest ratio. It is the ratio of the total number of shares held short to the average daily trading volume of the past month. If the ratio is in the 1.7 to 2.0 range, it is considered bullish. Anything over 2.0 is considered *definitely* bullish. In the period 1965–1970, each time the short interest ratio rose above the 2.0 mark, it presaged a market advance.

Market Diary

Under this heading, *The Wall Street Journal* every day gives a report on yesterday's *breadth of the market*. How many issues were traded? How many advanced or declined or remained unchanged? Suppose on a given day 1,595 issues were traded on the Exchange and 929 advanced, 368 declined, and 298 were unchanged. In that case, the market would be deemed technically strong. I think such statistics are far more meaningful than the Dow-Jones industrial averages on 30 industrial stocks in a service economy. The breadth of the market gives a picture of the demand and supply conditions for *all* listed stocks.

Another item of importance is the *new highs* and *new lows*. If the market were to show for a few days consistently 30 to 40 new highs and only 5 or fewer new lows, it would be interpreted as a show of great strength. Here again, a *caveat:* Very often these figures include a lot of preferred stocks that, like bonds, rise or fall with interest rate changes. An allowance for this should be made when looking at the daily new highs and lows.

The Breadth Index

You can easily compute your own breadth index. All you need to do is take the number of advances and declines for each week from the *Market Diary*, measure the difference, and divide this difference by the number of stocks that were unchanged. The total is cumulated. Suppose last week 3,300 stocks advanced, 2,100 declined, and 1,000 were unchanged. The computation would be $3,300 - 2,100 = 1,200$, which, divided by 1,000, gives 1.2. This is added to the previous week's total since more stocks advanced than declined. Had more stocks declined than advanced, the difference would have to be subtracted from the previous week's total.

The importance of the breadth index is in its confirmation or nonconfirmation of peaks in the Dow-Jones industrial averages. Generally speaking, when market breadth confirms peaks, market leadership is broad enough so that no decline in the market seems imminent. On the other hand, when the breadth index does not confirm a new high in the averages, the market advance is limited to a small number of stocks and a decline seems to be around the corner.

The Odd-Lot Figures

There are those in the Street who think the odd-lot trading figures indicate market trends. The case for bullishness of the odd-lot statistics rests basically on the fact that the odd-lot investors are selling on balance, selling more shares than they buy. If the reverse is the case, it would be considered bearish. The normal tendency of the odd-lotters, say the protagonists of the theory, is to sell on a rally and buy on a decline. Odd-lot behavior, they continue, when viewed in conjunction with other technical indicators, can be meaningful.

There are all kinds of refinements to the theory. For example, some market analysts follow the behavior of the odd-lot short sellers during sustained market breaks. Their theory: A large amount of short selling by odd-lotters may help to signal the bottom of a market break. Other Wall Streeters, however, notably partners in the odd-lot houses, pooh-pooh the whole theory. They say the buying and selling patterns of the small investor are meaningless as a key to market trends.

Share Volume

Investors and traders are too often only price-conscious. Worse, some buy simply because the price of the stock is low or they sell short simply because the price is high. Such a mistake can easily be compounded when stocks are bought with a very large volume of shares outstanding and the unrealized capital gains are then used in the margin account to buy more, or they sell short stocks with a small volume of stock outstanding. The latter can easily turn around and advance sharply on a small buying volume. The former will require a heavy buying volume to push up the price some more.

The question of volume, in an individual situation or for the market as a whole, is probably more important than any other technical factor. When volume increases on rallies and declines on sell-offs, the market is considered technically strong. But if the volume declines on rallies and increases on sell-offs, the market is technically weak. From scholarly studies that have been made, it would seem that volume is of much greater use in analyzing short time periods down to one day or even hourly rather than using it over an entire stock cycle.

Volume can, however, indicate that a stock is being distributed rather than accumulated. Great activity in the stock, indicating distribution, presages a decline in the stock's price.

Stock Charts

Charts can be of inestimable help to both investors and traders, particularly traders. They are graphic pictures of numerical data. They save a lot of time and prevent misunderstandings that so often stem from a verbal or written report. One quick look will show important changes in a stock's price or market movements and the trend over a period of time.

Don't be interested in too many stocks. You won't know any of them. Concentrate on a few issues and really know their fundamentals and their charts. By trading in *your* stocks, long or short, you will be far more successful than by just playing the field. Follow a few simple rules: If, from your chart, you are not sure what the trend is, don't trade—don't buy or sell. Confine yourself to active stocks; stay away from slow, inactive stocks. Above all, don't use limit orders; buy or sell at the market. If fundamentals tell you XYZ is the stock to buy, there is no reason you should buy it when the stock's volume is declining on the up side. Unless volume picks up, the stock will come down. Like an airplane, it is losing power; it cannot climb any higher and has to come down to a lower altitude.

A *line chart* is easy to make. The Dow-Jones averages are shown thus in *The Wall Street Journal* every day. Take a look and let them guide you. On a vertical axis to the left, mark off dollar figures and divide them into eighths. If the stock is currently in the forties, your zero point at the bottom, where it joins a horizontal line, need not be less than perhaps 25. It may be very questionable whether this stock, on which you are bullish, would ever come down to 25. On the bottom, on the horizontal line mark off days and the daily volume.

Let's say that Motorola opened yesterday at 47; the high was 48, the low 47, and the close 48. Draw next to your vertical axis a vertical line between 48 and 47, and at the top make a tiny horizontal bar. This shows you at a glance that the stock was yesterday high at 48, low at 47, and it closed at the high for the day. If it closed at 47, a small horizontal bar would be drawn at 47, at the bottom of your vertical line illustrating the day's trading in the stock. Tomorrow move over a little to the right and draw the next day's trading. Don't forget the date and the *volume.* Try to figure out why the stock rose or declined on volume or whatever happened. Line charts are easy to make and take little time. Everything you need is right there every day in your newspaper.

To make a line chart requires no higher mathematics. Anybody can do it. If you know a little about statistics, try your hand at a *semilogarithmic scale.* The trouble with line charts is that they show the same quantitative change whether a stock moved from 10 to 20, a 100-percent rise, or from 50 to 60, a 20-percent rise. A "log" chart shows *rates* of change instead of equal changes in dollar amounts. On such a chart, if a stock is rising 20 percent a year over a period of years, it would be depicted as a straight trend line. This is what makes comparisons dramatic. If you plot three stocks, the one that has the greatest percentage gain will show the steepest line. Depending on fundamentals and your projections, maybe that is then the stock to buy with all your funds, compounded by leverage through margin. Diversification has its role to play, but there is nothing wrong, at times, with putting all your eggs in one basket and then watching the basket. Charts will help you do that.

Another type of chart is the *point and figure chart.* Prices of the stock are plotted not in the form of a continuous line but by a series of Xs. Depending on whether it is a one-point, two-point, or even a five-point chart, nothing is done, no X is entered, unless the stock moves one, two, or five points. Volume is of no interest to the point and figure chartist, nor is the time interval. He concentrates on the development of formations and patterns indicating major price movements. You won't know every time your stock moves one or more points, and therefore you can't make such charts. There are good chart services that are happy to sell them to you. Try the R. W. Mansfield Company. Transparent overlays will enable you to compare your stock's performance with the averages or with other stocks in the same industry.

The great advantage of point and figure charts over other types of charts is that they enable the chartist not only to draw trend lines and search out areas of support and resistance but also to make a "count" or congestion area analysis.

When a stock fluctuates between an upper and lower resistance level, say between 40 and 50, a so-called congestion area is formed on a one-point figure chart. These congestion areas are also usually separated by "walls," pronounced vertical moves to the left and right of such an area.

The point and figure chartist insists that there exists a direct relationship between the horizontal width of a congestion area and the extent of a subsequent vertical move, up or down. He counts thus across a congestion area and arrives at an up-side or down-side price target for the particular stock under study. The big question, of course, is: What are congestion areas, bases or tops? Do they predict an upward or downward movement in the stock? Of that the point and figure analyst can never be certain until a "breakout," upward or downward, occurs. But while he can never be certain, he can quite often derive important clues from the congestion area prior to the breakout.

Chart Formations

Stock charts show patterns. Although they deal with the past, what buying and selling has occurred, the patterns themselves are a valuable help in forecasting the future. There are endless chart formations, of which fourteen of the more basic formations are given in the illustration on page 294. The ones showing major distribution indicate the end of an upward movement in stock prices, if we use an individual stock's chart. Take the first one shown, the head and shoulders top. As the line forms the right shoulder, it fails to come up as high as the head and then turns down again. When the line goes through the neckline, after forming the right shoulder, this breakout presages a downward movement. Contrast this formation with the head and shoulders bottom, an accumulation pattern.

The Dow Theory

Around the turn of the century, Charles H. Dow, then editor of *The Wall Street Journal,* developed a theory that tries to forecast stock prices by interpreting the action of the Dow-Jones industrial and rail (now transportation) averages. It is based on the premise that the stock market shows at all times three movements: a primary or long-term, a secondary, and a daily movement. As far as the theory is concerned, daily movements are disregarded as being unimportant. The primary trend is the major bull or bear market, and secondary movements or reactions, lasting from two weeks to one month or more, help in forecasting the long-term trend. Secondary reactions are technical reactions; they are caused by profit taking, by shorts or longs. Over recent years, bull markets have lasted much longer than bear markets, a reflection, no doubt, of the increasing stability of the economy.

Common Basic Formations Indicating

Major Distributions   Major Accumulations

1. Head and shoulders top
2. The common downward turn (umbrella pattern)
3. Triangular top
4. Descending top
5. Double top
6. Complex top (1 and 5 together)
7. The broadening top

8. Head and shoulders bottom
9. The common upward turn (saucer pattern)
10. Triangular bottom
11. Ascending bottom
12. Double bottom
13. Complex bottom (8 and 12 together)
14. The broadening bottom

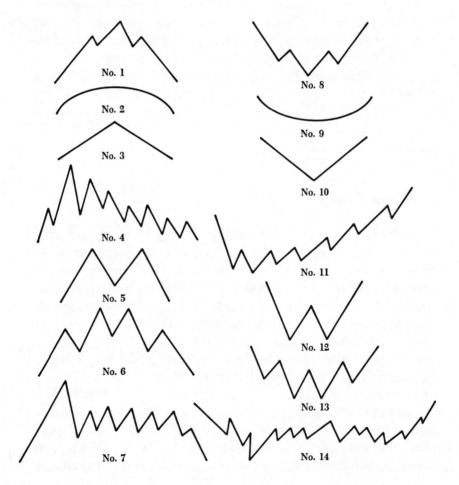

No. 1
No. 2
No. 3
No. 4
No. 5
No. 6
No. 7
No. 8
No. 9
No. 10
No. 11
No. 12
No. 13
No. 14

Originally, the Dow theory was really a business-cycle theory. The industrial averages show production and the rails, the movement of goods into industrial, wholesale, and retail channels. As long as goods were produced in high volume and moved smoothly into consumer channels without piling up as compulsory inventories, a state of prosperity existed and profits and dividends would be good. Therefore the industrial and rail averages, said Mr. Dow, discount all changes in production and transportation and in corporate earnings and dividends.

A bull or bear market is never definitely established until there is a "confirmation," that is, until both averages confirm the new primary trend. The time interval elapsing until a confirmation occurs plays no role. According to the confirmed Dow theorist, confirmations occur either by the two averages making lines and registering a breakout or by the averages registering new highs or new lows, that is, by technical reactions.

When an average, industrial or rail, is making a line, it means the demand for and the supply of stocks are in equilibrium. Suppose the rail (transportation) averages fluctuate between 207 and 212, and the industrials between 920 and 900. If both averages should push above 207 and 920, a definitely bullish signal is given. The breakouts could be weeks apart. If the breakout is on the down side, the signal would be bearish. There is no meaningful signal unless one average confirms that of the other.

Suppose we have an ascending bottom (chart formation No. 11 in our illustration). Here each rise exceeds the previous peak and each decline falls to a point less than the previous low. If the industrial and rail averages make a new high on each secondary reaction, the averages are said to confirm a continuation of the bull market trend. Should only one of the averages show such a pattern, the signal is considered meaningless. No confirmation has been given. Of course, a confirmation on the downside (figure No. 4) would indicate a bear market. There is again no time limit during which one average must confirm a primary movement, up or down.

What has been the record of the Dow theory? A big question mark. There are those who say, "Investors have a better chance by flipping coins (50–50) than by following the Dow theory." On the other side, there are highly regarded individuals like the late Edmund W. Tabell and his son, Anthony W. Tabell, who state that the theory's "ability to call major turning points in the market has been extremely good." But even they admit that the Dow theory has its real value only when long, wide upward or downward movements are involved. In sideways mar· kets, it is likely to give "whipsaw signals"—buying signals near the top of a trading range, and selling signals near the bottom of a trading range.

Perhaps this can be said: No matter how much or how little a theory is justified, if enough people accept it and act upon it, it is bound "to work." I have for years worked on an index based on how many people walk toward Trinity Church on Wall Street between 4:30 and 5:30 P.M. If more people walk on the right side of the Street, the market will unfailingly go up the next day. If more people walk on the left side, the market will unfailingly go down the next day. The index can even be weighted by the poundage of the walkers. If enough people act on my "theory" and the press gives it enough publicity, I shall go down in financial history as another Charlie Dow; it might be known as Lohman's axiom.

No matter how silly a theory is—and there have been some beauties in Wall Street over the years—if enough people act on it, it isn't silly any longer. Three things bug me about the *industrial* averages: (1) There are usually about 1,700 issues traded on the NYSE, but the Dow-Jones industrial averages consist of only 30 industrial stocks. This is why I think the breadth index is so significant. (2) The horribly inflated *point* index (if your broker tells you the averages are up five *dollars,* change brokers) is unweighted, a condition which the NYSE tried to remedy by introducing its own *dollar* index, weighted by the number of shares each company has listed. (3) We are no longer living in an industrial economy, but in a service economy. The service industry is today more important than manufacturing. So it all points to the fact, as our title indicates, that investing and trading in securities will remain an art; it will never descend to the category of mere mechanics. Keep this in mind when you read market letters and the opinions of "experts." Market letters are known in the inner circles of Wall Street as fly paper. The firm incurs the expenses of printing and mailing them because it hopes that customers and their orders will get stuck to them. I once wrote a *Principles of Economics* book with over seven hundred pages. Now I know it can be expressed more simply by saying that there is no such thing as a free lunch, particularly in Wall Street.

Summary

1. Fundamental economic and political plus technical factors, as well as the prevailing mood of investors, determine the prices of securities.

2. There is no one theory that can possibly tell you at what P/E ratio you should buy a stock. It will depend on the stock and market trends.

3. Some stocks will consistently reflect the growth in economic aggregates more than others. These are the stocks to buy.

4. Read the economic road signs. They will tell you when to get on or off the "turnpike."

5. Never sell stocks on strike news.

6. Economic news items are usually discounted; political factors are usually difficult to discount. They happen too quickly.

7. If the short interest ratio is over 2.0, *buy.*

8. The breadth index is a good check on the narrow Dow-Jones unweighted industrial averages.

9. Volume is important.

10. Make a line chart of your stock(s) and study it. If you want point and figure charts, you can easily buy them—at a price.

11. Study chart formations. No matter how bullish you are on a stock for the long term, it is silly to buy it if the chart shows a complex top (figure No. 6 on page 294).

12. Know what the Dow theory says. If a lot of people react on a confirmation, follow them. Don't fight the market, but park your chair close to an open door.

CHAPTER 18

The Role of the Money Market

The money market plays a crucial role in the determination of trends in securities markets and hence of securities prices. It has been—and for the overwhelming majority of investors it still is—a book with seven seals, and the topic receives scant attention in investment texts. This is why so many investors show such a bad sense of timing in going into or out of the stock market.

The money market, as the name indicates, deals with money. As was sketchily pointed out in Chapter 6, it is part of the over-the-counter securities market. While there is a certain interrelationship between the capital funds market and the money market, the former is primarily based on savings, and the latter on credit.

Money Is Nothing but a Ticket

Modern man has become entangled in the net of a ramified division of labor. Look around you. Everybody performs different tasks, but very few raise their own food, make their own clothing, or build their own shelter. We sell our goods and, largely, services, and in return we receive money in one form or another, usually in "bank money," which we exchange for the goods and services we need and want. Ask anybody whether his paycheck is money, and he will probably say, "Of course it is, you nut." But the check is not money. It is simply an order for money. The writer of the check orders his bank to pay out of his checking account x dollars to Mr. William J. Jones, the payee. The money is the bank demand deposit, not the check.

Money is a ticket. It doesn't matter of what it is made. People don't understand this either. That is why they have so often been so wrong about an increase in the price of gold when they decided to buy gold shares. When the price of gold eventually rises, as it inevitably must, they will miss the turn again.

Your laundry ticket entitles you to a specific performance on the part of society, namely, the return of your laundry. What happens if the laundry isn't on the shelf? Your laundry "money" is, at least temporarily, worthless. A twenty-dollar Federal Reserve Note or your check drawn on your bank demand deposit entitles you to a virtually unlimited variety of performances up to the value of twenty dollars. As a consumer you may spend it or save it, or you can translate it into goods and services or combinations thereof as you wish, subject to the prevailing law. As a producer you can hire labor and management, buy equipment and land, and produce something that others want. If the goods and services you want are not available, your money, like your laundry ticket, ceases to have much value. In the late fall of 1923, one dollar was the equivalent of 4.2 trillion German marks. Million-mark notes were lying in the gutter, and nobody bothered to pick them up, not even the street sweepers, because inflation had made them nearly worthless. Banks would bundle up "obsolete money" and sell it to a scrap dealer who bought old paper.

Saving and Spending

Usually we don't think of the two faces of money: the real side consisting of consumer and capital goods and services, and the other, the monetary side, in our society made up primarily of bank demand deposits, checking accounts, and to a much smaller degree, currency. When the relationship between the real and the monetary side, between goods and services and money, gets out of line, the division-of-labor machinery starts to sputter and miss or to overheat. Insufficient money means deflation, unemployment, and bear markets, and too much money spells inflation and a runaway market.

When a corporation sells bonds or stocks in the primary market, it competes for savings with the federal government, which might have to finance a deficit under conditions of high employment; with the states and local governments, which must raise money to finance public capital projects; with the mortgage market; and to some extent with consumers who want to buy durable consumer goods on time. Bonds and stocks are sold by the issuers because they want to exchange the proceeds, money, for goods and services to build highways or new plants, to buy new equipment and inventory, or to finance others to buy their goods. If these goods and services aren't there or are in scarce supply, they will bid more for them to get them away from others; up go prices and wages, and on we go toward a crackup. To make sure that the real side of the equation, the goods and services, is there, a sufficient volume of savings must exist.

When we save, we don't consume, and thus we create unwanted goods and services. With the money savings, new securities are bought in the primary market. The issuers now go out and use the money (the proceeds of the sale of the securities) to buy the goods and services made available by the savers. This is what is known as the process of capital formation. People who spend less than they receive are savers, whether they be individuals, corporations, or governments. Credit cannot be used to buy a twenty-year bond, because credit necessitates repayment much sooner. When a lot of unemployed people and resources exist, credit, up to a point, can be substituted for savings. But if the four basic resources of any society—land, labor, capital goods, and management—are not available in sufficient quantities, the substitution of credit for savings can only result in an inflationary mess.

We all want a higher per capita standard of living. This is a real concept, not a monetary one. With our rising population, this can only be accomplished by increasing our output of goods and services. I almost said "by increasing our GNP." Here again, guard yourself against being fooled. If we spend billions on cleaning up our environment, this will not directly contribute to a higher standard of living. Or a better illustration: Billions spent for defense will increase GNP, but not our per capita standard of living.

To produce more tomorrow, a high-employment society must take less today. We must consume less and save, so that resources become available that can be turned into private and public capital goods. A new machine, a highway, a power plant, flood control, and irrigation help to produce more tomorrow. This is a simple economic lesson that is so difficult for the emerging countries to learn, but even the allegedly mature countries have difficulties mastering it. Everybody always wants a bike, car, TV set, a steak this week rather than the week after next.

For analytical purposes, the description must be in black and white terms. Life doesn't know that; it only knows grays, lighter or darker grays. It is impossible to draw a clear dividing line between credit and savings, although on the whole things work the way I have described them. When a commercial bank cannot make all the loans it wants to make, it will buy government securities or municipal bonds. But it will not buy the very long maturities. The bank might also go into the money market in which we trade private and public debt instruments with a maturity of one day to one year.

The Nature of the Money Market

The money market has a threefold purpose: In it individuals, banks, corporations, and public bodies adjust their liquidity requirements; through it the Federal Reserve authorities change the nation's money supply; and the Treasury (re)finances itself.

If individuals and institutions are more liquid than they want to be, they will exchange nonearning cash for a short-term earning asset such as a Treasury bill. It has to be short-term in order to be riskless. In Chapter 13 the riskless aspect of a T-bill was discussed. Should the owners of short-term money market instruments need cash, they will sell them.

Whenever our national money managers, the Federal Reserve authorities, wish to influence the nation's money supply, they usually do it by buying and selling government securities in the money market.

As our economy expands, we shall need more money, particularly more bank money, bank demand deposits. Over 90 percent of all our transactions are settled through checks, through bank demand deposits. We must always try to keep the real side and the monetary side in balance. Too much money spells inflationary troubles; too little, deflationary headaches.

Back in December, 1941, the Federal Reserve banks had $2 billion in government securities. In the fall of 1971 they owned over $68 billion worth of them. By 1980 that figure will be still larger, because our expanding economy needs more money. Don't let the federal debt frighten you, as long as it is sensibly handled. Part of it, a lot, is needed to give our economy the liquidity it must have. And while the owners of the Federal Reserve banks, the member commercial banks, received in 1969 a measly $39,237,000 in a 6-percent fixed dividend, the Treasury got $3,019,161,000 from the "Fed." Here you have it: An expanding economy needs money, and the "Fed" supplies it by buying government securities in the market. But not directly from the Treasury because in that direction lies monetary chaos. As the "Fed's" amount of government securities owned increases, the Treasury gets more of a "kickback" from the interest payments.

Why does the Federal Reserve increase the money supply when it buys government bonds and decrease it when it sells? Simple. Just visualize the process; it is a kind of socialized bookkeeping. Let's say that the Federal Reserve Bank of New York, acting for the system, buys $10 million of T-bills from a government securities nonbank or bank dealer or from more than one. The dealer(s) will deliver the government securities to the "Fed" and receive payment in the form of a credit. The Federal Reserve Bank will credit on its books the reserve accounts, the deposits, of the banks concerned. The banks, in turn, will credit the dealers' accounts with the proceeds of the "cash" sale. Not only does a dealer like Salomon Brothers have the money to pay its client, the seller of the bills; SB's bank also has more money to lend and so has the entire banking system. And that is very important.

Member bank deposits, or reserves as they are usually called, at the Federal Reserve banks are "high-powered dollars," subject to multiple credit expansion through the operation of the banking system. Bank A has more money and makes a loan the proceeds of which flow into Bank B. It now has more money to lend, and so it goes. At the present time, each dollar the Federal Reserve provides through open-market buying can be expanded into about $6.50 of bank deposits in the country if we assume no leakage through an increased currency outflow from banks and maximum credit expansion. The "Fed" operates on a powerful leverage—on the buying or the selling side of the market.

On balance, since we are and must be an expanding economy, the "Fed" has been a buyer of government securities. Occasionally they sell or, more likely, throttle down the rate of monetary expansion. This is what gives the stock market the jitters. But you will always have an advance notice of market turns—if you read the signs. They will show you the range of action. Of course nobody can tell you the exact point of a turn. This chapter will give you signs so that you, too, can read the monetary scoreboard when it lights up—green, amber, or red. Sometimes the red lights are flashing and bells are ringing, but the stock market keeps merrily on its way up—for a while. Read carefully what I say here, and I can guarantee you that your sense of timing will improve.

The Treasury will be in the money market when it refinances a short-term debt or finances part of a new deficit with bills.

Will the "Fed" Ever Run out of Money?

As we march on toward our goal of the second trillion dollars in GNP, we shall need more "money." But what'll happen if the "Fed" ever runs out of money? That's one thing you won't have to worry about. The Federal Reserve system "manufactures" money, credit—any amount of it. There is no limit. It is not hobbled by legal reserve requirements, and we have cut the golden umbilical cord. But this makes it mandatory that the Treasury never get its hand into the credit cookie jar. Once the central bank loses its independence and becomes the errand boy of the Treasury, then hock your wife's jewels, go into debt as far as you can, and buy, buy, buy anything of value, for the worst kind of inflation is going to come that you ever saw or read about in American history books. European monetary history amply proves that point.

Interrelationships in Financial Markets

When things tighten up in the money market, the stock market has to come down—sooner or later. If it is later, the decline will be that much more severe. The "Fed" has a drum over on Liberty Street in New York, and when it beats on it, the reverberations go through the entire finance industry.

When it tightens the monetary screws, bank credit becomes costlier and more difficult to obtain. You will then read in the gossip column of *The Wall Street Journal* ("Abreast of the Market") that "banks are becoming more selective in extending credit." A merchant may be forced to sell stocks out of his portfolio to raise the cash he needs. Market makers pull in their horns and reduce positions. Interest rates rise in the money market, and bond prices come down. Smart people see the trend, sell their bonds, preferred stocks, and common stocks, and take refuge in the storm cellar of short-term public and private debt instruments. Even here not everything is always safe, as shown by the default of the Penn Central on its commercial paper.

Just as the money and securities markets are linked through the medium of expanding or contracting credit, so are capital funds markets and stock markets connected.

Almost until the end of the 1960s, individuals didn't buy bonds. The rates didn't particularly attract them. The bond market was primarily patronized by the institutional investors such as pension funds, insurance companies, the balanced mutual funds, and the trust departments of banks. Individuals were stock buyers primarily because their brokers, whose ignorance often matches that of the clients, had told them, "Buy common stocks. They are good inflation hedges." And then to put the lie to this much abused cliché, during one of the steepest inflationary developments in our history, the stock market went down and kept going down while bond interest rates went higher.

The individuals now disgusted with the stock market, not to say scared of it, and unhappy with the rate that savings institutions were paying decided to buy the luscious AAA and AA bonds with a coupon of 9 percent and even a little higher. While the "smart" professionals, the institutional investors, were sitting on the sidelines, individuals gobbled up bonds. Obviously this money did not go into the stock market, and thus the volume of trading had to come down by this extent. Whenever people's or institutions' savings go directly or indirectly into bonds or mortgages, the demand for stocks will suffer.

Sophisticated individuals will read the signs and temporarily go into the money market and buy the merchandise there. A lot of brokers wait. Their clients have losses. Instead of taking them out of the market with a bruise, they are afraid to call them. And so the clients ride the stocks down, finally become panicky, or need money desperately and sell—often just before the turn. A market turn will only be recognized *after* it has occurred. There is nothing you can do about that. But being able to read money market indicators will at least give you a range within which buying or selling seems advisable.

The Merchandise in the Money Market

Besides *short-term government securities,* which the Federal Reserve authorities might buy or sell outright or under a repurchase agreement, there are the federal agency short-term obligations such as those of the Federal Land Banks, Federal Home Loan Banks, or FNMA notes. There are also short-term municipal IOUs.

Commercial paper is to corporations, including bank holding companies, what T-bills are for the Treasury. By selling their IOUs, they are tapping the money market; corporations with surplus cash, and any other investor, are buying them for short-term investment with a maturity up to nine months. Between 1964 and the Penn Central default of its paper, the volume of commercial paper nearly quintupled, from $8.3 to nearly $40 billion at the beginning of June, 1970. Paper placed directly with a bank (for its trust department, for example) or other institutional investors will usually carry a somewhat lower yield than paper sold through a Wall Street house as dealer, because its maturities are adjusted to the convenience of the institutional investor.

Bankers' acceptances are primarily used in the financing of foreign trade. Through an irrevocable letter of credit, the bank permits a foreign exporter to draw on it. When the bank accepts the time draft, it becomes a banker's acceptance—a negotiable instrument that can be discounted by a money market dealer for resale to an investor. The use of such an acceptance enables the seller, or exporter, to receive immediate payment; he receives its discounted value. The buyer, or importer, of the goods need not pay until the goods are received or later. The advantage to investors is that they can buy commercial paper and bankers' acceptances and improve their yield by 1 percent or more over investing in T-bills.

Call loans represent short-term funds lent by commercial banks to securities houses to enable them to finance their margin customers. While technically the call provision allows termination of the loan arrangement by either the lender or the borrower on a one-day notice, in reality these loans are not money market loans at all. If a bank were to call a broker's loan, it would lose a lot of other brokerage accounts. What is, however, interesting to investors is the behavior of the stock market's activity, both as to volume and prices, when margin requirements are changed by the Federal Reserve.

Generally reductions in margin have tended to reverse pre-change patterns more than increases. When margin requirements are decreased, stock volume increases noticeably from three to six months prior to the change. It then tends to decline until a month after the decrease, and from there on market volume rises markedly. Stock prices show a tendency to reverse the trend after a margin reduction. But usually they tend to maintain their upward movement after a margin requirement increase.

In February, 1961, a Wall Street bank started to issue negotiable time certificates of deposits. Since then the *Certificates of Deposit* (CDs for short) have become a very important money market instrument, with over twenty billion dollars outstanding in the fall of 1970. This invention was a very successful defensive move on the part of banks. As interest rates started to rise from the low levels of the 1950s, corporations reduced their bank demand deposits and put funds into income-yielding money market instruments. Until 1961 banks did not accept corporate time deposits. The CD matures from thirty days to one year. Upon maturity the bank will pay the amount of the deposit plus interest to the bearer. This makes the CD readily negotiable and permits it to be traded on a discounted basis in the money market.

The CD enables a bank to attract funds and permits any investor to put large sums of money in a short-term instrument with a tailored maturity date at a substantially higher yield than T-bills. The banks, by raising or lowering the CD rates, can adjust their money inflow; however, how high the rate can be is set by the Board of Governors of the Federal Reserve System.

With the credit crunches of the late 1960s, banks developed still another money market instrument to obtain lendable funds. This was an international instrument—*the Euro-dollar.* Euro-dollars can be defined simply as dollar balances that are traded outside the United States. But the sources of Euro-dollars are not necessarily European; they could be from Latin America, the Middle East, Canada, or any other country of the world. Here is a pool of probably about fifty billion dollars that knows no frontiers; there are no national barriers in this money market sector. When the "Fed" set the CD rate below the yields available on other money market instruments, the banks lost funds heavily as the CDs matured, and corporations withdrew the funds and invested them elsewhere. To recoup these losses, the big American banks raided the Euro-dollar market.

Corporations are regular borrowers in the Euro-dollar market, usually with the American bank as a middleman; short-circuiting the bank would involve the company in a lot of time-consuming, costly trouble. A good United States company, with an AAA or AA rating, can get $100 or $200 million in one fell swoop. A New York banker says, "A good corporation borrower can get much more money easily with less restrictions" than at home. Euro-dollar rates are above the American prime rate, the rate that banks charge their borrowers with the highest credit rating.

The most actively traded items in the money market are

federal funds, Wall Street's "cashiest cash." Federal funds are funds on deposit at any of our twelve Federal Reserve banks and their twenty-four branches. They are good today. A New York bank draft is New York clearing-house money and good only on the next business day. A draft drawn on a San Francisco bank is good only after the second business day.

The federal funds rate is an important roadsign. It shows the pressure that exists in the money market, and particularly on banks. Every Wednesday the big banks must balance their legal reserve position with their respective Federal Reserve banks, since the law requires them to carry a certain legal reserve against their time and demand deposits. This reserve is primarily in the form of funds on deposit at the "Fed," and to a much, much lesser degree, currency in the banks' own vaults.

Suppose a bank is short $50 million on Wednesday forenoon. It can then go into the money market and buy federal funds from another bank that has excess reserves. In interbank transactions no physical transfer occurs. The "Fed" will debit the selling bank's reserve balance and credit the buyer's balance. The next day the bookkeeping transaction is reversed. The buyer of federal funds usually pays the interest in a separate transfer.

When a bank buys federal funds from another bank, it really borrows the other bank's excess reserves for a day, or rarely, over a weekend. The Federal Reserve banks pay no interest on the member banks' balances with them. Banks are therefore anxious to earn something on these deposits. A bank may have excess reserves only for a day or two before they are absorbed by a rise in deposits or lost through an adverse clearing balance. If it can get a day's interest, that is just so much found money. Banks from all over the country put such excess reserves into the New York money market through the "Fed's" own wire system to earn extra money.

The pressure in the money market can be tremendous on the weekly settlement day, and the stock market feels it. The legal reserve requirement is an average for the week, or for the smaller banks for two weeks. If a bank with $100 million deposits and a 10-percent reserve requirement is short $10 million one day, the next day the deficiency would be $20 million, and the third day $30 million. Saturdays and Sundays count too! A deficiency is cumulative, because every day a bank is supposed to have its legal reserve requirement covered.

In addition to federal funds trading to meet banks' legal reserve requirements, they are used as payment in transactions involving such other money market instruments as government securities, commercial paper, and time certificates of deposit. Federal funds are thus a basic factor in the money market, and their rate reflects pressure or ease. And the stock market wants to know how much money there is and how fast it turns over.

The Wall Street Journal gives a money rate table every day. Study it every day to establish a trend. If the federal funds rate is *consistently* substantially below the prime rate, you can be quite sure that a decrease in the prime rate is around the corner, no matter what a dozen bank presidents are saying. Such a decrease would be a very bullish factor for both the bond and the stock market. If the funds rate is consistently above the prime rate, there is a prime rate increase ahead as well as a decrease in stock market prices, at least initially.

The Tools of Our Money Managers

Our national money managers, the Federal Reserve authorities, have several control devices at their disposal. To restrict credit, they can do any of the following.

Sell government securities in the open market or slow down and decrease the rate of their buying of government securities.

Increase legal reserve requirements and impound more of the banks' money. The banking system's ability to expand credit has thus been reduced.

Increase the discount rate, the interest rate that member banks must pay when they borrow from their Federal Reserve banks.

Through moral suasion, an "open mouth" policy, tell member banks to reduce their lending activities. If banks are very tight, this can be quite effective, for borrowing from the "Fed" is still a privilege rather than a right.

Under Regulation Q decrease the interest rate that banks are permitted to pay on CDs.

Increase margin requirements—up to 100 percent if they wish. This does not affect the money supply, only the use of credit.

Any or all of these steps are bad news for the stock market. An easing of the money supply would, of course, be effected by reversing these steps. When this was done in 1970, it was good news for the stock market.

Monetary Indicators and the Friday Figures

Every Friday on the front page of *The Wall Street Journal* under "What's New—Business and Finance," there appears an item summarizing the trend in the so-called Friday bank figures, with a story on an inside page. These are the bank and money statistics as of the close of the preceding Wednesday. They are released by the Federal Reserve Bank of New York on Thursday afternoon and appear in Friday's newspapers.

Jot a few figures down every Friday. One or two weekly figures don't mean a thing. All sorts of fortuitous developments can occur. For example, the weather gets bad; airplanes don't fly, and checks are not collected. Banks in the East receive credit for checks deposited at Federal Reserve banks drawn on Far West banks before they are debited to the accounts. Result: The Far West banks still have the money and the Eastern banks have it too. The "float" has gone up, increasing the money supply. What is significant is the trend. To establish one will take anywhere from four to six weeks, at least. To buy stocks or bonds in the face of a steadily tightening money supply is flirting with trouble. The market may still continue to go up. Go ahead and trade, but park your chair close to an open door. When money gets tighter and tighter, this is the time to get out, take refuge with your dollars in short-term money market instruments, and *wait.*

Important items in the Friday figures are the following:

Member Bank Borrowings. They indicate how deep the banks are in hock to their Federal Reserve banks. A decreasing trend tells you that money is getting easier; a rising trend, that money is getting tighter. Flukes can occur. For example, a larger than anticipated currency outflow from the banks can leave them strapped. Rather than sell T-bills (banks, like everybody else, buy on the higher offer and sell at the lower bid price) and buy them back a couple of days later, banks prefer to borrow from their Federal Reserve bank. I repeat: It is difficult to spot a trend in less than a month or more. There is no hurry to act. The stock market adjusts to money market figures very slowly, but inexorably.

Net Borrowed Reserves or Net Free Reserves. They show how much money the member banks actually have. They are the difference between member banks' excess reserves, the funds in excess of required legal reserves, and member bank borrowings. If banks still have excess funds after deducting member bank borrowings, they are called net free reserves. If the figure is a minus item, they are called net borrowed reserves.

Let's say that as of a given Wednesday, member bank borrowings are $762 million and excess reserves $264 million; the net borrowed reserves would be $498 million. In other words, the banks really don't have any money over and above their required reserves. They could not have met them had they not borrowed.

The trend of net borrowed reserves was down between midsummer, 1969, and late summer, 1970. In July, 1969, net borrowed reserves were over $1 billion. For several months following, they stayed at a level somewhat below $1 billion. But from December on, there was a noticeable decrease. For several weeks in July, they shot up once again, owing to a number of more or less extraneous factors, to $1,451 million. This was the peak, and from there on the figures have steadily declined. By mid-September, 1970, the Federal Reserve authorities had apparently decided on a level of net borrowed reserves of $500 million. Undoubtedly, this trend was a big factor in the market's rally. If the money supply is steadily increased, the day must then come when net borrowed reserves become free reserves—when banks actually have more money than they need to meet their legal reserve requirements. Such a trend would be accompanied by lower interest rates and a rising stock market, the international situation permitting. By early spring of 1971, free reserves were again temporarily established. Money had indeed become easier. Stocks were *up*.

The movements in the reserve position of member banks have tended to show a rough parallelism with the movement in short-term interest rates. When they decline, there is a tendency for investors to go into the longer maturities to capture higher yields, and that in turn will bring the long-term rate down. But interest rates, particularly long-term rates, will stay for some time to come at a much higher level than we considered "normal" in the past.

The Money Supply. During much of the 1950s and 1960s, the Federal Reserve authorities tended to rely on the money market tone as guide for monetary policy. More recently, however, they said, ". . . increased stress should be placed on the objective of achieving modest growth in the monetary aggregates, with about equal weight being given to bank credit and the money stock." Therefore, every week, read what the money supply is doing, and keep track of it.

The money supply, narrowly defined, consists of the non-bank public's holding of coins and currency plus demand deposits, other than interbank deposits and United States Treasury deposits in banks. If we were to include interbank deposits, we would count deposits twice, and Treasury deposits behave quite differently from other deposits. Some economists, a minority, define the money supply more broadly and add time and savings deposits at commercial banks to it. For your purposes, it really doesn't matter what you pick up in the newspapers and use. Whatever figure you do use, follow it consistently.

The Bank Credit Proxy. This proxy for member banks uses total deposit liabilities of member banks to the approximate total bank loan and investment assets (or bank credit). Always look for a trend. All kinds of things can happen. For example, United States banks can borrow from their foreign branches, and banks may sell off loans to the parent one-bank holding companies. This would show up as an increase in the money supply, but has nothing to do with the trend in the money supply or Federal Reserve policy.

The three money aggregates—the money supplies both

broadly and narrowly defined and bank credit (the banks' total loans and investments)—have roughly an equal correlation with movements in Gross National Product and other economic measures, and these movements, of course, affect the stock market—after a lag.

Whatever you do, don't pay any attention to any other stories about Federal Reserve intent and policy except the Friday figures. What counts is the net effect on the money supply and bank figures of Federal Reserve action. There are times when the Federal Reserve will simply buy or sell government securities in order to offset a seasonal flow of currency.

Currency in circulation outside the banks increased between October 31, 1970, and December 31, 1970, from $55,020 million to $57,093 million. This reduced bank reserves—the high-powered dollars—by over $2 billion. Naturally, the "Fed" had to offset such a seasonal outflow by open-market purchases. To say that these purchases constitute a measure of Federal Reserve monetary policy is, of course, nonsense. Such purchases are "defensive" in nature. By the end of January, 1971, currency in circulation had dropped back almost to the October 31 level. The Federal Reserve would not want such an increase in member bank reserves, subject to multiple credit expansion; and to offset the currency inflow, it sold in the open market. Again this had no meaning as far as trends were concerned.

Summary

1. Within our country, money is merely a ticket; it is really social bookkeeping.

2. What makes us prosper is a proper relationship between saving and spending, between the supply of money and the availability of resources, the real side.

3. The money market is a place to adjust liquidity needs and take refuge.

4. The money market is also the vehicle through which the Federal Reserve authorities change the nation's money supply.

5. The Federal Reserve operates on leverage; member bank deposits at the Federal Reserve banks are "high-powered" dollars.

6. As the economy expands, it needs more money. The Federal Reserve will supply it and never run out of it.

7. When money gets tighter and keeps on getting tighter, think of getting out of the stock or bond market, and take refuge in high-yielding money market instruments.

8. The Federal Reserve authorities can increase or decrease the money supply through open market operations, moral suasion, and by changing legal reserve requirements and the discount rates. Regulation "Q," too, can play an important role.

9. Read the Friday figures regularly and jot them down.

10. Member bank borrowings and reserves indicate the pressure or ease that prevails in the banking system.

11. The money supply and bank credit roughly correlate with movements in the economy—output, income, employment, prices, and profits.

12. Watch trends in the money market and in money aggregates. They will indicate ranges of action when it may be wise to buy or sell stocks or bonds.

CHAPTER 19

What Can Be Done to Whittle Down

My Tax Bill?

Throughout the book, suggestions have been made as to ways to reduce or completely avoid a tax liability. I shall briefly summarize them here in the order in which they were originally given, and where necessary, I'll elaborate. In addition, proposals for sizable tax reductions will be presented.

Stock Dividends

Stock dividends that are paid in the same stock as that held by the investor are not taxable if kept. If the stock dividend is sold, he would be taxed on a long-term capital-gains basis on any portion of the selling price that represented a capital gain to him. It makes no difference what shares are sold, as long as the original stock was bought six months and a day or more ago. If the stock was held less than six months and one day, the gain would be short-term. Don't sell a stock dividend until you have held the original stock for over a six-month period if you want to avoid adding needlessly to your tax bill.

Stay clear of corporations that give shareholders the option of taking dividends in cash or in stock. Under the Tax Reform Act of 1969 a stock dividend (or its equivalent) is taxable if one class of common stockholders receives cash and another class of common stockholders gets a stock dividend (or its equivalent). The government says this is an arrangement that is tantamount to an election to receive cash or stock. Changes in conversion ratios that serve to increase the proportionate interest of a class of shareholders in a company are treated as a taxable stock dividend.

All stock distributions on preferred stock are considered a substitute for cash and are taxable.

If you don't own any common stocks and have your money in the savings bank at 5 percent or a little higher, take about $3,300 and buy 140 shares of the Ohio Edison Company, a very fine electric company. Your dividend on these shares will be a little over $200 a year, completely tax-free to any husband-and-wife team if the securities are registered in joint tenancy. Every individual has a $100 dividend exemption. If Junior files a tax return, why not increase his deductions by $100 through the purchase of a high-grade dividend-paying common stock? It is awfully easy for two people to throw $50 each year away if you're in the 25-percent income tax bracket. Don't do it. Fifty dollars invested annually over a period of 20 years is going to give you a fine vacation trip when you retire.

Corporate Investors

Corporate investors enjoy an 85-percent tax exemption on all corporate dividends, on common stock as well as on preferred stock. If a corporate business has temporarily idle surplus funds and can catch two or more quarterly dividend payments, I recommend investing temporarily in high-grade preferreds. The after-tax return to the company will be far more attractive on them than the completely taxable return from Treasury bills, commercial paper, or bank CDs. In view of the pronounced tendency of common stocks to fluctuate in value, they are unsuitable for the investment of temporarily idle corporate funds.

A Disappearing Opportunity

Over one hundred corporations, primarily utilities, have issued partially or wholly tax-exempt cash dividends. Any individual can still latch on to them until June 30, 1972. Ask your broker for a list of these companies.

Income Bonds

Since income bonds sell "flat," with the interest on until the annual ex-interest date, the interest accrual on an income bond bought right after the ex-interest day and sold prior to the next one is treated as a long-term capital gain. Unfortunately these bonds tend to have a rather high credit risk.

Government Securities

To reduce federal estate taxes, buy the deep-discount long-term United States Treasury bonds and put them into the estate prior to the owner's death. The Treasury is willing to accept them at par for the payment of any federal estate-tax liabilities.

The nonmarketable savings bonds have tax advantages that are often overlooked by their owners. Individuals who are not in a high tax bracket should declare the tax on each year's value appreciation. Those in higher tax brackets would be wise to carry the appreciation on the original bonds plus extensions over into the post-retirement period when income and taxes will be lower.

The accumulated value of E bonds can also be converted tax-free into ten-year H bonds. No tax will be payable on the accrued series E interest until such time as the bonds are being surrendered for cash or mature.

The New Housing Authority Bonds or Notes, issued in your state, are considered direct obligations of the United States Government. They are unique in that they are exempt from the federal as well as from the state and any local income taxes in your state. If you buy such securities issued in another state than the one you claim as your domicile, you must pay your state and local income taxes on the interest.

Municipal Securities

Municipal securities are exempt from the federal income tax as well as from any state and local income taxes if they were issued in the state that the investor claims as domicile. This tax exemption extends to income derived from the Municipal Investment Trusts.

Mutual Funds

No matter for how short a period you have been holding mutual fund shares, any long-term capital-gains distribution by the fund will be a long-term capital gain to you.

The capital shares of the dual purpose funds pay no income until the early 1980s. They are only entitled to capital gains made by the fund and therefore make extremely attractive vehicles for a practically assured substantial capital appreciation.

The Exchange Fund, or swap fund, was the greatest invention for postponing capital-gains taxes. Watch for it. Maybe it will come back.

Be on the lookout for mutual funds with large tax-credit carry-forwards, the result of the 1969–1970 bear market, when they took large losses like a lot of other investors. Instead of distributing any capital gains to the shareholders, these funds can now build up their net asset value much quicker since they don't incur any tax liability.

Subscription Warrants

No taxable income is received by a shareholder when he receives rights and exercises them. If he has held the stock less than six months and sells the rights, he should write the cost of his stock down by the amount he receives for the warrant. In so doing, he postpones the payment of a tax and, at the same time, converts a short-term gain into a long-term gain.

The Short Sale against the Box

Your stock is showing a tremendous appreciation this year, but next year your tax position will be much more favorable to you. If you sell the stock now, as you are tempted to do, the gains are thrown into the current year's income and you will get clipped. What can you do to save money? You can sell the stock short in December, and in January you can tell your broker to deliver the long stock to the lender of the stock. In so doing, you have closed out both your long and short positions, and you have carried over a short-term gain from one year into the next. Quit dreaming. You cannot carry over a long-term gain in this fashion.

Options

You can never make a long-term capital gain on a short sale. But you can buy a six-month-and-ten-day put option at the striking price at which you want to sell short. If you are right, you can sell the put option, the contract, back to the dealer after six months and one day, and your profit will be a long-term capital gain.

Option writers enjoy tax advantages. A premium received for an exercised call is treated as an increase in the price of the stock the writer must sell to the holder of the option. If the stock has been held longer than six months, such cash income is a long-term capital gain. Similarly, a premium received for an exercised put can become a long-term capital gain. It is treated as a reduction in the price of the stock put to the writer of the option. If the stock is sold profitably, later, after six months and one day, this cash income too becomes a long-term capital gain. The greatest tax advantage, of course, rests with the writer of straddles, since he continuously sells both calls and puts.

The Computation of Capital Gains and Losses

When there are long-term capital gains and losses, add your gains and subtract them from your losses, if any. Then do the same for your short-term gains and losses. If there is a net short-term gain, and no long-term net loss against which to offset it, it is added to your ordinary income. Don't forget. If there is a net short-term loss, deduct it from your long-term gains. For married couples filing joint returns, up to $50,000 of the net long-term gain will be taxed at the 25-percent rate.

Starting with 1973, one-half of the net long-term gain above the $50,000 will be included in ordinary income and taxed at the regular rates. There is a three-year phase-out period for the treatment of the excess. It will be taxed at 29½ percent for 1970 returns, 32½ percent for 1971, and 35 percent for 1972.

What happens if there is a net short-term capital loss in excess of net long-term capital gains? It may be used to offset ordinary income up to $1,000 in the year the loss is incurred and in each succeeding year until the loss is thus used up.

Only 50 percent of an individual's net long-term capital losses in excess of net short-term capital gains may be used to offset ordinary incomes up to $1,000.

Guidelines for Capital Gain and Loss Problems

1. Hold your securities, which appreciate in value until the gain, after six months and one day, becomes long-term. The chances are that you will be taxed at an appreciably lower rate.

2. Try to avoid taking long-term gains and losses in the same year. Long-term capital gains are taxed at a low rate, and a capital loss can be used as an offset to short-term gains or against income up to $1,000 per year.

3. Any security that threatens to become valueless should be sold before it is worthless in order to fix the year in which the loss occurred.

4. Should unrealized losses exist in your portfolio, take them. You can use such a realized loss as an offset to any short-term gain.

5. Beware of "wash sales." Assume you have bought 100 ABC at $40 and now the stock is $30. But you are still bullish on the stock and wish to retain it in your portfolio. Here is a good way to eat your cake and have it too: Double up. Buy another 100

shares at $30, and then wait 31 days before selling the other 100 shares. You must wait 31 days before repurchasing the same stock. If you buy back the stock within 30 days, the Internal Revenue Service calls it a "wash sale" and prevents you from using the loss as an offset.

As a result of doubling up, you still have 100 shares of ABC Company at $30, and you have a tax loss of $1,000 that you can use to offset a short-term gain. You have also protected yourself against a possible rise in the price of the stock during the required waiting period. Had you sold the original shares at $30 and waited 31 days before buying the stock back, the stock could have risen in price.

Substantially Identical Securities

If I sell ABC $1 convertible preferred stock at a loss and purchase the ABC common within 30 days *or* sell ABC common stock at a loss and purchase the ABC $1 convertible preferred within 30 days, may I use the loss on the transactions as an offset to a short-term gain? Or would the tax authorities consider these as wash sales?

The answer will turn on the interpretation of the phrase "substantially identical securities," for you cannot buy or sell a "substantially identical security" within 30 days and use the ensuing loss as an offset. But if the premium over conversion value is 15 percent or more, the convertible securities would not be considered "substantially identical" with the common stock. If a convertible security is involved with a conversion premium of around 10 percent, the Internal Revenue Service would probably consider the securities "substantially identical" and the transactions as wash sales. In cases where the conversion premium is less than 15 percent, it might be an excellent idea to discuss the matter with your tax man before you make the transaction.

The Reversionary Trust

A parent in the 50-percent income tax bracket wishes to set aside annually $1,000 in a savings account for the future educational expenses of his small son. Note that to accomplish this, $2,000 before taxes must be available. There is, however, a way in which a parent can set aside $1,800 for the child in 1971 without paying any tax whatsoever: a reversionary trust that must be set up for a minimum period of ten years and a day. During these years all income earned on the stocks in the trust will be distributed to the beneficiary. At the end of the period stipulated in the trust instrument, the securities will revert to the parent. If the stocks have meanwhile appreciated in value, as I think we can assume, no long-term capital-gains tax liability is incurred by him until he sells the securities and realizes such gains.

Under the Tax Reform Act of 1969, the child as a separate taxpayer would have, in 1971, a $650 personal exemption ($700 in 1972 and from 1973 on, $750).* He also has a standard deduction of $1,050 in 1971 ($1,000 from 1972 on) and a $100 dividend exclusion.

Personal exemption	$ 650
Standard deduction	1,050
Dividend exclusion	100
Tax-free income	$1,800

If a $45,000 trust were set up, invested in stocks and yielding a 4-percent income, $1,800 a year could be distributed to the child without incurring any tax liability if we assume, as is usually the case, that this $1,800 was the child's sole income. Ten years later, with the $1,800 annually placed conservatively in a 5-percent savings account, the youngster will have more than $23,000 after taxes. And that ought to be enough to educate him. Moreover, the funds could be invested in a higher-yielding high-grade bond.

To set aside $1,800 a year, the father would have needed an additional $3,600 before taxes. As long as he provides for the child's support, he can still claim the boy as a dependent and

* Under the bill signed by President Richard M. Nixon in December, 1971, the exemption is now $675 for 1971 and has been raised for the other years.

use the applicable support exemption ($750 from 1973 on) on his income tax return.

If there are more children, a so-called sprinkler-type trust can be set up—one trust instrument covering all. Each of the children covered would have the right to claim $1,800 in annual tax-free income.

There is one problem here, but it can easily be taken care of. Who is going to select the stocks for the portfolio? Manage and supervise it? I suggest you ask your broker to contact the local or regional representative of a firm like Calvin Bullock. They have a very fine suitable mutual fund for you and have experience along these lines. Your attorney and Calvin Bullock can work out all the details very easily once you have decided to avail yourself of an $1,800 annual tax-free income.

One final question: What happens should the fund make any capital-gains distributions as distinguished from income distribution? They would be taxable to the parent. But, I repeat, no tax is due on any undistributed, unrealized capital gains on the fund shares when they revert to the parent at the end of the stipulated trust period.

The Private Annuity

The private annuity has aroused a great deal of interest among tax and investment advisers as well as attorneys. Considerable tax savings can be achieved. Income, gift, and particularly the progressive estate taxes can be substantially reduced or avoided entirely.

Let's assume an individual has $100,000 worth of ABC stock, an electronics growth company, which cost originally $25,000 and pays a small cash dividend. He now contemplates retirement and wants a regular income; he also seeks diversification for protection. Above all, he does not want to pay the capital-gains tax due on the $75,000 appreciation in order to keep his capital base intact. From 1973 on, he will have to pay 25 percent on $50,000 capital gains, and in addition $12,500, half of the remaining $25,000 gain, will be included in his income.

Avoiding the Capital-Gains Tax

In order to avoid the capital-gains tax completely, the man's, or woman's, attorney draws up a private annuity agreement between the parent and an adult son or daughter. Under this agreement, the parent *sells* the ABC stock to the son for his promise to pay him, or her, an annuity for the remainder of his life. It has been ruled that the unsecured promise of an individual to pay an annuity, as determined under a regular annuity table, does not have a fair market value. There is thus no capital-gains tax payable on the sale of the ABC stock to the son.

This is a sale and not a gift; therefore it would not jeopardize any of the distributions of an estate that can be made under the gift tax exemptions.

Under the Standard Annuity Table, a male aged 65 has about 16 years to live. Based on the parent's age, an annuity is worked out that would equal in value the $100,000 of the ABC stock. What type of annuity is to be set up will, of course, depend on the financial problems that will have to be solved. For example, if both parents are living a joint-and-last-survivor annuity may be deemed best. Under this annuity, income continues as long as either parent lives. Under a straight life annuity, income payments are made that continue only as long as the annuitant lives, but stop upon his death. In the case of only one parent living, this may be appropriate, since the biggest monthly payments can be made under this type of annuity. On the other hand, if another child or grandchild is to be protected, a refund annuity might be considered. In the case of a 10-year certain annuity, payments are guaranteed for a period of 10 years. Should the annual payments be $7,000 and the annuitant die after 5 years, a balance of $35,000, 5 years' payments, would be available for distribution to the estate or a designated beneficiary. If the annuitant lives beyond 10 years, he will continue to receive his monthly annuity check as long as he lives, but nothing would be available for distribution when death occurs. However, while he is alive, he can take care of the child's needs.

The son's cost basis for the ABC stock would not be the parent's $25,000 original cost basis, but a new basis of $100,000.

For that is the current value of the annuity payments the son will make over the parent's life span.

But how can the son be sure he will have the money to pay out each year? The answer is quite simple. Since his cost basis for the stock is $100,000, he may now sell the stock without incurring any capital-gains tax liability. An electronics growth stock is definitely not for older people; the risk is too high. In order to obtain diversification and professional management, he can reinvest the $100,000, the proceeds of the sale, in a good mutual fund, such as one of the Calvin Bullock funds, and set up a withdrawal program with the fund's bank. Assuming the annuity payments are $7,000 a year, under the withdrawal program a monthly check of about $583 would be mailed by the bank to the parent.

What happens should the annuitant die after payments of $70,000 have been made? The son's cost basis is then changed from $100,000 to $70,000, and he would have to pay a long-term capital-gains tax on $30,000 in the year the annuitant dies. It is important that the son hold the ABC stock for at least six months and one day before selling it. For if the parent should die during these six months, the son would have a long-term holding period; he would incur only a long-term capital-gains tax liability. If he sells the stock at once and the parent dies prematurely, he could saddle himself needlessly with a short-term capital-gains tax burden. If the sale is made in January, the annuity payments could then commence in July in order to take care of that "waiting period."

Additional Tax Relief

By purchasing such a private annuity, the parent can substantially reduce the federal estate tax because the estate has been reduced by $100,000. Since the federal estate tax is a rather steeply progressive tax, the difference in the tax burden between a $300,000 and a $200,000 gross estate could easily be $25,000 or better, depending on the debts outstanding against the estate and the amount of administrative expenses. Saving $25,000 or more in estate taxes is quite a bit of money! You can even save more if you take our advice and buy some long-term, deep-discount U.S. Treasury bonds.

While the annuitant lives, there is also an appreciable relief from the federal income tax. In order to recover his original cost basis of $25,000, part of each annual payment of $7,000 would be entirely tax-free and another large part would be taxable only as long-term capital gain. The exact amounts coming under this favored tax treatment will depend on the annuitant's life expectancy. Perhaps as much as half of the $7,000 could come under either recovery of cost basis or long-term capital-gains tax treatment.

If the annuitant outlives his life expectancy, there should be a big appreciation of the mutual fund shares that were purchased to make the monthly payments.

The setting up of a private annuity requires the services of a competent attorney. Should your attorney be unfamiliar with such a private annuity, go to your broker and ask him to contact the wholesale representative of a proper mutual fund. The document can be drawn up by legally trained officers of the fund. There is usually no charge for this service. Your attorney's fee will be the only expense incurred by you. The best time to contact your attorney for such estate-planning work is in the summer or early fall. Once his tax work gets heavy, he most likely will give you less time or turn you over to a junior partner.

Recent Changes in the Federal Estate Tax

In view of the changes in the federal estate tax, which went into effect on January 1, 1971, it will be even more advisable than formerly to have deep-discount U.S. Treasury bonds in the estate. Heirs now must pay the tax within nine months of death rather than within fifteen months, as under the old law. This creates a need for adequate liquidity in the estate. The bonds can be given to the Treasury at par for the estate tax due; stocks might have to be sold at low prices if the market took a downward turn, and other bonds might have to be sold at the wrong time in the interest rate cycle. You may, however, ask for an extension up to twelve months (formerly six months) from the date fixed for the payment of the estate tax. How liberal the

Treasury will be in granting such extensions is another question.

Another change is the payment of capital-gains taxes by heirs. Previously a son could inherit stock from a parent without paying any capital-gains tax on the appreciation of the stock while it was in the parent's possession. From 1971 on, the son must pay the tax on such gains. Long-term capital-gain or loss treatment for securities or other property included in its owner's estate may be taken even if the property is sold within six months of his death. Make sure, therefore, that proper records are kept to show when the stock was bought and at what price. This capital-gains-tax problem for heirs highlights the advantage of the private annuity and the installment sale as a means of avoiding or reducing such tax liabilities.

The Installment Sale

Let's now go back to our previous illustration of the ABC stock, which was bought at $25,000 and is now worth $100,000. Again the owner of the securities wants to sell the stock, but hates to pay a large capital-gains tax. The installment sale is another way of avoiding such tax payments.

With the help of an attorney, an installment contract is drawn up with the son, who agrees to buy the stock. Like under any other installment sales contract, his payments are spread equally over a period of years. The son could make monthly or quarterly payments, as convenient. Every payment made by him to his father will result in a payment of interest and a payment of principal.

During the early years of the installment sales contract, a large part of each payment will be interest. The interest portion of each payment gives the son an income tax deduction in the years the payments are made. Of course, as with all installment payments, as more and more of the principal becomes paid, the interest charges on the unpaid principal portion decrease.

What is the tax effect to the father? The interest part of each payment the son makes is, of course, taxable income to him. Since the father's cost basis was $25,000, a quarter of the principal portion of each payment is tax-free. The remaining 75 percent of each payment's principal portion is taxable to the father as long-term capital gain. As the payments come in, there will be less and less taxable income to him, since the interest portion of the payments is continuously decreasing and the long-term capital-gains portion is ever increasing. The father thus receives an assured regular income that is taxed on a far more favorable basis than ordinary income.

Since the cost basis of the stock to the son is $100,000 the son can sell the stock without incurring a sizable capital-gains tax liability. The proceeds of the sale could then be invested in a diversified, professionally managed mutual fund. Under a withdrawal program monthly or quarterly payments could be made to the father. The fund's bank would mail the checks directly to the father, freeing the son of any administrative chores regarding the installment sales contract.

When the father dies, only the current value of any remaining installment payments is included in his estate; the payments could continue to be paid to the estate, or more likely, to a designated beneficiary.

Income Averaging

Under the Tax Reform Act of 1969, income averaging will result in even bigger tax savings than before. Under income averaging, a taxpayer can considerably reduce the effect of the progressive income tax rates on sharply fluctuating annual incomes.

Beginning with 1970, the income fluctuations don't need to be as great as they did in the past. Any taxable income in excess of 120 percent of the taxpayer's average taxable income for the preceding four years can be averaged and will be thus taxed at lower rates than would otherwise have to be paid.

As long as your excess income exceeds three thousand dollars and your current annual income is 20 percent greater than your average income for the past four years, you may average. Net capital-gains income, the one-half of the excess of net long-term capital gains over net short-term capital losses included in your reported gross income, money received in a lottery or from any other wager, and income from gifts—all these are now eligible for income averaging.

Gifts to Minors

In view of the progressive nature of both the federal income tax and the federal estate tax, it would also be wise to consider making gifts to minors of securities or money that a custodian may manage and invest. But you must set it up right, or a tax liability could easily hit you.

The Uniform Gifts to Minors Act offers an opportunity of giving securities and/or money to a child and thus getting both the principal and the income away from the donor. The minor will receive permanent possession of the securities at age twenty-one. But if the donor is unwise enough to name himself or herself as custodian and dies before the minor reaches twenty-one, the entire gift or gifts are taxed to the estate, throwing them most likely into a higher estate tax bracket.

Lifetime Gifts to Children, Spouse, or Others

It is very advantageous to make such gifts. They remove the conveyed property from the top bracket of the progressive estate tax. Either they fall under the liberal allowed deductions and are therefore tax-free, or if in excess of the allowances, they will be taxed under the much lower gift tax. Gifts will also result in taking income away from the donor who is presumably in a higher tax bracket than the recipient of the gift.

An individual may give away up to $3,000 annually to as many people as he likes. If the conveyed property is owned jointly by husband and wife, this annual gift allowance is doubled to $6,000.

In addition to this $3,000, or $6,000, annual exemption, every individual is entitled to a lifetime exemption of $30,000, or if the property is owned jointly, of $60,000. This provision is cumulative. An individual is free to use up his lifetime exemption in one year, or he may spread it over a period of years. A husband and wife together could give up to $66,000 to one person in one year, tax-free. They could give $12,000 each year over a 10-year period to a son or daughter or any other person.

Under the marital deduction allowance, the taxpayer may deduct 50 percent of the value of the gift made to his wife in estimating his gift tax liability. This deduction is in addition to the annual exclusion and the lifetime exemption. He can thus give his wife $6,000 annually and pay no taxes, since the marital deduction brings the amount down to $3,000, which is his annual exclusion.

The annual exclusion applies only when the gift is of "a present interest." In other words, you can claim this deduction only when the recipient benefits at once from the gift. Should a gift be made in trust to a beneficiary who does not have the right to its income or principal at once, a gift "of a future interest" has been made. It does not qualify for the annual gift exclusion.

There is also a marital deduction in connection with the estate. A husband may give his wife (or a wife to her husband) up to 50 percent of the value of the estate tax-free. In view of the progressive nature of the estate tax, it can be easily appreciated that the marital deduction here is probably the most valuable single tool for easing the estate tax burden.

Watch out for one thing when making gifts: Payment of the gift tax is due on or before the fifteenth of the second month following the close of the calendar quarter in which the gift was made.

Suppose a $2,500 gift is made by a father to his son or daughter in February. No tax payment need be made since it is well within the $3,000 annual exemption. But now he makes another gift of $2,500 in May. A gift tax return is due, in this case, on August 15, reporting a gift of $2,000 ($5,000 total gifts minus the $3,000 exemption). It may thus become necessary for you to change the timing of your gift-making should the required quarterly payment of the gift tax impose a financial drain on you. Moreover, there may be income lost on the money used to pay the quarterly gift tax unless you defer the gift until the final quarter of the year.

Always Look

Always be on the lookout for tax savings. Suppose you own a municipal bond that you bought some years ago. The chances are it will sell at a substantial discount from par since the interest rates are now higher than, say, in the 1950s. Sell the deep-discount municipal bond and buy another deep-discount municipal issue of the same quality, with about the same yield to maturity since current income is not desired, and same maturity. You can now sell your ABC stock, which you also bought years ago and have always hesitated to sell because of the capital-gains tax. You can use the loss on the municipal bond to offset the gains on the stock, repurchase the ABC shares, and establish a new higher cost basis. Even if the long-term capital loss should exceed your gains, you're ahead, for you can save these excess losses for the future. Such a loss can be carried over indefinitely under present tax laws.

A Will Is a Must

If you fail to draw up a will, your estate may have to pay otherwise unnecessary taxes because your wife receives less than the amount she could have been given tax-free. Many other complications can arise. But do not draw your own will. Your attorney should prepare it.

Summary

1. Stock dividends, unless sold, are not taxable. If they are sold, a long- or short-term capital-gains tax will be due, depending on the holding period of the original stock.

2. Corporate investors enjoy an 85-percent tax exemption on all corporate dividends.

3. Via a short sale against the box, you can carry over a short-term gain into the next year.

4. Option writers enjoy great tax advantages.

5. Always be on the lookout for unrealized losses in your portfolio. Take them and use them as offsets to gains.

6. Beware of wash sales. Watch out for "substantially identical securities."

7. If you want to put money aside for a child's college or graduate school educational expenses, the reversionary trust is ideally designed for such a purpose.

INDEX

333

Just Like
Beverly

Vicki Conrad

Illustrated by

David Hohn

little bigfoot
an imprint of sasquatch books
seattle, wa

On a farm near Yamhill, Oregon, lived a girl named Beverly Bunn.
She had no siblings and there were no other children nearby, so her
playmates were farm animals. She fed baby birds, climbed trees,
and followed horses around the fields.

Beverly loved stories, but she had only two books. Her mother read them out loud over and over. Beverly was so starved for new stories, she made up her own.

She made up stories about the fluffy yellow chick in a magazine ad. She recited *Goldilocks and the Three Bears* over and over and dreamed up adventures about the Campbell's Soup Kids.

In Yamhill, other children needed books too. Beverly's mother decided to start a children's library in town. When she asked the Yamhill community for donations, a pile of adult books arrived.

Where are the books for kids like me? Beverly wondered.

Beverly's mother wrote an article for the newspaper about Yamhill's need for books. To her surprise, crates of books arrived from the State Library of Oregon in Salem. Sixty-two beautiful children's books in a cupboard in an empty room above the bank became Yamhill's first children's library.

Finally, Beverly had new stories. She sat on her mother's lap and listened to book after book. Fairy tales and Beatrix Potter's stories about bunnies and squirrels were her favorites.

When Beverly turned six, her family moved to Portland, Oregon. There she found playmates—neighborhood children just like her. They had games and toys! Parcheesi, Tinkertoys, Old Maid, and dollhouses.

Everyone owned roller skates—except Beverly. She sat on the front steps of her house, longing for her own pair.

Her father came home from work one day with the perfect gift.

At last Beverly felt like part of the neighborhood, skating up
and down the hills with skinned knees.

Beverly and her friends had fun inventing games. They made "perfume" by pounding rose petals and soaking them in water. They played "brick factory" by smashing old bricks into dust with rocks. They clanked around on stilts made from coffee cans until they fell over laughing.

To teach her to be graceful, Beverly's mother enrolled her in ballet. She danced around the studio, trying to learn steps that sounded like "gallop" and "sauté."

Soon, it was time for Beverly to attend Fernwood Grammar School. Her father brought home two first-grade readers.

"I'll teach you to read," her mother said.

Beverly shook her head no. She wanted to learn at school.

The first day at Fernwood was a blur of children. A whistle blew and everyone marched into class. Beverly pumped her knees and followed. Before lessons, the class sang about "the dawnzer lee light."

What kind of light is a *dawnzer*? she wondered.

Everything was strange to Beverly:
the songs, the Pledge of Allegiance,
the rules, the desks all in rows. She
felt small and nervous.

Math lessons were easy for her. She could already add and subtract. With real numbers, not counters. Her teacher, Miss Falb, never noticed. When Beverly wrote with her left hand, Miss Falb noticed.

"You must always hold your pencil in your right hand," she scolded. Now writing was painful and hard.

Beverly began to read small words, like *mamma*, *kitty*, and *see*.

City of Portland
Health Department

WARNING
SMALLPOX

Then Beverly got sick with smallpox.

This was a serious sickness. A red sign on her lawn warned the
neighbors and the milkman to keep away. Even her father had
to leave until she was well again.

When she returned to class after weeks and weeks, reading was harder. Miss Falb put everyone into reading groups: bluebirds, redbirds, and blackbirds. The bluebirds were the best readers; the blackbirds, the worst. Beverly was assigned to the blackbirds.

Beverly dreaded reading circle, when each blackbird had to stand and read aloud. All eyes watched her struggle, her tongue tripping over the sounds. She hoped for easy words she already knew, like *party* and *baby*. As she stood for her turn, Beverly's stomach twisted, and her voice was small as a mouse.

Besides, the reading books were boring. The children in the stories never did anything interesting, and they weren't funny like her friends.

"Tom and Pam go to the seashore," she read. Beverly knew everyone in Oregon went to the *beach*. No one said *seashore*.

Where were the books about kids like her?

Once, when Miss Falb caught Beverly daydreaming, she whipped her hands with a switch. The stinging was unbearable. Another time, she banished Beverly to the coatroom. She sat on the floor and cried.

School was not the happy place she had imagined.

At the end of the year,
Beverly's grades were bad
and she could barely read.

All summer she dreaded going back, worried she
would have to repeat first grade with Miss Falb!

But something wonderful happened the next year. Beverly went on to second grade and got a new teacher. Miss Marius was patient and encouraging.

"Beverly, come to my desk with your book." Side by side, Miss Marius pointed to letters and hinted at their sound. Soon Beverly could read every word.

Finally, she was happy and confident at school. She was proud in a way she had never been before. She could read, but the books were too boring.

So, Beverly decided she would read *only* for Miss Marius, the teacher she loved.

One day, Beverly's mother found a box of old books in a church basement and brought two home for her.

I will never read these, Beverly thought.

But on a rainy, boring Sunday afternoon, she picked one up, just to look at the pictures. It was called *The Dutch Twins*.

Beverly read a few pages. Then she read a few more pages. And a few more. Before she knew it, the whole afternoon was gone.

At last, Beverly understood the magic of books. The children in *The Dutch Twins* were just like her. They were funny and had adventures. She started the next book right away. For the first time ever, her mother put off bedtime.

From that day on, Beverly was a reader. She endured the gloomy Oregon winters curled up in the public library.

Beverly's love of reading led to writing. A newspaper offered a free book to any child who wrote a review. Her mother suggested she try it.

The newspaper gave her *The Story of Doctor Dolittle*. They published her book review in the paper, along with her photograph. Suddenly, Beverly was the school celebrity.

When Beverly was in fourth grade, the store across the street from school held an essay contest. The best animal essay would win a two-dollar prize! Beverly chose an excellent topic—the Oregon beaver, of course!

Her father brought home green scratch paper from his job at the bank, and Beverly used it to write her essay.

Beverly was nervous—so many of her classmates planned to enter. But she did her best and turned her essay in early. On the last day of the contest, she raced to the store.

Beverly won! Mr. Abendroth handed her the prize money. She couldn't believe it! Two whole dollars!

"You *were* the only one who entered," he said with a chuckle.

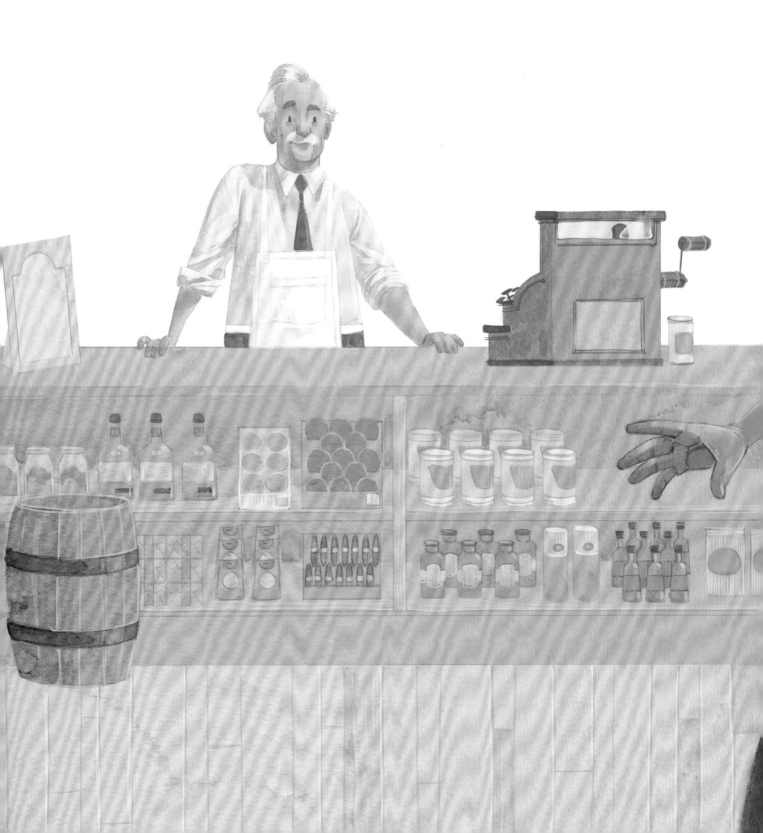

Beverly was still thrilled. In fact, she learned a powerful lesson: Try! Anyone can talk about writing, but only those who sit down and do it will succeed.

In seventh grade, Beverly wrote stories in her reading class. Her teacher, Miss Smith, was impressed. She read one of Beverly's stories out loud and announced, "When Beverly grows up, she should write children's books."

Beverly dreamed of being a writer. She even found the spot on the library shelf where her books would go someday.

After finishing high school, she went to college in California. At a party, a kind man named Clarence Cleary asked her to dance. They soon became friends, and as college ended, Clarence promised to marry her.

But Beverly needed to follow her dreams of becoming a librarian.

So, while Clarence stayed in California, she moved to Seattle to study library science at the University of Washington. Then she got a job as a children's librarian in Yakima, Washington.

Beverly missed Clarence, but she loved her job. Once a week, a group of rowdy boys came in looking for books. She struggled to find something just right for them. One exasperated boy asked her, "Where are the books about kids like us?" Beverly didn't have an answer.

She thought about her own childhood reading boring books. She remembered how she longed for funny stories about children in her neighborhood—children just like her.

So, with her first paycheck as a librarian, she bought a typewriter to write the stories she wished she'd had as a girl. But her librarian duties and writing letters to Clarence ate up all of her time.

After a year, Clarence came to Yakima and surprised her with a ring. Beverly was overjoyed.

They got married and moved to California, where, staying true to her love of books, she worked as an army librarian and bookstore clerk.

As Beverly's life changed, she still longed to write her own stories.

One day, in the closet of their new home, she and Clarence found a ream of paper.

"I guess I'll have to write a book," joked Beverly.

"Why don't you?" asked Clarence, quite seriously.

Beverly laughed. "We never have any sharp pencils!"

The next day, Clarence came home with a present.

Beverly remembered her lesson from the essay contest. She had to try. She was determined to write a story of her own.

As she stared at the paper in the typewriter, she wasn't sure how to begin. Was it all a foolish dream?

She thought about the boys at the library. She thought about her childhood, roller-skating on Hancock Street. She would write the story she longed for as a child.

Beverly remembered hearing a funny story about a boy and his dog riding the streetcar. She wrote her first sentence: "Henry Huggins was in the third grade."

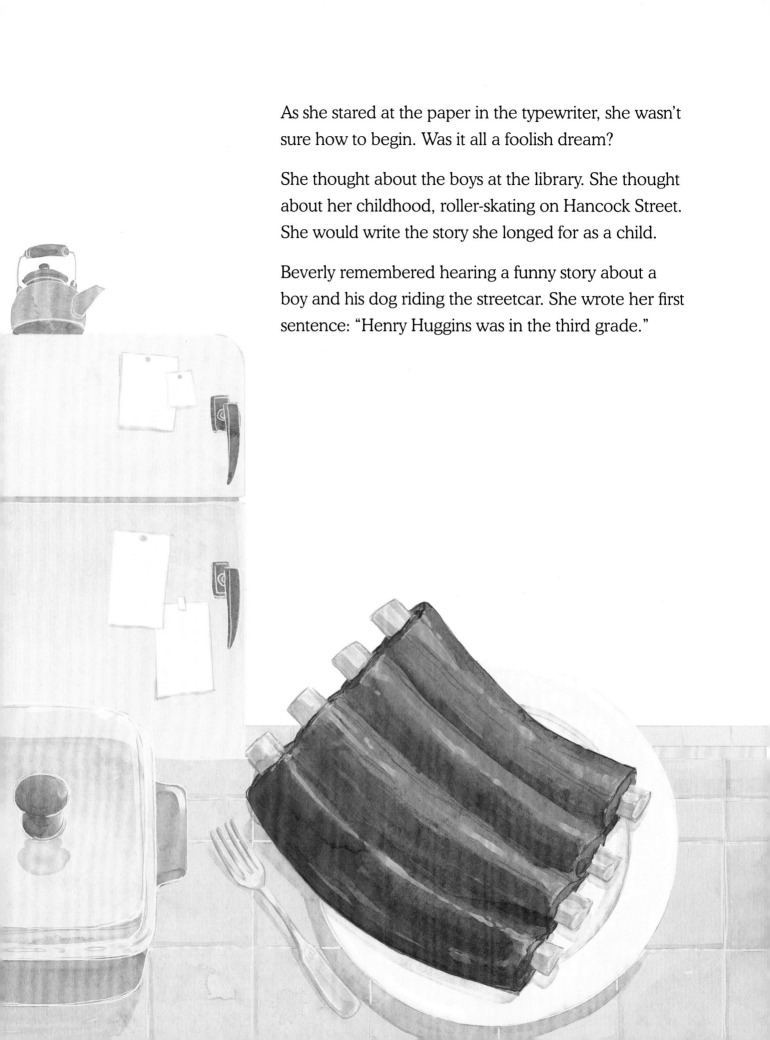

What will I call the dog? she wondered.

Glancing toward the kitchen, it came to her: Spareribs!

Beverly completed her first short story, naming it "Spareribs and Henry." She sent it off to publishers and waited.

She checked the mail every day. Finally, a postcard came that read: "Your manuscript has been received."

She kept waiting.

Every afternoon for six long weeks, she trimmed the rose bushes in her yard, waiting for the mailman. Beverly explained she was waiting for good news.

At last, the mailman came running. "It's here!" he called.

Beverly celebrated with Clarence.

Spareribs became Ribsy, and two years later, *Henry Huggins* became her first published book. It was a huge success.

She wrote many more books inspired by her childhood.
Each story was filled with characters who lived and
played on Klickitat Street.

Beverly's character Ramona Quimby
loved playing "brick factory," wearing
coffee can stilts, and roller-skating.

She wondered about the "dawnzer
lee light," just like Beverly.

Henry Huggins was just like the boys who came into the library.

Beverly Cleary, the struggling blackbird reader, wrote more than forty books for children. She became one of the most celebrated authors in the world by writing for children just like her.

How **Beverly** Bloomed

Beverly Atlee Bunn was born on April 12, 1916, in McMinnville, Oregon. She lived on a farm in Yamhill, Oregon, until she was six. She was able to run wild and free, but as an only child, she always dreamed of having siblings and playmates. Beverly's parents dreamed of escaping the struggle of farm life, so they moved their family to the big city: Portland, Oregon.

The city was full of new experiences and different adventures for Beverly. She rode streetcars over the Willamette River. Their neighborhood was paradise. She had playmates, sidewalks for roller-skating, and freedom to play all day long.

The memories Beverly made during her elementary years would later become the material for the funny stories in the books she wrote. Her childhood struggles with learning to read and being forced to read

boring books motivated her to write for children. As she overcame her difficulties with reading, Beverly's storytelling talent came to life—she had a gift that continued emerging as she got older.

She began to write seriously in the seventh grade when a school librarian recognized her promise. The librarian, Miss Smith, also taught reading and writing. She was an unusual teacher because she encouraged students to be creative.

During Beverly's school years, there were strict rules: no reading ahead and no reading for pleasure in class. When writing a paper, students were usually asked only to summarize their assigned reading. Using your imagination was not encouraged. Miss Smith's assignments required imagination.

When Miss Smith instructed her class to write a letter pretending they lived in George Washington's time, Beverly wrote about having to sacrifice a pet chicken to feed the troops at Valley Forge. Miss Smith praised Beverly by reading her letter out loud. And her classmates, who had been stumped for ideas, began writing copycat chicken stories. For the first time, she was allowed to use her imagination, and it felt glorious.

Miss Smith's next assignment was to write about a favorite storybook character. Beverly couldn't think of just one, so she wrote a story about visiting all of her favorite characters in a place called Bookland. As she wrote on a rainy winter afternoon, the same magical peace came over her that she experienced when she first got lost in a book at the age of eight. She got lost in the wonder of writing.

Beverly didn't think her story was superb. However, Miss Smith loved it and read it out loud, encouraging Beverly to write children's books. Beverly was not used to being praised, especially in front of her peers. Those words were powerful, and they gave her a direction that she followed into adulthood.

Beverly attended college from 1934 to 1938, in the middle of the Great Depression. Life was hard during this time. Few jobs were available, and money was scarce for most people.

She depended on family to afford college and lived with her mother's cousin in Ontario, California, for two years while she attended a junior college.

She went on to attend the University of California at Berkeley. This was her dream school because of its graduate School of Librarianship program. Beverly refused to be a financial burden on her parents, so she worked very hard through school to pay her own expenses. She babysat to earn extra money. When she realized her sewing skills were superior to that of her classmates, she began hemming their skirts for fifty cents apiece.

Her gift for writing bloomed in her college years. An essay she wrote about her early reading experiences earned an A. The essay was so well written, her professor read it aloud in class. Without knowing it, Beverly had begun to write the story of her life.

Each week, Beverly attended dances at Berkeley. One evening, a kind young man who stood out from the rest asked her to dance. This is how she met her future husband, Clarence Cleary. They were close friends all through her college years, and the weekend

of her graduation, he expressed his desire to marry her. But first, Beverly wanted to pursue a career.

Her pursuit of this dream was shaped by her early school experience. Once she discovered a love of reading, Beverly wanted to surround herself with books and pass this love on to others. She wanted to write but didn't believe she could make a living from it.

After college, she returned to the Northwest to complete the Librarianship program at the University of Washington in Seattle, while Clarence stayed in California.

She soon realized that the best place in any library was the children's section; she also realized that cataloging was boring and not her natural talent. To Beverly, the library represented freedom. It provided a safe place where children were free to come and go, and they could discover the magic of books.

Her first job was as a children's librarian in Yakima, Washington. Reading at story hour was nerve-racking at first, but when she focused on the children's faces, her nerves went away. Once, on a school visit, she read *Horton Hatches the Egg*, and a child laughed so hard he fell out of his chair. That's when she discovered the joy of sharing the right story with the right children.

With her first paycheck, Beverly bought herself pajamas, underwear, and a typewriter, to fulfill her dream of writing. She did not know what to write, so she read a lot of books and wrote many letters to Clarence in California.

Beverly's parents did not approve of Clarence, but she married him anyway. He came to Yakima and surprised her with a ring. After they got married, they moved to California together.

Clarence was the biggest supporter of Beverly pursuing a writing career—he encouraged her every step of the way.

While living in San Francisco, Beverly worked at the Sather Gate Book Shop. Selling children's books gave her a stronger drive to write for children. She felt that many books for children were dull, and the children were not drawn to the children's books. This inspired her to offer something better.

Beverly began writing her first story, about Henry Huggins, based on her childhood and her playmates in Portland on Hancock Street, where she grew up. Beezus and Ramona were smaller characters in the Henry and Ribsy series. She eventually expanded the girls' stories into her most famous series: the Ramona books. Her characters played the same games as Beverly and her friends.

She thought about the stories she wanted to read in her childhood as she wrote, and she took her mother's writing advice to keep it simple and make it funny.

Five years after Henry Huggins was published, Beverly and Clarence had twins, Malcolm and Marianne. Beverly drew from their lives for writing inspiration. When her son had reading struggles, she created Ralph S. Mouse to help him read. After she watched

Malcolm play with a handful of toy cars, she wrote *The Mouse and the Motorcycle*.

During her long and successful career, Beverly has written more than forty books. Her work has received thirty-five state awards, as well as many other honors, including the Laura Ingalls Wilder Award and Newbery Medal.

The lives of Beverly's ordinary characters resonate deeply with children across generations. In recognition of this, she was given the Library of Congress' "Living Legend" award in 2000 for her many outstanding contributions to children's literature. Also, on Beverly's ninetieth birthday, HarperCollins established National Drop Everything and Read (D.E.A.R.) Day in her honor, and April was declared D.E.A.R. Month in 2013.

Portland, Oregon, honored its beloved author by creating the Beverly Cleary Sculpture Garden in Grant Park. Statues of Ramona Quimby, Henry Huggins, and Ribsy were built in Beverly's honor. The elementary school she attended and wrote about in her stories is now called the Beverly Cleary School.

Beverly Cleary lives in Carmel, California, and celebrated her hundredth birthday on April 12, 2016.

Timeline

1916

Beverly Bunn is born in McMinnville, Oregon, and lives on a farm in nearby Yamhill

1922 – 1934

Moves with parents to Portland, Oregon, and attends Fernwood Grammar School and Grant High School

1938

Earns a bachelor's degree in English from the University of California at Berkeley and meets Clarence Cleary

1948

Begins writing her first book, inspired by her childhood experiences in Portland

1950

Henry Huggins is published by William Morrow and Company

1955

Gives birth to twins, Malcolm James and Marianne Elizabeth, and publishes *Beezus and Ramona*, the first book in her most well-known series

1981

Wins the National Book Award in the children's fiction category for the paperback release of *Ramona and Her Mother*

1982

Ramona Quimby, Age 8 is named a Newbery Honor Book

1995

Beverly Cleary Sculpture Garden is dedicated at Grant Park in Portland, Oregon, near where Beverly grew up and set many of her stories

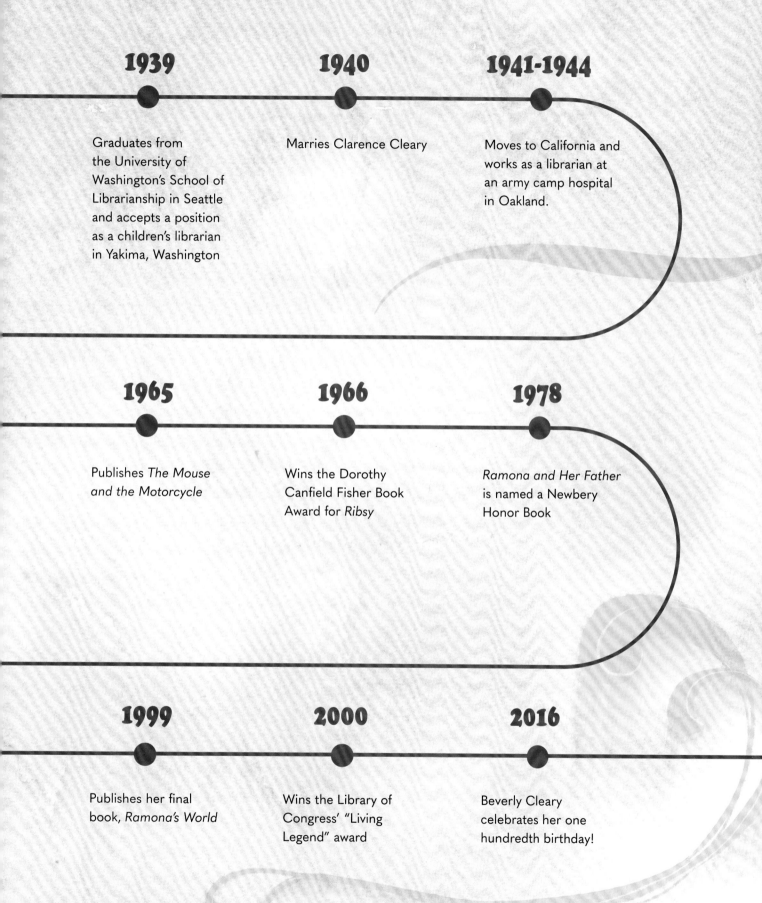

1939

Graduates from the University of Washington's School of Librarianship in Seattle and accepts a position as a children's librarian in Yakima, Washington

1940

Marries Clarence Cleary

1941-1944

Moves to California and works as a librarian at an army camp hospital in Oakland.

1965

Publishes *The Mouse and the Motorcycle*

1966

Wins the Dorothy Canfield Fisher Book Award for *Ribsy*

1978

Ramona and Her Father is named a Newbery Honor Book

1999

Publishes her final book, *Ramona's World*

2000

Wins the Library of Congress' "Living Legend" award

2016

Beverly Cleary celebrates her one hundredth birthday!

Dedicated to children. May you find
yourself reflected in the pages of a book.
If you don't, write that book. —VC

Thank you to Michelle McCann, Christy Cox, and everyone at Sasquatch Books. Michelle, your belief
in this story put it into print. Christy, thank you for the thoughtful and wise edits through all of the
drafts. Thank you to the Tuesday night writers; your support and friendship mean the world to me.
Thank you to every friend and coworker who cheered me on through the waiting and wondering.
Thanks, Mom, for all the Beverly Cleary book order purchases. Thank you, Beverly, for writing the
books about kids just like me. —VC

Copyright © 2019 by Vicki Conrad
Illustrations copyright © 2019 by David Hohn

Manufactured in China by C&C Offset Printing Co. Ltd. Shenzhen,
Guangdong Province, in May 2019

LITTLE BIGFOOT with colophon is a registered trademark of
Penguin Random House LLC

23 22 21 20 19   9 8 7 6 5 4 3 2 1
Editors: Michelle McCann, Christy Cox
Production editor: Bridget Sweet
Design: Tony Ong
Copyeditor: Rachelle Longé McGhee

Beverly Cleary photo on page 40: © Archive PL / Alamy Stock Photo

Library of Congress Cataloging-in-Publication Data

Names: Conrad, Vicki, author. | Hohn, David, 1974- illustrator.
Title: Just like Beverly : a biography of Beverly Cleary / Vicki Conrad ;
    illustrated by David Hohn.
Description: [Seattle, Washington] : Little Bigfoot, [2019] | Series: Growing
    to greatness | Audience: Ages 5-9. | Audience: Grades K-3.
Identifiers: LCCN 2019003937 | ISBN 9781632172228 (hardcover)
Subjects: LCSH: Cleary, Beverly--Juvenile literature. | Women authors,
    American--20th century--Biography--Juvenile literature. | Women
    librarians--United States--Biography--Juvenile literature.
Classification: LCC PS3553.L3914 Z5913 2019 | DDC 813/.54 [B] --dc23
LC record available at https://lccn.loc.gov/2019003937

ISBN: 978-1-63217-222-8

Sasquatch Books
1904 Third Avenue, Suite 710
Seattle, WA 98101
SasquatchBooks.com